GOD HERE AND NOW

Spiritual Exercises for Personal Growth

Hedwig Lewis, S.J.

GUJARAT SAHITYA PRAKASH ANAND

2005
GUJARAT SAHITYA PRAKASH
POST BOX 70
ANAND
GUJARAT, 388 001
INDIA

2nd Reprint : 2005

ISBN 81-87886-62-5

Price: $ 12.00

Published by K.T. Mathew, S.J., GUJARAT SAHITYA PRAKASH
P.B. 70, ANAND, Gujarat, 388 001, India.
Laser-set and printed by S. Abril, S.J., ANAND PRESS, P.B. 95.
GAMDI-ANAND, Gujarat, 388 001, India.

FOREWORD

The story goes that a man who advocated atheism had a big poster framed on his drawing-room wall which said: ***GOD IS NOWHERE***. One day, while he was in the room with the newspaper, his little daughter, who was sitting next to him doing her school assignment, suddenly turned her gaze to the poster and began reading it aloud, GOD... IS... **NOW**...**HERE**! And she beamed for having successfully gone through the statement.

Her father was about to correct her to say "nowhere" but some instinct prevented him from doing so. And, as grace would have it, his daughter's reading of the poster made on impact on him. Somehow, every time he looked at it, he could only read: GOD IS NOW HERE... and he eventually came to believe it!

GOD HERE AND NOW is a prayer-manual based on the *Spiritual Exercises* of St Ignatius Loyola, which leads a person step by prayerful step to encounter God in the here-and-now, and to experience his Presence in all creation.

The *Spiritual Exercises* is highly structured, progressively leading one from "knowing about God" to "knowing God", from head-knowledge to heart-convictions.

Though intensively programmed, the *Spiritual Exercises* is not a time-bound 'project' but a 'Spirit-guided' adventure into the heart of God. The emphasis is on quality rather than quantity: not all the points on the proposed topics need be finished at one session. One is constantly coaxed into using both one's 'wings' – "doing" and "being" – in order to soar to the heights: 'exercises' necessarily entail "doing"; 'contemplation' is "being" present before the God who is present in the here and now. One is also repeatedly reminded that one must make allowances for those 'gracious' moments when one may not need the wings: God sweeps one off ones feet into a loving embrace!

This book is an off-shoot of the popular prayer-guide ***At Home With God***. It contains hundreds of thought-provoking stories, anecdotes, and poems as well as inspirational quotes from Scripture and other sources in keeping with the theme of the day.

God Here And Now will appeal to all who yearn for God in prayer and are enthusiastic about leading God-centred lives. The inspirational inputs, simple prayer techniques and spiritual exercises will strengthen, intensify and deepen their relationship with God.

In the process they will discover their own inner resources and be motivated to use their insights and experiences in a constructive way for the building up of the Kingdom of God. They will increase their desire to love God with their whole heart, mind, soul and strength, and to love their neighbour as they love themselves.

They will become aware of God's presence in all things, persons, events and places! They will learn to be 'contemplatives in action', transforming every one of their activities into 'spiritual exercises' and thus being in contact with God – "praying" always – in the here-and-now! H.L.

CONTENTS

STRUCTURE OF THE BOOK

God Here And Now is based on the *Spiritual Exercises* of St Ignatius. [See the Appendix, at the end of this book, for an understanding of the *Spiritual Exercises*].

St Ignatius follows the "logic of the heart" more than the "logic of the head". The prayer-exercises must be done for personal experience, focusing more on 'knowing' God experientially rather than 'knowing about' God theoretically. All our thoughts/actions, though they may appear as our initiative, are in truth initiated by God's grace. One must, of course, make oneself more and more open-hearted to receive God's gifts.

The book is well-structured:

A **Section** contains the general thrust of a particular stage within the dynamics of the *Spiritual Exercises.*

A **Phase** contains a specific theme within the section. A phase consists of **seven units**. One may begin a phase on any day of the week... and take as many days as necessary for each unit. One need not finish a phase within a week.

The **topic** for each day contains several inputs that contribute towards the theme specified. Remember, the topics are just 'signposts' indicating the direction you must proceed. A topic may help you get started in prayer for the day. Therefore it is important that you stay alert to the 'movements' of God's Spirit in your heart, and proceed according to its dictates.

Do not become anxious about completing all the inputs suggests for the day's prayer. Prayer is not a 'project', remember, but an 'experience'. Relish the experience for as long as it lasts.

There are **introductions** to each section and phase.

GUIDELINES FOR FORMAL PRAYER

[See NOTES at the end of this book, for detailed guidelines].

1. **Prepare for prayer**. Glance at the topics for each day's prayer either before you retire at night or when you wake up in the morning. This will help make easier the transition to prayer later in the day.

2. Choose a **time** and **place** conducive to prayer; that is, relatively free of distractions and disturbances. For psychological and practical purposes, it may be good to keep the same time and place every day, if possible. It would also be helpful to have some simple objects – a cross, a candle, a holy picture..., to support your concentration.

> "The absence of external noise is not enough. It can even reveal our inner hubbub. It would be an illusion to hope to empty our mind of all its clutter by all sorts of preliminary techniques. Praying is not about *creating a vacuum!* Praying means to be authentic and present. It means to be united with the living God, just as I am, with all that I am and all that I carry with me. *God doesn't join us in a 'sterilised' part of ourselves.* I become calm, quiet in faith, I become aware of Him Whom I want to encounter in love." Bethy Oudot

3. **Plan** on spending at least 30 minutes to an hour in formal prayer. Planning ahead is like making an important 'appointment' – it helps prepare you interiorly. Remember, the time should be long enough so as to give you sufficient time to recover from your previous activity and get into the 'mood' for prayer. It will also prevent you from getting anxious if there are pressing matters on hand which you have not scheduled in advance.

4. Keep your **Bible** at hand for easy reference.

5. Since your body 'accompanies' you at prayer, take a **bodily posture** that lends itself to prayer (kneeling, squatting, sitting, lying prostrate). Have your hands folded or

placed across your breast or in your lap, or keep your arms outstretched. Resist frequent change of posture or physical restlessness. A proper posture is one that combines reverence before God who is present, physical relaxation, mental peace. Do a few body relaxation exercises if they help.

6. Make an "**Act of Presence**" at the start of every prayer. That is, through a gesture (like deep-bowing your body) or endearing words ("Your presence fills me with joy and brings me pleasure forever"- Ps 16.1; "I have come to You to take Your touch... Let your eyes rest upon my eyes for a while" - Tagore), or moments of recollected silence..., acknowledge God who is present.

7. Proceed with the **topic** of the day.

8. **Ask** for grace of the day's prayer. When you 'ask' it means you are ready to receive. In asking, you acknowledge that everything comes from God, even prayer is a gift from God.

> "Asking forces me to sort through my desires and to recognise humbly the one I need today in order to be open to God. It is directing my desires towards God, listening to what is really in my heart, and looking beyond myself to find the Lord, the Source of all desires. In asking for the grace I need I can no longer cheat either myself or God.... At the heart of every petition, there is hidden praise, the acknowledgement that He can give what is asked for."
>
> Bethy Oudet

8. **Conclude** your prayer-period with the Our Father – which contains the core of our Faith: the purpose for which we are created and the goal towards which we are all striving – the praise, the reverence, and the service of God.

We acknowledge God as our Father and Provider, and we pray that we may live in harmony with one another.

9. **Review** your prayer. For details, see *Guidelines For Formal Prayer* in NOTES at the end of this book.

Keep this structure all through the programme.

AT HOME WITH GOD

Reserve a half-hour (at least)
on your busy schedule
to be at home wtih God!
Give top priority to this 'appointment',
deciding to be with no one else,
with nothing else,
and nowhere else
except at home with God!

Sit at the Master's feet,
rest a cheek on His knee
play with the hem of His garment,
feeling His loving caress
as He lays a hand on your head,
experiencing the power of His words,
as your heart burns within
you while He speaks.

To His silent queries:
Do you love Me?
Do you love Me more than your life?
Do you really love Me
with an ever-growing love?
Let your whole being explode
in a response of joy and generosity:
Yes I do! You know I do!

Make the Lord feel at home with you.
Feel at home with God. H.L.

SECTION ONE

GOD OUR FOUNDATION

GOD OUR FOUNDATION

There is an ancient Chinese Taoist story about a farmer in a poor village. People considered him wealthy because he owned a horse which he used for ploughing and transportation. One day the horse escaped into the hills. The neighbours sympathised with the farmer over his bad luck.

The farmer replied, "*Bad* luck? *Good* luck? Who knows?"

A couple of days later the horse returned to the farm with a herd of wild horses following its trail. The farmer locked the horses in his stable. When the neighbours heard of it they rushed to the farm and congratulated the farmer on his good luck.

The farmer said: "*Good* luck? *Bad* luck? Who knows?"

The following day the farmer's only son mounted one of the wild horses and was thrown off, fracturing his legs. Once again the neighbours called on the farmer to express their sorrow at his bad luck.

The farmer replied, "*Bad* luck? *Good* luck? Who knows?"

The following week conscription officers arrived at the village to recruit all the able-bodied young men because of a war that had started. They, of course, had to leave the farmer's son behind. When the neighbours told the farmer how much in luck he was he replied: "*Good* luck? *Bad* luck? Who knows?"....

Every event takes on a particular meaning depending on the context in which you perceive it. By changing the context, you change the meaning. To possess two extra horses is a good thing, until it is seen in the context of the son's injury. The broken leg seems to be bad in the context of his inability to help the farmer, but in the context of conscription and war, it suddenly becomes good.

In this book you will discover the art of 'contextualising' your life. You will learn to perceive yourself and others, all of created reality and every event, in the context of God. God will become the focal point of reference for everything. Thus, all things will take on new meaning. Correspondingly, your responses and behaviour, your attitudes and actions, too, will be affected. You will become more and more God-centred.

"Who created you?"
"God created me."

The drilling you received in your catechism classes in childhood may have stuck in your mind and heart. "God created me!" When you come to think of it deeply, this is not a complete response to your origin. It is not as though, after breathing life into you at conception, God handed you over to your parents, as their responsibility. No. God continues to keep you alive. He is very much part of your growth process.

You depend on Him every single moment of your life. Day by day, moment to moment, He continues breathing new life into you, enabling you to develop your 'personality' – providing you with the talents and qualities you possess.

Why is God so interested in *ME*? The answer is simple as it is profound: because I am His child, HE LOVES ME! "God is Love." He shares with me His very Nature, He has created me in His 'image and likeness'. I may have not always felt this way, or lived up to this image, but God continues sustaining me with His love. Just as God created the world "out of chaos", bringing order into disorder, God's grace is working in me, in a variety of ways, transforming my own 'disorders' into 'order' – making my life meaningful and harmonious.

The involvement of God will last my entire life. God continues challenging me out of darkness, selfishness, slavery to unhealthy habits and unproductive attachments... into light and love and freedom. Through me, with me and in me, God is bringing about His Kingdom on earth, to the extent that I cooperate by remaining open and generous with His love.

I must realise that just as my own life is a gift of God and is continually sustained by God, so is the whole of creation. The universe and all created reality are a reflection of God's own presence and providence everywhere, at all times. "In Him we move and move and exist" (Acts 17.28). I am in God and God is in me. God is present in flesh through His Son Jesus, who is "Immanuel", a name which means 'God-is-with-us' (Mt 1.23). Christ "is everything and he is in everything" (Col 3.11). "The kingdom of God is among you" (Lk 17.12).

In the daily prayer sessions of the next four phases you will focus on the mystery of God's love. You will consider God as the Foundation of all creation. You will dwell on His innumerable gifts to you and seek ways of making a whole-hearted response.

FOUNDATIONAL PRAYER

Lord, my God, You created me out of Your great love for me. Every time I have responded to Your love, I have experienced Your life filling my heart to overflowing. May I become more and more aware of how Your Unconditional Love has been sustaining me from the beginning of my life up to this very moment.

Father, all the things You have created, You have lovingly presented to me as gifts, so that I may recognise You more easily in them, cherish them and enjoy Your goodness everywhere, at all times, and offer You praise and thanksgiving.

Teach me to use these gifts wisely so as to deepen my love for You. Let me not get carried away by their attractiveness or make them the main focus of my life. For I desire to have You, Lord, as the centre of my being. My goal in life is to be with You forever.

Enable me, with Your love and grace, to develop a heart and mind that enjoys such total freedom as to take a balanced view of all reality. Let me not be unduly preoccupied with either health or sickness, wealth or poverty, a long life or a short one. Let me live by the conviction that I am safe in Your hands.

Let me grow in the awareness that everything You created and anything that comes my way, can be for me a revelation of Your love if I am open to see You present everywhere. Let my choices always be in favour of things that lead me to You, against those which do not, so that I may experience Your Spirit in me in all its fulness shaping me into the image of Your Son. Amen. (H. L.)

PHASE ONE

WARM~UP

> One day, a professor discussing the marvels of creation, confessed to his wife how, in spirit of his being a specialist in many fields, his knowledge was yet so limited. "I tend to take a lot of things for granted. For instance,"he confided, "I am ashamed to admit that I don't even know how the electric bulb works."
>
> "That's unbelievable," exclaimed his wife. "Why, it's so simple, dear," she said, "you *press a switch*, that's all!'"

In the spiritual life, we, too, tend to take many things for granted: God's omnipresence, power, providence, prayer. Figuratively speaking, we press many 'switches' to get things done in life, little realising the 'power' at their sources which make them work! "Prayer is like the turning of an electric switch. It does not create the current; it simply provides the channel through which the electric current may flow." Max Handel

"For while love is the wiring that connects our souls with His, faith is the switch that turns on the power. Our homes are full of things that are run by electricity: lights, irons, sewing machines, toasters... Just believing that there is a power called electricity is not enough to make these things work for us. Every time that we want one of them to work, we must touch the button that releases the power in that one. Just believing a set of facts about God does not necessarily turn on the power in a single one of our prayer-objectives. In order to do that, we must believe this, we will naturally rejoice and give thanks for it. And when our belief is weak, the act of rejoicing and giving thanks will awaken our faith." Agnes Sanford

To deepen your awareness of God's presence and power, you will spend the next seven days reviewing your relationship with God and Jesus Christ, as well as assessing your life of prayer. The topics in the following units will help you examine your relationship with God and Jesus Christ, as well as your approaches to prayer and the spiritual life.

The Three Step Prayer

It is normally said in the morning. In the first step, you focus on the day ahead; in the second, on yourself, and in the third, on the mystery of life. You begin by standing still and centring yourself. The size and type of steps you take are entirely up to you.

With the ***first step***, you greet the day and everything that will be given to you. A prayer for this first step might be: "O Great God, You have given me this day as a special gift. In taking this step, I accept every-thing it will bring, whether it is part of my plan or not. Teach me to accept every gift that comes my way today. Help me to use each gift wisely, to love my brothers and sisters, and to care for my Mother the Earth."

The ***second-step*** prayer might go like this: "O Great God, You have created me as I am. In taking this step, I accept myself as I am now, as I have been in the past, and I will be in the future. I ask to be true to the way You made me."

Step three involves mystery: "O Great God, You have created me and everything around me with a sense of mystery. I now step into that mystery and put my arms around it. Help me to accept the things that I do not – and cannot – understand. May my encounter with them bring me nearer to You and closer to living a holy life."

Sr Jose Hobday, O.S.F

I have come to thee to take thy touch
before I begin my day.
Let thy eyes rest upon my eyes for awhile.
Let me take to my work the assurance
of thy comradeship, my friend.
Fill my mind with thy music
to last through the desert of noise!
Let thy Love's sunshine kiss the peaks
of my thoughts and linger
in my life's valley
where the harvest ripens.

Tagore

1/1*

Making space for God

The Father knocks at my door seeking a home for his Son.
Rent is cheap, I say.
I don't want to rent. I want to buy, says God.
I'm not sure I want to sell,
but you might come in to look around.
I think I will, says God.
I might let you have a room or two.
I like it, says God. I'll take the two. You might decide
to give me more some day. I can wait, says God.
I'd like to give you more, but it's a bit
difficult; I need some space for me.
I know, says God, but I'll wait. I like what I see.
Hm, maybe I can let you have another room.
I really don't need that much.
Thanks, says God. I'll take it. I like what I see.
I'd like to give you the whole house
but I'm not sure –
Think on it, says God. I wouldn't put you out. Your
house would be mine and my son would live in it.
You'd have more space than you'd ever had before.
I don't understand at all.
I know, says God, but I can't tell you about that.
You'll have to discover it for yourself. That can
only happen if you let him have the whole house.
A bit risky, I say.
Yes, says God, but try me.
I'm not sure – I'll let you know.
I can wait, says God. I like what I see.

Margaret Halsaka, O.S.F.

Listen! I stand at the door and knock;
if anyone hears my voice and opens
the door, I will come into his/her house.

Rev 3.20

---

* The first number stands for the 'Phase' and the second for the unit.

Suggestions

Have you used the above 'fantasy' method in prayer?

Do a fantasy exercise: Close your eyes, still the body, silence the mind. You hear a knock on the door. On opening it you find God there. What is your immediate reaction? Welcome Him in. Offer Him a seat. Start a conversation. Speak to Him about your expectations, desires, plans, fears... regarding this prayer programme you are just beginning. Listen to what he says, then respond.

If you run out of words, do not get impatient or anxious. He understands. Silently observe Him looking at you, and wait for Him to speak again.

Read meditatively **2 Cor 5.1-10**.
Pray in the words of **Ps 84**.

Ask the Lord to give you courage to offer him your entire heart! Pray that you may always feel at home with God!

To be there before you,
Lord, that's all.
To shut the eyes of my body.
To shut the eyes of my soul,
And to be still and silent,
To expose myself to you
Who are there, exposed to me.
To be there before you,
The Eternal Presence.
I am willing to feel nothing, Lord,
To see nothing, to hear nothing.
Empty of all ideas, of all images,
In the darkness. Here simply
To meet you without obstacles,
In the silence of faith,
Before you, Lord.

Michel Quoist

Visualising MY God

The parish priest, a tall man, well built and athletic, was standing at the Church entrance greeting people as they walked out from Mass. Along came a little girl, hardly two feet tall, a human cherub, if there ever was one. She looked up at the giant priest and said something he could not hear. He bent over, way down, as if he were going to touch his toes, and asked her to repeat what she said. In a piping voice she asked, "What colour are God's eyes?"

Without a moment's hesitation the priest replied, "Blue, just like yours." Tiny as she was the little girl was flattered. She blinked, smiled, and then toddled away to tell her mother.

The Lord is my shepherd. Ps 23.1

Suggestions

What are the various ways in which you have visualised God since your childhood? Have there been different 'images'. Why? What is your present 'image' of God. How does this 'image' affect, influence, your relationship with God?

Pray in the words of **Ps 23**.

Is 43.1-5 is rightly considered by many as God's "love letter"to his beloved. Read it prayerfully, absorbing the love which resounds in each phrase.

Ask for the grace to become more and more aware of your relationship with God.

God is like a mirror. The mirror never changes but everybody who looks at it sees something different. Harold Kushner

1/3 Reviewing my spiritual journey

One night I dreamed I was walking along the beach with the Lord. Across the sky flashed scenes from my life. For each scene, I noticed two sets of footprints in the sand; one belonging to me, the other belonging to the Lord. When the last scene of my life flashed before me, I looked back at the footprints in the sand. I noticed that many times along the path of my life there was only one set of footprints, and that it happened at the very lowest and saddest times in my life...

This really bothered me and I questioned the Lord about it. "Lord, you said that once I decided to follow you, you'd walk with me all the way. But during the most troublesome times in my life, there is only one set of footprints. I don't understand why when I needed you most you would leave me." The Lord replied, "My precious, precious child. I love you and I would never leave you. During your times of trial and suffering, when you see only one set of footprints, it was then that I carried you in my arms."

God says: "I picked them up and held them to my cheek." Hos 11.4

Suggestions

How often have you experienced God very close to you? Reflect on your relationship with God from as early in your childhood as your can: what others have told you about your 'prayer' before you were old enough to do your own reasoning. Note the times you felt close to God, and the times you felt you had moved away from God.

Pray in the words of **Ps 138**.
Read about God's loving invitation and care in **Is 55.1-11**.

Thank God for making you aware of his on-going presence in your life; ask for the grace to deepen your love for God.

Assessing my prayer

St Benedict was once travelling on horseback. He came across a peasant who was trudging along wearily on foot. The monk dismounted to exchange pleasantries. "You are very fortunate to have a horse," said the peasant with envy. "If I had given my life to prayer, I'm sure I would not have to journey on foot."
"Do you think you could manage as a man of prayer?"
"Why ask? Isn't it simple enough?"

"Let's strike a bargain. If you are able to complete one *Our Father* without an interruption, I will give you my horse."
"That's an easy bargain," said the astonished peasant. "So here I go."
He immediately stood still, folded his hands, closed his eyes, and began the recitation of the Lord's Prayer. *"Our Father in heaven, holy be your name, your...."*

He cut it short, raised his eye-brows and inquired of the saint, "will you give me the horse with its saddle and bridle, too?" Only too late did he realise he had lost the bet!

> **These people, says God, honour me with their words, but their heart is really far away from me.** Mt 15.8

Suggestions

How do you feel about the way you pray to God? Does prayer come easy? Is your heart in your prayer mostly? Today you must trace the evolution of your prayer life: Who taught you to pray? ... Do your prefer saying prayers you have memorised, or do you pray spontaneously? Do you feel a need to change the pattern or quality of your prayer?

Pray in the words of **Ps 139.1-12**. Feel God's nearness.

Ask for grace to be attuned to the Spirit within you that enables you to pray with deep faith and trust in God.

Relating prayer to life

I knelt to pray when day was done,
And prayed, "O, Lord, bless everyone;
I knelt to pray when day was done,
Lift from each saddened heart the pain
And let the sick be well again."
        And then I woke another day
        And carelessly went on my way.
        The whole day long I did not try
        To wipe a tear from any eye;
I did not try to share the load
I did not even go to see
The sick man just next door to me.
Yet once again when day was done,
I prayed, "O, Lord, bless everyone."
        But as I prayed, into my ear
        There came a voice that whispered clear,
        "Pause, hypocrite, before you pray;
        Whom have you tried to bless today?
        God's sweetest blessings always go
        By hands that serve him here below."
And then I hid my face and cried,
"Forgive me, God, for I have lied;
Let me but live another day,
And I will live the way I pray."   Anon

Pray on every occasion. Eph 6.18

Suggestions

Does your life flow over from your prayer? Or is there a mis-match?

Read meditatively **1 Jn 4.7-21** or **Jas 2.14-24**.

Ask for the grace to let your prayer become fruitful in service.

1/6 My need for solitude

A teacher in a hill-station school noticed that a colleague, instead of going straight home at the end of the day, used to retreat into a wooded area behind the building. One day, he followed him at a distance. He observed that when his colleague reached a little clearing in the lonely forest, he sat down on a flat rock, hand clasped together, head bowed. He understood that he was in prayer.

The teacher left, but the next day, after disclosing that he had followed his colleague, he asked: "Were you praying?"
"I was," replied the teacher.
"But why go to that lonely spot?"
"Because I feel close to God there."
"God can be found everywhere," said the concerned colleague. "Besides, isn't God the same everywhere?"

"God is," replied the teacher, "but I am not."

Be still and know that I am God.
Ps 46.10

Suggestions

Have you experienced the joys and benefits of solitude? Do you make time for it? How often? Do you find it easy to still the body and handle your distractions while at prayer?

Pray **Ps 63.1-8**.

Ask for the grace to genuinely relate to God in the intimacy of your heart.

Only in quiet waters things mirror themselves undistracted. Only in a quiet mind is adequate perception of the world. Hans Margalius

My friendship with Jesus

The world, I thought, belonged to me,
Goods, gold and people, land and sea,
Where'er I walked beneath God's sky,
In those days the word was *'I'*.

Years later, in my pathway clear,
Flashed the Vision of a fragment dear;
My former word no more sufficed,
And what I was was *'I and Christ'*.

But oh! the more I thought of Him,
His glory grew while mine grew dim,
I shrank so small, He towered so high,
And what I said was *'Christ and I'*.

Years passed. The Vision held its place
And stared me steadily in the face,
I speak now in a humbler tone,
And what I say is *'Christ alone'*. Anon

I call you friends... Jn 15.15

Suggestions

Has your attachment to, your friendship with Jesus Christ grown over the years? How does it show?

Read meditatively **Lk 5. 27-32**. Observe how Jesus visits the homes of sinners and mingles so freely with them. Sense Jesus' desire to make you his dear friend, overlooking your limitations and failures. Tell him of your desire to get more intimate with him.

Ask for the grace to become more and more aware of Jesus as your brother and friend.

PHASE TWO GOD IN CREATION

Eighteen-year-old Amanda, unusually simple-hearted and deeply religious, decided, in one of her pious moods, to write a letter to God. Taking her best stationery she wrote, *"I LOVE YOU"* and addressed the envelope to "Mr A. God" (*A* for Almighty), Bliss Project, Paradise." She did not put a return address, in case the letter was returned and people would think her crazy. But she waited for an answer nevertheless.

Days, weeks, a whole month passed, but no letter came. She consulted an old priest who was amused at her novel way of approaching God, and told her, "Don't worry, Mandy. God's answer will come in due time. But you'll have to be patient. He's a shy lover, you know."

Amanda decided to wait for her lover's answer, even if it would take years. But despite her resolution she often felt hurt by God's silence. One day, while sitting near a brook, she thought she heard a voice nearby. Looking around, she saw nobody. She bent over the brook and listened deeply. Then she heard the water say very distinctly, "I love you, too!" God was answering her letter!

After this incident Amanda trained her ear to listen to Nature, and heard the words "I love you, too" in the sigh of the breeze, the whisper of the tree, the rustle of the dry leaves, the twittering of the birds. She even found the sky proclaiming the message in clouds which formed the letters: I love you, too.

In disbelief she murmured, "Gosh, Lord, for a shy lover you certainly know how to express yourself."

(Nil Guillemette, S.J., *The Shy Lover* – condensed)

> The Creator has put man in creation, charging him to administer it for the sake of the good of all, thanks to his intelligence and his reason. We can be certain that even a person's tiny good actions have a mysterious effect of social change and contribute to the growth of all. On the basis of the covenant with the Creator, towards whom man is called over and over to return, each one is invited to a deep personal conversion in his or her relationship with others and with nature.
>
> Pope John Paul II

In this unit you will spend your prayer-periods, as well as the time outside prayer, marvelling at God's Creation, bathing in the warm sunshine of his love, recalling with gratitude His many gifts, and our responsibility toward them. You will delve into the mystery of God's love for you – because you are special, unique. Your response to God's love will be "praise, reverence, and service". Praise will flow out of you intimate experiences of God in created reality. Reverence will be reflected in your attitudes towards God-self-others. Service will be expressed in good deeds.

Dear Lord, your presence fills me with joy.
It is my earnest desire to direct all my efforts – physical and mental – during this time of prayer solely to your greater glory.
Father, I want you to be the centre of my being.
Deepen this desire so that I may be
fully united with you, my Creator and Master,
at all times and in all places.
I want to praise you and bring you honour
all the days of my life.
Increase my spirit of generosity.
Make me large-hearted enough
to freely offer you all that I am and have,
so that you may use me in whichever way you please,
and enable me to do your holy will in all things
in a spirit of loving service. (H. L.)

2/1 Perceiving God's reflection

At the peak of a popular hill-resort is a large hotel. About half-way up the slopes, there is a clearing that offers a breath-taking view of the winding road, the plains with its forests, shining rivers and lakes, and the range of hills in the distance. It is an attractive stop-over spot for vacationers. The Hotel owners who had cleared the area for the view, put a large sign-post:

SIGHT-SEEING POINT

ENJOY NATURE'S WONDERS

Courtesy of Hilltop Hotel

One visitor, who was clearly upset by the presumptuous statement, added this comment below the last line, in dark charcoal letters:

"And a little help from God."

Lord, you have made many things!
How wisely you have made them all!
Ps 104.24

Suggestions

How often have you felt close to God through Nature? Recall those experiences?

Everyone, at some time or other, has experienced the wonder of creation: a breathtaking sunrise/sunset, a star-filled sky, gorgeous flowers... *Recall* such experiences, one by one, slowly, without haste. *Relish* the memories, that is, so not merely think about them but let your emotions come to play as you visualise the scene.

Pray **Ps 104**. Or read meditatively **Job 37**.

Ask God to help you maintain your sense of wonder at the beauty you see around – in nature, in people.... Praise God for the wonders of creation.

Acknowledging God's gifts

Pundit Bholabhai was on a vacation in the countryside. He rented a bungalow near a Bird Sanctuary. A variety of birds sang merrily outside his window all day long. Bholabhai was so thrilled that every time he stepped out of the house he thanked the birds loudly for their enchanting melodies. One day the landlord followed him out and protested:
"You don't suppose those birds are singing for you?"
"Why, of course I do," the Pundit asserted.
"Well, you are sadly mistaken; the birds are singing for me!"

They got into such a serious argument that they decided to settle it in court. The judge heard the case carefully, then, to their utter amazement, asked each of them to pay a penalty.
"Why?" queried Bholabhai.
"Because," declared the judge solemnly, "because you are both mistaken. Those birds have always been singing only for me!"

As long as I live I will sing praises to my God. Ps 104.33

Suggestions

Creation is God's special gift to me. Do you feel God would have created the universe even if you happened to be the only human being on earth? If you believe so, what are the implications for your life?

Pray in the words of **Ps 19** or **Is 40.25-31**.

Ask God to grant you an understanding of how the whole of Creation is His gift to you. Respond with praise and thanks.

2/3 Recognising God's presence

One Sunday a group of bullies parked themselves at the entrance of a church and kept teasing the little ones as they trickled out after Catechism class. They stopped a smart-looking boy.
"What did you learn in class today," one of the bullies asked. "Oh, things," he lad replied swiftly, " lot of things."
"Like what?" pressed the older fellow.
"About God?" said the boy smartly.
"God, ah. Okay," said the bully pulling out a 25 paisa coin from his pocket. "I'll give you this if you can tell me *where* God can be found."
The bright lad stared at the shiny bit of silver, thought for a moment, then suddenly pulled out a round rupee from his shirt pocket, and pointing it to his challenger said, "And I'll give you this if you can tell me where God *cannot* be found."
There was stunned silence for a moment. So, grabbing the quarter from the bully's frozen palm, the little fellow hopped away cheerfully.

O Lord, our Lord, your greatness
is seen in all the world. Ps 8.1

Suggestions

Are you convinced that, like the atmosphere that covers the earth, God's presence pervades the universe?

Meditate on **Ps 139.7-12**.

Praise God for his loving presence; ask for the grace to continue responding in love and service.

I have sought Your nearness;
with all my heart have I called You,
And going out to meet You
I found You coming toward me.
Yehuda Halevit

God's special creation: ME

There was a gala banquet held to honour the renowned poet Carl Sandburg on his 75th birthday. Several celebrities waxed eloquent on the merits of the poet.

A well-known photographer is reported to have remarked: "On the day God made Carl, he didn't do anything else that day but just sit around and feel good."

You are precious in my eyes.
Is 43.4

Suggestions

How often have you reflected on the fact that you are 'precious' to God? Isn't it God who gives you the gift of life, and the freedom to choose good?

Meditate on **Ps 139.13-18**.

Next, complete this statement:
On the day I was born, God felt so .... that he ....

How do you feel towards God today?

Praise and thank God for gifting you with his life, and presenting you as a gift to the world. Ask for greater openness to his unconditional love for you.

Whenever God creates a person He whispers to the infant: "You are my favourite, I have never made such a beautiful person before. I'm not going to make another so beautiful again. You are simply unique!"
Arabian proverb

2/5 My uniqueness and growth

An art student once asked a friend if he could paint the friend's portrait for a class assignment. The friend agreed, and the art student painted and submitted the portrait, only to receive a low grade.

The art student approached the professor to ask why the grade was so poor. The teacher told him that the proportions in the painting were incorrect. "The head is too big." the professor explained. "The shoulders are too wide, and the feet are enormous."

The next day, the art student brought his friend to see the professor. He took one look at his friend, and realised how accurate the portrait was to the reality!

"Okay, Excellent," he said. I will up-grade your work.

You are my Lord, all the good things I have come from you. Ps 16.2

Suggestions

Are you aware that God has created you as a unique being?

God is compared to a Potter in the work of creation. Read meditatively **Jer 18.1-6**. In what ways do you reflect the image, the love, the creativity of God?

Ask for the grace to make yourself as soft as clay so as to allow God to mould you into the image of his Son.

If then you are the work of God, offer him your heart, soft and tractable, and keep the form in which the artist has fashioned you. Let your clay be moist, lest you grow hard and loses the imprint of his fingers. St Iraneus

Sharing earth's resources

Two families asked the village's rabbi to settle a dispute about the boundaries of their land. The rabbi listened to the members of one family recount how they inherited the land from their ancestors and how it had been in the family for many generations; they produced maps and papers to prove their claim.

Then the rabbi listened to the other family describe how they had lived on the land for many years, working it and harvesting it. They claimed that they knew the land intimately; they had no papers to prove their claim, only their calloused hands and sore backs and the harvest they reaped from the land. After presenting their cases, the families said, "Decide, rabbi, who owns this land."

The rabbi said nothing. He knelt down on the land and put his ear to the ground. He listened for some time. He then stood up and said to the families, "I have listened to both of you, but I had to listen to the land, the centre of the dispute, and the land has spoken. It has told me this: 'Neither of you owns the land you stand on. It is the *land* that owns *you*.'"

> **Your land must not be sold on a permanent basis, because you do not own it: it belongs to God.** Lev 25.23

Suggestions

Do you believe that natural resources are meant to be shared for the mutual betterment of our earth and its peoples?

Read meditatively **Ps 8**.

Ask for the grace to realise your responsibility towards God's creation and to ensure that you behave in accordance with it.

Revering creation

A traveller was on the roads under the hot sun.
He begged for shade.
The tree gave it and then the traveller felt like staying with the tree and to build his home near it.
He needed wood for his home. His eyes fell on the tree.
He looked for an axe to cut the tree.
Then he begged for a handle for his axe from the tree and the tree gave it.
After he made the axe, he cut the tree and built his house. But when the house was built, the traveller cried and felt lonely and hot.
Then he left that place in search of shade. Anon

God looked at everything he had made,
and he was very pleased. Gen 1.31

Suggestions

Do you feel indebted to and responsible for Nature's bounty? Are you concerned about the universal exploitation and destruction of Nature for selfish human gains?

Read meditatively **Rom 1.19-21**.

Ask for the grace to co-operate in re-creating creation and reconciling it with God again, so that he might rejoice in it.

As humans we are called to reverence and respect that uniqueness (of each entity in the universe). All that exists does so within the sacred web of life, within the earth's community. As humans we are called to live responsibly and creatively within the communion.

John Surette, S.J.

GOD'S GRATITUDE

I heard God say one word today.
I thought He was playing pranks.
I scratched my head, 'cause the word He said,
Was "Thanks, my little one, thanks."

"Thanks for what?" I mused and mused
And urged Him to explain.
"Thanks for all you are to me
In sunshine and in rain.

Thanks for accepting my limitless love
Thanks for trusting in me.
Thanks for accepting my infinite care
When it's difficult to see.

Thanks for giving your burdens to me,
Mistakes and all the rest.
Thanks for overlooking the past
And believing that I know best.

Thanks for noting my gifts to you.
Thanks for resting awhile.
Thanks for turning now and then
To give your companions a smile.

And while I'm at it, thanks so much
For leaving the future to me..."

Sr Joan Metzner, M.M.

PHASE THREE

EXPERIENCING GOD

A salt doll journeyed for thousands of miles and stopped on the edge of the sea. It was fascinated by this moving liquid mass, so unlike anything it had seen before.

"What are you?" said the salt doll to the sea.
"Come in and see," said the sea with a smile.

So the doll waded in. The further it went the more it dissolved till there was only a pinch of it left. Before that last bit dissolved, the doll exclaimed in wonder, "Now I know what I am!"

To experience God....well, you must just "let go, and let God". For, as you have reflected in the past week, God surrounds you, fills you.... His love penetrates every fibre of your being. But it is your 'self' that comes in the way of experiencing God fully.

However genuine your desires to remain in contact with God, and however sincere your efforts, you may find yourself failing to keep God in focus all the time. You must realise that your quest for God is, in a sense, an 'ideal' you are striving at. Different people experience God at different levels, at different stages of their life. There is no need to feel ashamed, discouraged or frustrated if, according to you, you are still far from this 'ideal'.

It is a life-long process. It is important that you do not give up the desire of being more open to God's presence, of experiencing His love. Of course, the fact that you are going through this programme is evidence of the deliberate choice you have made to experience God at a deeper level.

When I don't feel as close to God,
As I did in childhood, I admit
It is I who have done the moving
God hasn't moved a bit. E.J. Toner, S.J.

The “experience” of God is a 24-hour affair! It is not restricted only to times of formal prayer. It demands constant awareness of His presence all through the day and night.

> “My deepest moments of intimacy with the Lord have always been in the struggle to remain available to him, faithful in moments of darkness, defeat, frustration, weariness, in the big and small rebellions of every day when I have tried to impose my wisdom and my ways. I continue to find him more intimately when he proves stronger in the daily demands for availability and service than in times of formal prayer which are often ‘empty’ and dry, lived in faith and the natural feeling of wasting time. Ignatius’ note in the ‘Exercises’ which can appear cold and negative has become positive for me and an experience of ‘devotion’: “For everyone ought to reflect that in all spiritual matters, the more one divests oneself of self-love, self-will and self-interests, the more progress one will make.” The Lord’s companion, Peter, discovered this, and with him I too can only say, “To whom should I go? You have the words of eternal life, and I believe. I know that you are the Holy One of God.” Cecil McGarry, S.J.

The reflections of this unit are intended to help you reflect on the extent and depth of your awareness of God’s Presence in your life. You will examine the demands of faith, the need for silence and simplicity. You will come to realise that instead of you ‘seeking’ God – as if He were some place else, he is always available near you, if you are open-minded, open-hearted to His presence. He will reveal to you His will.

Remember, though, it is not proper of you to want to *feel* God’s presence – because a *sensible* awareness of God’s presence is a gift. You cannot force it; you can only keep an open heart to receive it when God chooses to offer it to you.

Ask God to sharpen your eyes of faith so that you may see him with your heart at every moment of the day, and experience his loving presence and be obedient to his will.

In faith

A Seeker set out early one morn in quest of God. She came upon a high tower which seemed to kiss the sky. A Voice beckoned her to enter. She opened the creaking door and peered into the darkness. A tiny glow from far above revealed a spiral stairway. Determined and daring, and trusting in the Lord, she began the ascent. Step upon step she climbed higher and higher.

The tower seemed endless. Doubt and anxiety slackened her pace. Hope gave in to fear in her heart. Shouldn't she go back down? She stopped, ready for the descent. As she let her foot down she got the shock of her life. She could feel no supporting step below. She then realised that with every step she had taken up, the step below had fallen away leaving a void. She gazed up once again. The glow still beckoned, and the stairway seemed endless...

Fear not, I will help you. Is 41.13

Suggestions

Do you have a 'vision' in your quest for God? Do your realise that uncertainties, anxieties, obstacles... often accompany the search? Do you tend to give up – or to carry on with full faith in God?

Read about the strong assurances of God in **Is 41.1-20**

Ask for the grace never to lose heart in your quest to know God more deeply, intimately.

I can take my telescope and look millions of miles into space. But I can also lay it aside and go to my room, shut the door, get down on my knees and see more of heaven, and get closer to God than I can assisted by all the telescopes and all the material things on earth.

Isaac Newton

Pundit Bholabhai thought his wife Anita was losing her hearing, so one day he decided to test it. He walked in quietly through the front door and stood there hidden from her view. She was seated on a sofa busy with her knitting. "Anita," he said, "can you hear me?" There was no response, so he moved to six metres behind her. "Anita," he repeated, "can you hear me?" Still no reply. He advanced three metres and asked, "Now can you hear me?"
"Yes, dear," Anita replied gently. "For the third time, yes!"

I pray to you, O God, because you answer me, so turn to me and listen to my words. Ps 17.6

Suggestions

How attuned are you to God's 'whispers? 'Read about how God contacts the prophet Elijah in quietude: **1Kgs 19.10-12**. Reflect on your experience of prayer. You must realise that silence and stillness help you get in touch with God more easily than noise and restlessness.

Read about how the Lord appears and speaks to Samuel in **1 Sam 3.1-10**. Then **hear God speak your name**. By what name does he call you? (Full name, or first name, nickname, or some term of endearment?). What is the tone of his voice as he pronounces your name? (Pleasant, gentle, urgent, pleasing...?) Listen in silence, absorbing his love. Then repeat the words of Samuel: *"Speak, Lord, your servant is listening."*

Ask for the grace to be attentive to the Lord at all times as he speaks to you — in your heart, or through people, events....

Silence enlarges the heart until it is capable of containing God gift of himself.

In simplicity

St Teresa of the Child Jesus, popularly known as "The Little Flower" joined the convent when she was 15 years old. Some nuns thought it was wrong to admit "a mere child" Outwardly her life was ordinary, for she worked in the laundry, the sacristy, the dining-room, and as assistant novice mistress, but her inner life was one of spiritual beauty. She followed a path which she called "he little way of spiritual childhood, the way of trust and complete self-surrender," a way that led to the heights by the loving performance of the small duties of everyday life, and the silent, heroic bearing of annoyances and hardships.

Teresa wrote in her *Autobiography*: "I want to seek a way to heaven, a new way, very short, very straight, a little path. I would like to find a lift to raise me to Jesus, for I am too little to climb the steep steps of perfection." She did climb these steps rapidly, but by the steady and exact observance of the Rule, weaving the tapestry of her life thread by thread out of deeds too small for notice.

When you pray, do not use a lot of meaningless words. Mt 6.7

Suggestions

What are the 'simple ways' by which you get in touch with God during the day?

Read Jesus' teaching about simplicity in prayer: **Mt 6.5-13**. How simple and genuine is your prayer generally? Spend some time evaluating it.

Ask the Lord to help you understand the need for 'simplicity' your dealings with him.

In prayer, reason little, love much.

In the heart

At the time of Creation, God called upon his archangels and asked them to help him decide where to put the Secret of Life. One suggested to bury it in the ground; another, to put it on the bottom of the sea; and still another, to hide it in the mountains.

God said, "These places are beyond the reach of most people. The Secret of Life must be accessible to EVERYONE."

One archangel suggested: "Put it in each man's heart."

God took the suggestion. And there lies the Secret of Life to this day. But how many actually find it there?

The kingdom of God is within you.
Lk 17.21

Suggestions

Are you convinced that your heart contains the "secret of life"? What is that 'secret'?
God has created you in his own "image" (Gen 1.27), and breathed his "life-giving breath" (Gen 2.7) into you.

Read reflectively **Gen 1.26-31**.

Ask for the grace to grow in the awareness of God presence in your heart, in your whole being.

How gently and lovingly
You wake in my heart,
Where in secret you dwell alone;
And by your sweet breathing,
Filled with good and glory,
How tenderly you swell my heart
with love St John of the Cross

In expansiveness

A woodcutter found it difficult to make ends meet. He often went to bed hungry, and could not afford oil for his lamp. However, when an itinerant sage once asked for shelter, the man took him in and offered hospitality according to his means. While leaving, the wise man looked into the eyes of the woodcutter and said, as if letting him onto a secret: "Go farther."
The woodcutter wondered what that could mean. Should he go 'farther' into the forest? He decided to take the risk, and to his surprise, he came upon a dense grove of Sandalwood trees. He chopped them and sold them at the market at a good price. Soon he had enough to eat, and barrels of oil for his lamp. He was happy with his new-found wealth, and settled down comfortably.
Months later, the Sage's word struck him again: Go farther. Had he gone far enough? No, he must explore the territory beyond the grove. When he did so, he was in for another surprise. He found a copper mine. He soon bought the land, organised help, and started excavating. Eventually he became very rich, built a huge mansion, got married, and had several happy children. When he was again beginning to settle down, the Sage's words hit him like a magic wand. He decided he must go farther... You guessed right: this time he found a gold mine!

O God... my whole being desires you.
Ps 63.1,5

Suggestions

Do you realise that the search for the mysteries of God is a never-ending process? How 'adventurous' are you?

Pray again **Ps 63**.

Ask God to give you the grace of perseverance, so that you will never cease yearning for him.

I don't know how to say it, but somehow it seems to me
That maybe we are stationed, where God wants us to be;
The little place I'm filling is the reason for my birth,
And just to do the work I do, he sent me down on earth.
If God had wanted otherwise, I reckon he'd have made
Me just a little different, of a worse or better grade;
Since God understands all things of land and sea,
I fancy that he placed me here, just where he wanted me.

Sometimes, I get to thinking, as my labours I review,
That I'd like a higher place with greater things to do;
But I come to the conclusion, when the envying is stilled,
That the post God sent me, is the post he wanted filled.
So I plod along in the hope, when day is through
That I'm really necessary to the things God wants to do;
And there isn't any service which I should scorn,
For it may be just the reason God allowed that I be born.

Anon

God is always at work in you to make you willing and able to obey his own purpose. Phil 2.13

Suggestions

Are you fully open to the will of God for you? Have you accepted it? Does it bring meaning to your daily life? Or do you avoid it or compromise with your own conveniences?

Pray meditatively **Ps 40**.
Review the past level. Which day's prayer did you find most satisfying and inspiring? Go over it once again. If you have time, take up some of the other points that brought you great joy in prayer.

Ask for the grace and strength to be obedient to the will of God under all circumstances.

One of the worst fires in the history of California destroyed over 600 houses in June 1990. Pico Iyer, a journalist, barely had time to escape – with only a nearly completed book manuscript. When he returned to the site of the tragedy the following day, all that was left of his home was "a mass of ashes". He then made this insightful observation:

"As smoke hissed out of the charred rubble, I knew, I really knew, that what was precious to me was irreplaceable.... The insurance would cover everything but what I had really lost... Reduced to bare essentials, the clothes on my back and a pad of paper, I gained a quickened sense of what to be thankful for, not least my life itself, and the providence that watched over me. I now know exactly what I value most, because I have lost everything else."

Ever since God created the world, his invisible qualities... are perceived in the things that God has made. Rom 1.20

Suggestions

Are you open-minded in your quest for God, so as to find God in the most unexpected places, circumstances, events?

Read meditatively **Rom 11.33-38**.

Ask for the grace to increase your sense of wonder and to recognise God wherever and whenever he reveals himself.

God's greatest gifts fall into empty hearts.
St John of the Cross

An Integrated Personality

O sweet Mother Mary,
give me a heart that is fresh and open
as the heart of a child, and
as transparent as the waters of a clear spring.
Give me a generous heart
that does not brood over the unpleasant things
it has encountered.
A magnanimous heart that gladly gives itself.
A heart that knowing its own weakness,
understands and becomes more deeply sympathetic
towards the weaknesses of others.
A deep and grateful heart
that does not overlook small things.

Give me a heart that is gentle and humble
and loves without expecting love in return;
that gladly leaves another's heart
to give way to your Son.
A noble and buoyant heart that will not
become embittered by disappointments;
that because of its faults
will not become ungenerous in its sacrifices;
that will not be paralysed by trials;
that will not be irritated by neglect;
and that will not be discouraged by indifference.

But give me a heart that in its love of Jesus
will be drawn by an irresistible current
towards the further honour and glory of Jesus Christ,
and will find no rest until I enter into Heaven. Anon

PHASE FOUR

THE UNDIVIDED HEART

A young man displayed his heart, one day. It was a sight to behold – without a single flaw. "The most beautiful heart in town", he proclaimed, and attracted the crowds to admire it. Then an aged man joined the big group. "Why, my heart is beautiful, too," he said quietly. All eyes turned to see his heart. It was beating strongly, but had innumerable scars, patches, deep gouges and several jagged edges. The people stared. How can he claim to have a 'beautiful' heart, they wondered.

The young man remarked: "You must be joking. My heart is perfect and yours is a mess of scars and patches."

"Well," said the old fellow, "The heart's worth is measured by Love. In giving love, you tear out a piece of your heart; that leaves a gouge – which is patched up when you receive love. If you give more than you receive, then gouges remain, and can be painful – but that is the risk you take....

Inspired by the true symbol of the heart, the young man, ripped off a piece of his heart and offered it with trembling hand to the old wise man; then he patched the gouge with the large piece the old man gave him. They embraced each other. As the crowd watched in awe. Then each one in the crowd began to examine his or her heart.

* * *

The above story is interesting. It speaks of the 'wear and tear' involved in the transactions of the heart, and the risks involved. It explains the 'divided heart theory'.

The Theory

The 'divided heart theory' goes like this. Many of us tend to create clear-cut compartments in our 'heart': we reserve a large chunk of our heart, so to speak. (Some give only a corner of their heart to God!). The rest we use for our relationships to people or our 'love' towards things.

According to this theory, a person who has given space to God may be compared to someone who has rented out a room or two (see 1/1) to God in one's house. That is, a person who gives space in his/her life for spiritual activities: prayer, devotions, Eucharist, acts of mercy, charity, etc. Then uses the rest of the time for his/her involvement in life – of which he/she believes God is not a part of.

God is seeking occupation of the 'whole house', though – of an undivided heart. This is possible only if one does not compartmentalise one's life into "sacred" and "secular". Everything in life is "sacred" when God is present in it. Everything must be placed in a 'divine context'. Thus, we must surrender our whole heart to God and make our life God-centred.

> "Everything you love for its own sake, outside of God alone, blinds your intellect and ruins your judgement of moral values, and vitiates your choices, so that you cannot clearly distinguish good from evil and you do not truly know God's will, And when you love and desire things for their own sakes, even though you may understand general moral principles, you do not know how to apply them. Even when your application of principles is formally correct, there will probably be a hidden circumstance you have overlooked, which will spoil your most virtuous actions with some imperfection." Thomas Merton

The Practice

> **I was going to Darjeeling to make my retreat. It was in that train that I heard the call to give up all and follow him to the slums and serve him amongst the poorest of the poor. It was an order.**
>
> Mother Teresa

All that you are and have – are "gifts" of God intended for the service of others. These include your body, your character, your talents, qualities, abilities, your money, work, responsibilities..., and people.

All these things are neither good nor bad in themselves; it is the way you relate to them which give life to or restrains you from fulfilling your human vocation. You can only reach God – your goal – through created reality. God has created you free – so you may make the right choices to achieve my goal.

> **Our one desire and choice should be what is more conducive to the end for which we are created.**
>
> St Ignatius Loyola

In this unit you will examine your heart. Have you given it completely over to God? Or have you given Him only a little room? Are there persons, possessions, or perceptions (toward sickness, death, honours,....) preventing God from gaining full control over you?

Ask for the grace to live a life of freedom and to have healthy ambitions and attitudes in life, so that you can offer your whole heart to God.

Attachments

An itinerant *sannyasi* (holy man) found a diamond which he placed in his little bag. One morning, as he was resting under a tree in the outskirts of a village, a man came rushing up to him and said he had dreamed that the sannyasi possessed a precious stone; and if that were true, would he give it to him. Without a moment's hesitation, the *sannyasi* pulled out the diamond from his bag and handed it over to the man. The villager couldn't believe his eyes. Being a jeweller, he immediately recognised the value of the precious stone. He thanked the holy man for his generosity and left.

Strangely, instead of rejoicing over his good fortune, the jeweller – a God-fearing man – was troubled. He was restless through the night, and as soon as it was light, he rushed to the boundaries of the village. But the holy man was nowhere around. Upon enquiries, he followed the path the sannyasi had taken and managed to track him down. Falling at his feet, he pleaded, "Take away this diamond.... Give me, instead, that valuable spirit of detachment which enabled you to give away the precious stone."

Your heart will always be
where your riches are. Lk 12.34

Suggestions

How do you relate to things God has entrusted to you? Do you act as if they had nothing to do with God, or do you treat them as gifts received? Are there things so are so attached to that they take away from your complete heart-surrender to God?

Read meditatively **Gen 22.1-19** on how Abraham was willing to sacrifice the most precious possession God himself had given him.

Ask God to give you the power to let go of your attachments, and to use things only in so far as they lead you to God.

Possessiveness

Leo Buscaglia, the popular American 'love doctor' once told an interesting experience of what he called the family 'misery dinner'. One evening Leo's father returned home from work, gathered the family together and informed them that his partner had absconded with everything and that he was heading for bankruptcy. Everyone felt shocked and sad at the tragedy.

The next day when his father came home, again despondent, and the whole family came home really wondering what they would eat, they had the most incredible dinner. It was like a Christmas dinner. Leo's mother had sold some jewellery to prepare the meal. Leo's father was clearly upset. he demanded to know whether his wife had gone crazy. To which Leo's mother replied: "The time for joy is now, when we need it, not next week."

With that, the family began to pull together. Leo, though still very young, offered to sell magazines. His sister decided to work overtime. The mood changed completely, from sadness to a determination to succeed, thanks to the wisdom of Mrs Buscaglia.

Let hope keep you joyful, be patient in your troubles. Rom 12.12

Suggestions

What is your attitude toward wealth, toward your possessions? Do you realise that money cannot buy happiness? Do you make decisions involving money in the 'context' of God?

Read meditatively **Lk 18.18-25**: the Rich Young Man.

Ask the Lord to fill you with wisdom so that you show a holy indifferce to both possessions poverty.

Ambitions

In the opening scene of Robert Bolt's *A Man For All Seasons*, Richard Rich, a bright but desperately ambitious young man, petitions Thomas More, the king's humble and saintly chancellor, for a position among the glitterati at the court of Henry VIII. More tells Rich that he can offer him a position, not as a courtier, but as a simple teacher.

The young man is crestfallen, and More tries to cheer him up, "You'd be a fine teacher. Perhaps a great one." Rich fires back, "And if I was, who would know it?"

The ever patient More responds: "You, your pupils, your friends, God. Not a bad public, that."

> **Everyone who makes himself great will be humbled, and everyone who humbles himself will be made great.** Lk 14.11

Suggestions

How sensitive are you about receiving recognition for your work, or how preoccupied about your status or 'honours' are you? You may not aspire to great honours or spectacular awards, but it may be the nagging need to be 'made to feel great' in small, public demonstrations, or undue recognition for your painstaking or creative contributions.

Read meditatively **Lk 9.46-48**.

Ask for the grace to be able to put your life and occupations into perspective and seek only the greater glory of God.

> **Hallowed be Thy name, *not mine*, Thy Kingdom come, *not mine*, Thy will be done, *not mine*.** Dag Hammarskjold

Desires

A lady saw three old men sitting forlornly in her front yard. She said, "Please come in and have something to eat." "We do not go into a house together," they replied. "His name is Wealth," one explained, pointing out, "his Success and mine Love. Please discuss with your husband which one of us you want in your home."

"Let us invite Wealth, said her husband, "he will fill our home with riches!"

"Well, I think it would be better to invite Success," said his wife.

Their daughter-in-law, who was listening, jumped in with her own suggestion: "Why not Love? Our home will then be filled with Love!"

After some debate the all agreed to invite Love as their guest. The lady approached the three strangers and said, "We want Love to be our guest." Love immediately got up and started walking toward the house. The other two also stood up and followed him. Surprised, the lady asked them, "I only invited Love; are you coming in, too?"

They replied: "Yes. If you had invited either of us – Wealth or Success -- Love would have gone alone. But wherever Love is invited, we accompany him!"

It is love, then, that you should strive for. 1Cor 14.1

Suggestions

Are your desires in accordance with the will of God for you? Do your choices indicate your attitude of God-centeredness?

Read meditatively **Rom 8.5-9**.

Ask for the grace to purify your desires so that you may seek God in all things.

A good relationship has a pattern like a dance and is built on some of the same rules. Partners do not need to hold on tightly, because they move confidently in the same pattern, intricate but gay and swift and free, like a country dance of Mozart's. To touch heavily would be to arrest the pattern and freeze the movement, to check the endlessly changing beauty of its unfolding.

There is no place here for the possessive clutch, the clinging arm, the heavy hand; only the barest touch in passing. Now arm in arm, now face to face, now back to back – it does not matter which. Because they know they are partners moving to the same rhythm, creating a pattern together, and being invisible nourished by it. Anne Morrow Lindbergh

I become all things to all men.
1Cor 9.22

Suggestions

How are your relationships with people? Are you too attached to anyone? Do you respect everyone's freedom? Are you prepared to give up a relationship that is proving to be an obstacle to giving your whole heart to God?

Evaluate your relations in the light of St Paul's practical definition of Love: **1 Cor 13.1-7**.

Ask for the grace to love everyone as you love yourself and God.

Love is more easily demonstrated than defined.

In *A Voice Over The Water*, the author, Fr William Breault tells of a newly ordained priest's visit to a paralysed 11-year-old blind girl, Judy, in a hospital. Judy's mother told him she had worked out a simple method of communication. Judy could move only an eyelid and the little finger of her right hand. So the mother would speak into Judy's ears, and ask questions; Judy would move her eyelid to signify 'yes', and her little finger to signify 'no'. The priest put his face close to the girl's ear. "Judy, can you hear me?" There was a slight movement of the girl's eyelid. "Yes."
Slowly, the priest told Judy the story of Jesus' life, putting into it a lot of colour and action – of how Jesus loved everyone with all his heart. "Do you understand, Judy?" Again the flutter of the eyelid. "Yes." The priest continued to tell Judy stories, day after day, as she grew more feeble. One day he asked her, "You hurt a lot inside, don't you, Judy?" The answer, "Yes."
"Do you know that the Lord loved children in a special way?" The eyelid moved. "Do you know that he loves you in a very special way?" There was a pause, and then the eyelid moved again. Yes, she knew that! Surrounded by darkness, rooted in pain, unable to move, Judy knew that Jesus Christ loved her!

All I want us to know Christ and...
to share in his sufferings. Phil 3.10

Suggestions

What is your attitude toward suffering, sickness, pain? Do you show an acceptance of God's will for you?

Read meditatively **Rom 2.18-25**.

Ask for the grace to understand health and sickness, so so as to accept either for God's greater glory.

In his column *"Parables for Today"*, in *The New Leader*, Fr Joe Mannath, SDB, cited a gripping story taken from the Tamil daily *Malaimurasu* (Oct 10, 1998). Sixteen-year-old Rajalakshmi, a standard XI student in Tiruvannamalai, was riding a bicycle with a lunch-box for her father, a daily labourer, when she was knocked down by a lorry. Both her legs were crushed. She was rushed to the Government hospital.
Just before she succumbed to her injuries, though she was writhing in agony, Rajalakshmi made three requests. One, that her parents stop quarrelling and live in harmony. Two, that her eyes be donated to her cousin Bhuvana. And three, that the Collector, Ms Kannagi, who had helped her with text-books, be called so that she could express her gratitude. She died before the Collector arrived.

On the threshold of death, Rajalakshmi's thoughts were not on herself. There was no remorse or regret, no bitterness or complaint. Her last breaths and final heartbeats were for others.

Death, where is your victory? Death, where is your sting? 1Cor 15.55

Suggestions

Do you reflect on 'death' sometimes? Your own? Do you pray for a 'long life' or a 'fruitful life'? Are you prepared to leave life and death in the hands of God?

Read the moving story of the three young men who were condemned to be burned alive for their faith: **Daniel chapter 3**.

Ask God for the grace to deepen you understanding of the mysteries of life and death, and to give you a balanced attitude toward both.

SECTION TWO

GOD'S FORE-GIVING LOVE

GOD'S FORE-GIVING LOVE

> In his book *He Touched Me*, Fr John Powell, tells the story of a sinful woman who believed her life was a failure and decided to end it by drowning in the sea. She walked along a deserted beach, sobbing her goodbyes to the world. Suddenly, she heard an inner voice that told her to look back. When she did, she observed how the waves were washing away her footprints. That brought her the realisation that God's love and mercy were wiping out all her past failings. The voice seemed to urge her not to die. She turned back and began a new life.

God loved and loves you even though you are a sinner. This is important to understand: Otherwise you may conceive God as bad, demanding, dreadful... and you will fear him, develop guilt feelings, even resent him. You are a sinner who is loved by God! God's love makes life worth living. It challenges you to live life on a higher plane by responding to that love.

God's love is unconditional: it has no "ifs" in it. God does not make any demands – that we should give up our evil ways, stop sinning... in order to receive his love. In fact, Jesus himself pointed out that his Father "makes his sun to shine on bad and good people alike, and gives rain to those who do good and to those who do evil" (Mt 5.45). God's love is "fore-given" – even before we can turn our hearts to him and ask for his love and mercy, it is already present.

> "God has shown us how much he loves us – it was while we were still sinners that Christ died for us. By his death we are now put right with God." Rom 5.8-9

> Precisely because this Father is love He will everlastingly bestow the gifts that sustain us in being whether we use them rightly or wrongly. The sun will rise on us whether we use the day for good or ill; the rain will come to our parched souls whether we love or hate. We with our actions cannot make this relentless love less warm or tender; we may turn away, but God's love, like the sun and rain, will not. Francis Baur, O.F.M

The unfortunate fact is that most of us are slow in availing ourselves of this love and grace. We succumb to the gravitational pull of the earth and do not allow our spirits to soar. Like a mega-magnet, the "world" attracts us to its values which often go contrary to the values of God. "There are many whose lives make them enemies of Christ's death on the cross. They are going to end up in hell, because their god is their bodily pleasures. They are proud of what they should be ashamed of, and they think only of things that belong to the world" (Phil 3.18-19).

Quality of life

You must come to grips with the essence of sinfulness. It is something *personal*: it is the snapping of your relationship with God, with your 'neighbour' and even with your true self. You must not be preoccupied only with your "sins of commission" – the 'quantity of evil you do: for example, "I told lies twelve times since my last confession"; but you must also consider the 'quality' of your life, your attitudes and values: "I still hold a grudge against...", "I didn't stand up for my co-worker in a case of injustice...", "I failed to fulfil my personal responsibilities as a Christian." Some of these are termed "sins of omission".

The vital question you must ask is: Am I going to reinforce the effects of sin in myself, in my neighbourhood, in the world at large, or am I going to do whatever I can to create, with God's grace, a world of peace and love? Am I going to make myself and others free from the slavery of sin and enjoy freedom as God's children?

The first step toward answering the questions is to make yourself aware of the nature of sin, of sinfulness in all its dimensions – personal, social, universal. You must place your life in the context of God unconditional, fore-given love. You must see that love reflected in the Christ crucified – the symbol of God's total self-giving.

Co-creators

In the past weeks you have prayed over God's gifts of Creation, and His special creation - YOU. You are a unique individual with special gifts and talents. You have the power within you to grow and develop. Therefore, you have pledged your life, as co-creator, to be obedient to the will of God and to share in God's on-going creative mission.

'Sin' is refusal to develop the potential, failure to be what you can and ought to be. You are aware of certain 'blocks' in your life. Now you will take your reflections further: To understand the power of evil and the nature of 'sin'; to gain confidence in the over-powering and unconditional love of God; finding ways to heal yourself and the world.

During the next four 'phases', you will keep your eyes constantly on Jesus outstretched on the cross – the focus of God's unconditional love – while you examine your 'attractions', to see in which directions you are pulled, and put things right before God and men. In the process you may experience 'shame' at your sinful state, and the spread of evil in the world – of which you are a part. You will feel "confused" when you contrast your 'sins' with the overwhelming love of God, and will wonder why God has been so good to you in spite of your evil tendencies. You will express "wonder" at God's kindness, mercy, and fore-given love.

The symbol of love

> "God loved the world so much that he gave his only Son, ... to be its saviour." (Jn 3.16-17)

God's unconditional love is strikingly reflected in the crucifix: Jesus died for us while we were still sinners. This means that he does no give us his saving grace only *after* we repent. It is already present, available to us in order that we make ourselves whole.

> A truly Christian conversion does not come from looking at sin, but from looking at Christ. It is not a deeper insight into evil but a higher insight into good. One discovers the beauty of a whole new plane of values, the plane of God Himself; the values one saw before will never seem adequate again.
>
> David Knight

Jesus taught that sin was failing others, neglecting to respond to the material and emotional needs of people. Neglecting the hungry or thirsty, the naked or the sick or the imprisoned... is seen the evil which cuts you off from others and damages your relationship with God. (Mt 25) Sin, according to Jesus, is also the failure to forgive others (Mt 18.21-35), failure to respect others (Lk 18.9-14), and tempting others to sin (Mt 18.6-7).

When you grapple with the reality of evil in the world and in yourself, you may feel helpless and cry out: Who will free me from bondage to evil that is dragging me to my death? And you will find the answer in prayer: The love of God in Jesus has made me free. Then you will realise that though you are a sinner you have been saved, loved, called by Christ. You will respond by resolving to commit yourself whole-heartedly to the service of Christ by asking yourself:

What have I done for you, Christ?
What am I doing for you, Christ?
What more ought I to do for you, Christ?

O Jesus, my divine Spouse!
Let me never lose
the second robe of my Baptism!
Take my heart before I can make
the slightest voluntary sin.
Let me always seek and find you alone,
let creatures be nothing to me
and I nothing to them,
but you Jesus be ALL!...
Let not the things of the earth
ever disturb my soul,
let nothing disturb my peace.
Jesus, I only ask of you peace,
and also love, infinite love
without any limit other than you...
love that is no more myself but yourself,
my Jesus.
Jesus let me die a martyr for you,
the martyrdom of the heart*
or of the body, or rather of both...

St Teresa of the Child Jesus

[*That is, to love Jesus without feeling one's love, and also these little sufferings which no one sees]

Glorious Jesus, my Lord! Oh, how glorious you are!
Unworthy as I am, I come to you
to sing a hymn of thanksgiving and repentance.
Like the woman in the crowd, I reach out,
knowing that you will make me whole;
like the Canaanite woman, I call to you;
like the blind man, I ask for healing,
so that I may say to you: Alleluia!
O Jesus, healing Fire
whose touch no one can feel and remain unchanged;
O Jesus, shining light who enlightens those in darkness,
O Jesus, heavenly Music, true Song to my soul:
You healed the woman who touched you,
you converted Paul who persecuted you,
you loved Mary who listened to you.
In like manner, heal my infirmities,
and shed light upon my darkness,
let me sit at your feet and sing to you:
Jesus, my powerful King,
Jesus, my mighty God,
Jesus, Fire in my heart!
Jesus, my eternal Lord,
Jesus, my glorious Creator,
Jesus, Light of my eyes!
Jesus, my Guide most gentle,
Jesus, my Pastor most caring,
Jesus whose touch is my health!
Jesus, my Master most compassionate,
Jesus, my Saviour most merciful,
Jesus who leads me to peace.
Jesus, burn in my heart with your cleansing flame.
Jesus shine in the darkness within me.
Jesus, restore me who am worn down by sin.
Jesus, rid my mind of every vain thought.
Jesus, shield my heart against evil desires.
Jesus, guard my will against self-love.
Jesus, Son of the Living God,
Have mercy on me a sinner!

Archbishop Joseph Rava

PHASE FIVE

OUTSIDE LOVE'S CIRCLE

West Side Story is an entertaining movie. One little scene in it is quite thought-provoking. The members of a gang have assembled at a drug-store, and brag in audible tones about a horrible crime they had attempted to commit. The old man who runs the store and listens in to the conversation feels disgusted by the callousness of the men to crime. No longer able to contain himself, he shouts out to the men: "You make this world lousy." One of the young gangsters turns to him and says indifferently: "We found it that way!"

We are born into a world that has strayed from God's original plan after the "Fall from grace" of our first parents – Adam and Eve in the garden of Eden. (Gen 3) When God made the world, he saw that everything was good. Down the ages, as civilisation advance, together with the marvellous inventions and discoveries, humans seem to be resorting to newer and more dangerous and disastrous forms of evil. They cause inconceivable harm to fellow-humans and incalculable damage to the environment: materialism, communalism, injustice, discrimination, oppression, corruption, pollution, deforestation.... are words that occur daily in our newspapers. Besides there are personal evil tendencies that add to the degradation of family life, society, and the world at large.

In spite of all, we live in hope. For Jesus said, "The world will make you suffer. But be brave! I have defeated the world." (Jn 16.33)

In this phase you must spend your prayer-time reflecting on the power of evil in you and in the world around. You must check for whatever distracts or separates you, – by making you worldly and vain, – from the love of God, from Christ.

5/1 Potential evil

In his autobiography, *Original Sin*, the movie superstar Anthony Quinn recalls a boyhood experience:
Once, when my sister Stella was six years old and I was nine, I saw a man dragging her to a tunnel near our house where a stream of water ran under the street. I drew near crawling on all fours, and I saw he was caressing her between the legs. I ran home and took a hatchet. I approached stealthily and hit him over the head with the back of the hatchet. I hit him again and again. My sister saw the blood and screamed. People came, help me back and took the man to the hospital. He was half dead.

That night, when my father came back home, my mother told him hat had happened.... My father came to me and told me, "Let's get out for a moment." He held me by the arm and said: "I am proud of you; you have acted like a brave man. I'm immensely glad that you have saved your sister; but I'm going to whip you." He took out his own belt. "The first time you hit the man you did it because of what he was doing to your sister. The second time you hit him out of indignation, and that too could have been alright. But the third and the fourth time you hit him show that you are a potential murderer, and I'm going to whip you so that you never again lose your temper to the extreme that you may kill somebody." I received the whipping like a man.

From his heart come the evil desires which lead him to kill. Mt 15.19

Suggestions

How powerful are the evil tendencies within you? How often do they surface and in what ways?

Pray in the words of **Ps 51**.

Gaze lovingly at the crucifix. Ask for the grace to overcome the evil within you.

Selfish choices

In *Living, Loving & Learning*, Leo Buscaglia tells of an interesting sociological experiment with the students of a midwestern university in the U.S. concerning sharing and giving. Students were asked to produce a dime (ten-cent coin) and were given three choices.

In the first instant, they were told there was a plague in India, people were starving and were in great need of help. If they felt like helping, they should put the dime in an envelope and write on it 'India.' The second choice: There is a family in the neighbourhood ghetto that really needs groceries to live now. Those who felt like helping them should put the dime in the envelope and mark it 'poor family.'

The third choice: the university was in need of a photocopier so that papers and manuscripts could be copied and made easily accessible to the students. If they wanted to give to this, they should mark their envelope 'copier'. Eighty percent of that money went to a photocopy machine.

> **Those who get rich fall into temptation and are caught in the trap of many foolish and harmful desires.** 1Tim 6.9

Suggestions

How do you respond when you have to choose between acquiring some superfluous, luxury items for yourself and reaching out to a neighbour struggling to make ends meet?

Read reflectively the parable of the Rich Fool in **Lk 12.16-21**. Follow up this reflection by reading **1Tim 6.17-19**.

Ask for the grace to be as "self-emptying" as Christ was, in order to respond generously to God's love.

Destructive ambitions

Somebody had re-written the Bible "story" about creation and Adam and Eve. Nine months after Adam and Eve expressed their love in sex, a child mysteriously emerged from Eve. They were amazed and cried: "Like God, we have created a human being!" They were happier than ever with all the good things they had. Until they recognized the good things they did NOT have. Eve said: "I wish I could swim like the fish." Adam said: "I wish I could fly like the eagle." So Eve dove into the whirlpool and drowned; Adam flew from a tall tree and crashed to his death. God looked at the lonely child and said: "It is not good to be alone in the world....there is no paradise, nor perfect world. There is just you and I and how we treat each other in the real world. Let us live together in love in our own world."

They heard the Lord God walking in the garden, and they hid from him among the trees. Gen 3.8

Suggestions

Have you felt ashamed of your misdeeds and tried to 'hide' or run away from God?

Read about the ambitions, the deceptions, and the eventual disobedience of our first parents in **Gen 3**. Pray in the words of **Ps 101**.

Ask for the grace to be always obedient to the will of God, as Christ was.

After their Fall, Adam and Eve were ashamed to face their Creator. It is God who takes the initiative gently to call them out of hiding. Divine justice casts them out of the garden, but with a touch of kindness: "The Lord God made clothes out of animal skin for Adam and his wife, and he clothed them."

Attitudes to evil

Upon his retirement from the U.S. Air Force, General Paul Tibbets, pilot of *Enola Gay* the aircraft which dropped the first atomic bomb upon Hiroshima, commented:

"I look back on it purely as a job I was assigned to do. We knew the effects that bomb would have when we dropped it. We looked down from the plane and we could see the havoc it was making. Of course, I think it was right to drop the bomb. I don't think about the effects of it, though. If you start doing that you would go insane."

If we say we have no sin, we deceive ourselves. 1 Jn 1.8

Suggestions

What is your reaction to the Pilot's attitude? How would you respond if you were asked to do something harmful to society by someone in authority over you?

Read meditatively **Jn 1.8-2.6**.

You may reflect on some of the 'terrorist' attacks that have destroyed precious lives in our own state, country, the world.

Gaze at the crucified Lord. Ask for the grace to have a sensitive conscience and not trample on people, especially the innocent.

If you are neutral in situations of injustice, you have chosen the side of the oppressor.

Spreading evil

On 27 February 2002, the Sabarmati Express carrying Hindu pilgrims was attacked by Muslims owing to some provocation. One compartment of that train was burned down, charring to death about 60 children, women and men. In retaliation, the Hindus took to widespread rioting, looting, murder in Gujarat. At first the "communal carnage" was restricted to the major cities, but eventually spiralled to even remote hamlets, some having only a single muslim family. Hundreds of people (including women and children), were stabbed, murdered, burned alive.

Besides, there were some shocking reports in the newspapers. Certain people took the opportunity of the mayhem to make money. They started gambling on the riots. Regular bookies too on all kinds of bets: where the violence will break out next, will curfew be imposed, how many rounds of cartridges will be fired by the police, will there be any private firing, what will be the death toll on a given day... And, concluded the reporter wryly, "this is one business which is not divided on communal lines"!

Evil people look for ways to harm others. Prov 16.27

Suggestions

Are you aware of how evil-minded people are? Have there been times when you have taken advantage of the vulnerability of others for your own personal gain? Have you joined hands with others in doing so?

Read meditatively **Mk 9.42-48**; **Eph 4.17-32**.
Focus on the crucifix, the symbol of oppressed humanity today.

Ask for the grace of sensitivity to the marginalised, the powerless, the persecuted, and a clear conscience in your dealings with them.

5/6

Sins of omission

A few years ago I was travelling from Royapettah to Mylapore – two important landmarks in Chennai. In between, a middle-aged man, ill-clad in a soiled shirt and dhoti, boarded the bus and asked for a ticket to Luz Corner, giving the conductor a 50 paise for the ticket. The angered conductor yelled at him and ordered him to get down when he found that the poor man had no more money on hand. The frustrated passenger was shame-facedly getting down at the next stop when the conductor stayed him with his out-stretched hand.

"My dear fellow, get in and occupy any vacant seat. I was only waiting to find out whether any of these big men would offer you 25 paise. Don't you bother." He took 25 paise out of his shirt pocket and threw it into his leather bag, tore a ticket and handing it over to the surprised passenger, went his way to the other end of the bus without waiting for any thanks. At that moment the conductor appeared to me the tallest man in the bus, and I was kicking myself for my failure to offer help. R. Saroja

They have eyes, but they are blind,
they have ears, but they are deaf.
Is 43.8

Suggestions

Do you turn a blind eye to those who need help?

Read meditatively **Lk 16.19-31**.

Gaze at Christ on the cross who did not shirk the mission given by the Father but stuck out his neck and sacrificed his life.

Those who live for themselves do
not have very much to live for.

Hardened hearts

There is a scene in Bruce Marshall's novel *Father Malachy's Miracle*, which is very revealing. An old sailor is on the point of death; a priest is helping him make a good confession. The problem is that the sailor has no regrets for the wrongs he has done in the past. He looks on the many affairs he has had in different ports as justifiable outlets for the hard life he had to face on deck.

The priest, who is unable to elicit any repentance, finally says to the dying man, "Are you sorry, at least, that you're not sorry?"

Harden not your hearts. Ps 95.8

Suggestions

Do you tend to justify all your evil deeds, big and small? Is your conscience blunted?

Are there disordered tendencies in your heart? These may show up in certain of your behaviours and approaches that directly affect others, like: expressing yourself in overpowering ways, rigidly expecting conformity, bullying, judging, grasping, cheating, nagging, demanding, etc. Perhaps you are not aware or only semiaware of them: "...the things I do, I don't want to do" (Rom 7:15).

Read meditatively **Lk 23.39-43**: the attitudes of two criminals.

Pray that the Lord take away your stony heart and give you a heart of flesh. (Ez 36.23)

The worse thing in the world is not sin; it is the denial of sin by a false conscience for that attitude makes forgiveness impossible.

PHASE SIX

MISSING THE TARGET

Sin is an unfashionable word these days. People prefer to use terms such as crimes, atrocities, mistakes, errors... for realities that simply mean 'sin' in the 'old' understanding. Whatever the term used, sin is a real part of life. It was, in fact, the central concern of Jesus, our Saviour from sin: "It is not the healthy who need the doctor, but the sick. I did not come to call the virtuous, but sinners." Mk 2.17

Off target

For Jesus, as for the Jews of his time, 'sin' was understood in the Greek context of *hamartia* the term used in New Testament scriptures. which meant "missing the target"– as in archery. (Today, however, *hamartia* has come to mean 'tragic flaw' or even a moral fault, as used in literary criticism).

God created us good. So being evil was considered as missing the goal or target of creation. For the Jew, the whole purpose of life was to be true to self and others, and in so doing to be faithful to God. To sin, therefore, means to be selfish and hateful, to turn away from God and others, rather than to strive to shape oneself into the image and likeness of God!

Jesus our model

St Paul informs us that Jesus was like us in everything except sin. Some wonder how Jesus, being human, could also be sinless. It was possible in Jesus' case because his life was always "on target". The goal of his life was to remain closely united with his Heavenly Father and to fulfil the mission entrusted to him. Jesus never deviated from this goal into some sidetrack of selfish pleasure or search for personal power, honours, and wealth.

However, it is true that as a human being, Jesus was capable of sinning. That is, he was free to make sinful decisions, if he so willed. And we know that Jesus "was tempted in every way that we are, but did not sin" (Heb 4.15), because he always chose to do good and to be faithful to his Father's will. In this Jesus stands out of the human race – as our Model! He is the Way, the Truth, the Life... that enables us to reach our target.

In the last unit you meditated on different aspects of 'sin'. In this unit you will reflect on the consequences of sin – the harm that sin does to the sinner, to society and to the world at large. Once again, you will focus your heart on Christ on the cross – the symbol of God's unconditional love, for inspiration, and ask yourself:

How have I responded to Christ's love in the past?
How am I responding to it currently?
What more is Christ challenging me to do for him?

Voice of Jesus, call us when we stray.
Eyes of Jesus, look upon us
when we need encouragement.
Face of Jesus, smile upon us
when we need assurance.
Hands of Jesus, anoint us
when we grow weary.
Arms of Jesus, lift us up when we stumble.
Blood of Jesus,
wash us clean when we get soiled.
Body of Jesus, feed us when we are hungry.
Heart of Jesus, help us to love one another
as you have loved us. Anon

Evil's backlash

A contractor for a construction company used to routinely cheat on materials that went into the houses that he built. But he made the exteriors look so attractive that none of the owners suspected he had used inferior materials.

Before his retirement he was given his final construction project. It was to be a luxury home. Since this was his last opportunity to make money, he cheated on it gloriously, using as much inferior material as possible, and inflating all the bills.

When the house was completed the manager of the company came to inspect it. It looked fantastic. He congratulated the contractor. Then he called the construction workers together and said he had a very special announcement to make.

"Our contractor is about to retire. As a mark of gratitude for his many years of service," he said, turning to the contractor, "the company has decided to gift him with this luxury house which he himself has constructed!" The contractor almost collapsed!

The wages of sin is death. Rom 6.23

Suggestions

It is often said that "cheaters prosper"; what is your opinion?

Reflect on the 'evil' of corruption, bribery, cheating... that infest all levels of society. Ask yourself how much of a part you play in it, however insignificant. Read meditatively **Jas 4.1-10** or **Ps 14**.

Ask the Lord for grace to become more and more aware of the evils of society and for strength to lead an upright life.

Deadly repercussions

A scorpion being a very poor swimmer, asked a turtle to carry him on his back across the river. "You must be out of your mind," said the turtle. "How can I do that? You'll sting me while I'm swimming and I'll drown."

"My dear turtle," laughed the scorpion, "if I were to sting you, you would drown and I would go down with you. Now, where is the logic in that?"

The turtle agreed, asked the scorpion to get on its back, and crawled into the river. Halfway across the deep waters, the scorpion gave the turtle a mighty sting, and they both began to sink. Resignedly, the turtle asked the scorpion, "Where's the logic now? Why did you do it?"

"My stinging has nothing to do with logic," the drowning scorpion sadly replied, "It's just my character."

If I do what I don't want to do...
I am no longer the one who does it;
instead, it is the sin that lives in me.
Rom 7.20

Suggestions

Are you aware of the kinds of 'evil' that have become part of your nature and ultimately cause you yourself harm in different ways and in varying degrees?

Read meditatively **Rom 7.14-23**.

Ask for the grace to conquer evil by doing good and deepening your respect for your fellow beings.

One cannot be isolated from sin,
but one can be insulated against it.

Uneasy conscience

There is a legend about Leonardo da Vinci of the time when he was painting *The Last Supper*. One day he is said to have had a big quarrel with someone. Afterward, he went to his studio and began to paint the face of Jesus. But he found, to his utter dismay, that there was a strange feeling in his hand, and it became impossible to use the brush with any effect. He immediately left the place, went to the man he had fought with, and asked his forgiveness.

When he returned to the studio and resumed painting the face of Jesus, he could paint with ease.

Forgive others, and you will be forgiven. Lk 6.37

Suggestions

Have you felt miserable after having wronged someone? What was your response? Are you aware that remorse causes discomfort?

Read meditatively **Lk 15.11-32**.

Gaze lovingly at the crucifix. Ask for the grace of courage to reconcile with those you have wronged.

Forgiveness means looking steadily
at the sin, the sin that is left over
without any excuse, after
all allowances have been made,
and seeing it in all its horror,
dirt, meanness and malice, and
nevertheless being wholly reconciled
to the person who has done it.
And only that is forgiveness. C.S. Lewis

6/4 Pangs of guilt

As a schoolboy, the English author C.S. Lewis was often victimised by a teacher. He felt deeply hurt, and carried a scar for most of his life. Every now and again he would feel the sting, and give in to unpleasant thoughts about the teacher.

As Lewis matured, he realised that the wound would heal only if he forgave the teacher from his heart. He tried hard to reconcile himself to what had happened in childhood, yet he just could not get himself to forgive the wrong done to him. To make matters worse, he suffered from severe guilt-feelings because of his inability to forgive.

Finally, shortly before his death, Lewis wrote to a friend: "Only a few weeks ago, I suddenly realised that I had at last forgiven the schoolmaster who so darkened my childhood. I'd been trying to do it for years and each time I thought I'd done it, I found it had to be attempted again. But this time, I feel sure it is the real thing."

> **"Lord... how many times do I have to forgive him? Seven times?" "No,..." answered Jesus, "seventy times seven."** Mt 18.21

Suggestions

Have you had difficulty in forgiving? Have you been torn apart by guilt?

Read meditatively the Parable of the Unforgiving Servant in **Mt 18. 21-35**. Or **Jer 31.31-34**.

Gaze at the crucified Saviour and ask pardon for the many times you have failed to forgive others in spite of having experienced God's forgiveness so often in your life.

Our neighbourhood has a high concentration of migrants... How do they survive? First, they spend as little as possible. They eat beans and, when available, rice, cereal, and eggs... Clothes and shoes they buy on rare occasions... Living here is difficult... Residents hole up where they can... There are five persons to a room and to families to a shack. Living as they do, piled on top of each other, there is no place to throw their garbage. The water supply comers from the creek where the sewage goes. All the water is contaminated. Who could be healthy under such circumstances? They work hard, eat less, live like animals, and put up with all this filth. Who could stand it? They are subjected to all the diseases of the poor: worms, malnutrition, dehydration, tuberculosis, bronchial pneumonia, meningitis. One disease is added to another and the net result is a short life-span... (A Basic Christian Community report)

If you... oppress the poor to get rich, you will become poor yourself. Prov 22.16

Suggestions

Are you aware that poverty is the consequence of unequal distribution of wealth – attributed to human selfishness?

If possible, spend today's prayer-time outside a slum or a poor residential area. Observe the goings-on carefully. Do not overlook the misery and squalor, the under-nourished faces...Feel the effects of 'sin' all around.

Read meditatively **Amos 5.10-17**.

Ask for the grace to be ever sensitive to the poor and of your responsibility of contributing toward the establishment of a just human order.

Virtual hell

In the thirteenth century, Dante Alighieri wrote an epic poem called *The Divine Comedy*. It has all the ingredients of science fiction and fantasy movies. In brief, Dante takes his audience on an imaginary journey through the circles of hell, into purgatory and then, finally, into heaven.

Fr Andrew Costello, a noted Redemptorist author, commenting on the poem in *Markings* (1988) said: "Ours is the century of the here and now. Ours is the century of the denial of death... of hell.... Ours is the century of two world wars, Hiroshima and Auschwitz, Korea and Vietnam, millions of abortions and millions of people starving to death. All we have to do is open our eyes and we can see hell." We could add the 'terrorist wars' of the new millennium for good measure!

Dante wrote with pictures and images. He visualised hell, purgatory and heaven for us. He had a great imagination – but he also said: "I found the origin of my hell in the world which we inhabit."

What human nature does is plain. It shows itself in immoral, filthy and indecent actions.
Gal 5.16

Suggestions

How concerned are you about the 'sinful' state of the world, of the creation of "new hells" instead of "heavens"?

Read meditatively **Jas 4.1-10**.

Gaze fervently at our Saviour on the cross and ask for the grace to be an effective 'co-redeemer', in his service.

What is hell? I maintain that it is the suffering of being unable to love. Dostoevsky

Tragic alienation

There is a bizarre story entitled *Metamorphosis*, by the celebrated Czechoslovakian writer Franz Kafka (1883-1941). It is about an unmarried man, Gregor, who lives with his parents and sister. Gregor works as a clerk in a store. As a good salesman, he tries to project a pleasant image to his customers, but he is a deeply unhappy man. He suffers much from an over-powering boss and an unsympathetic family – both treating him like an insect. Eventually he begins to have nightmares about his insectlike life. One morning he wakes up to discover that his nightmares have become a reality: he has been transformed into an insect – a giant cockroach!

Just as fairy tales go, Gregor can become human again only if he is loved and nurtured by humans, particularly members of his family. However, since his appearance is revolting, this does not happen. Gregor makes several pathetic efforts to express himself to his family, to appeal to them to show some affection, all in vain. Ultimately, he simply gives up and dies, remaining a cockroach until the end.

> **I am a worm, despised and scorned by everyone!** Ps 22.6

Suggestions

Do you understand the "alienation" people experience in the context of widespread selfishness, indifference, lack of compassion?

Read meditatively **Ps 22.1-21**.

Ask for the grace of com-passion that flows from the cross of Christ.

> **If you want to see how alienated we've become, watch when a door of an elevator opens. Everyone's standing like zombies, facing straight forward, hands to the sides.** Leo Buscaglia

FORGIVENESS

Forgiveness is letting go
of the pain
and accepting what has happened,
because it will not change.

Forgiveness is dismissing the blame.
Choices were made that
caused the hurt;
we each could have chosen
differently, but we didn't.

Forgiveness is looking at the pain,
learning the lessons
it has produced,
and understanding
what we have learned.

Forgiveness allows us to move on
towards a better understanding
of universal love
and our true purpose.

Forgiveness is knowing that love
is the answer to all questions,
and that we all
are in some way connected.

Forgiveness is starting over
with the knowledge
that we have gained.
I forgive you, and I forgive myself.
I hope you can do the same.

Judith Mammay

PHASE SEVEN

A CO-OPERATIVE HEART

One evening a parishioner was conversing with a priest in a park, while his little son was flying a kite. The man said: "Father, we cannot see God and hear Him, so how do you know for sure that God called you to the priesthood?"

The pastor lifted his eyes to the skies, as if expecting an answer. Then a sudden smile flashed across his face. He turned to the lad flying the kite.

"Say Chris," he called out, "is your kite still there?"
"Of course, Father," the boy replied, as he gave the taut string a few tugs.
"How come we don't see it?"
"It's behind the clouds, Father," said Chris without shifting his eyes from the sky.
"But how can you be sure the kite's still there?"
"I can feel the pull," shouted Chris emphatically.

The priest turned to the man and said, "I knew for sure that God called me because I felt His pull.... And I still do feel it!"

* * *

If sin is 'missing the target' – overshooting your goal, as it were, for selfish purposes, repentance is placing your life 'back on track' every time you move away from God. To do this effectively you must nurture a sensitive conscience – one that can "feel the pull of God" at all times. It is important to develop a listening heart, too, so that you can respond instantly to the oftentimes quiet voice of God.

You have been meditating on the "fore-given love" of God. You have become more aware that God is always present, always knocking on our door, calling you to greater intimacy. But often you have moved away from God for lack of generosity or out of fear of the demands and responsibilities that cooperating with God entails.

God still keeps calling you to cooperate with him in building up a better world (Gen 1.27-28). To respond whole-heartedly to God's call will serve you as a positive, constructive, and an effective way of counteracting the evil that oppresses you. More, it will also prove to be a sacred and exciting mission and responsibility that you will relish. For it calls for greater and more creative approaches to life, in keeping with the advances made in the fields of science and technology.

So, as you have been reflecting over the past weeks, the challenge is for you to place God at the centre of your life, and submit yourself fully to his holy will. A total surrender would give a new depth, a greater urgency and a transcendental value to your human tasks. It would keep you away from the snares of evil.

> Isaac Rubin, a psychologist and popular author, in one of his books provides a 'strategy' for "falling out of love" – a 'love' that you are too attached to and want to get rid of. Rubin insists that it is necessary to create a distance between oneself and the object of one's love/infatuation. The distance should be physical, if possible, but certainly it should be psychological and emotional. In case one is extremely attached, then the only way to 'fall out of live' is to 'fall in love' with someone else.

To be an effective co-operator with God you must ensure that your body-mind-heart-soul work in sync. You know from experience that in the process of cultivating spiritual values, you have to battle with 'human issues' like failures, limitations, problems.... It is important that you develop sound attitudes towards these.

In this unit you must pray for the grace to be an effective 'co-creator': to make God the top priority of your life and prayer; to understand the breadth, the length, the height, and depth of God's plan for you, to accept life positively. You must ask very particularly for the grace of generosity and magnanimity in responding with your whole heart to God, so that you find joy in doing his will in all things, at all times. You must continue to seek inspiration for Christ on the cross. The crucifix is a reminder of what total cooperation with God's mission and complete surrender to God's will entail.

Help me to love, Lord,
not to waste my powers of love;
to love myself less in order
to love others more and more
that around me, no one should suffer
because I have stolen the love
they needed to live. Michel Quoist

I will be true, for there are those who trust me,
I will be pure, for there are those who care;
I will be strong, for there is much to suffer,
I will be brave, for there is much to dare.

I will be friend to all, the foe, the friendless,
I will be giving, and forget the gift;
I will be humble, for I know my weakness,
I will pray to God for help to love and LIVE.
Anon

7/1 Focusing on your goal

In the great Indian epic, *Mahabharata*, there is the gripping anecdote of Arjuna's skill at archery.

There was a tournament held to test one's marksmanship. On a high pole hung a wooden fist, with its eye serving as the target. A host of brave princes took up the challenge to shoot the fish's eye. Just before each one could let his arrow fly, to test his concentration, his guru would ask him what he saw, and all of them invariably replied that they saw a fish on a pole at a great height and went on to describe the head of the fish, or its colour, and so on. When Arjuna was asked the same question as he took aim, he replied, "I see nothing but the eye of the fish." And he was the only one who succeeded in piercing the target with is arrow!

> **Look straight ahead with honest confidence.... Don't go one step off the right way.** Prov 4.25, 27

Suggestions

Do you have your eye on God in all you do? Do all your activities have a single purpose? Is the realisation of God's Kingdom the aim of my life? Is 'vocation' or 'career' in accordance with God's will?

Pray in the words of **Ps 18. 20-34**.

Ask for the grace to have a single-minded purpose in life – after the example of Christ – for the greater glory, the praise, the service of God.

> **All men should learn before they die**
> **Where they are going to, from where**
> **and why.** Thurber

Giving God top priority

Sudas, the gardener, plucked from his tank the last lotus left by the ravage of winter and went to sell it to the King at the palace gate. There he met a traveller who said to him, "Ask your price for the last lotus, – I shall offer it to Lord Buddha."

Sudas said, "If you pay one golden *masha* it will be yours." The traveller paid it. At that moment the King came out and he wished to buy the flower, for he was on his way to see Lord Buddha... The King offered him ten (*mashas*), but the traveller doubled the price.

The gardener, being greedy, imagined a greater gain from him for whose sake they were bidding. He bowed and said, "I cannot sell this lotus."

In the hushed shade of the mango grove beyond the city wall Sudas stood before Lord Buddha... Sudas looked in his face and put the lotus at his feet and bowed his head to the dust. Buddha smiled and asked, "What is your wish, my son?" Sudas cried, "The least touch of your feet."

Tagore

To you, alone... must glory be given.

Ps 115.1

Suggestions

How confidently can you say that God has the topmost priority in your life? Why? Choose something most precious to you and make an offering of it to the Lord.

Read meditatively **Ps 115**.

Ask for the grace of generosity that you will give topmost priority to our cooperation with God in the building up of a just and loving world.

Refining God's image

A group of women were studying chapter three of the book of Malachi in the Bible. Verse three: *He will sit as a refiner and purifier of silver* – puzzled them. They wondered what this meant about the nature of God. One women offered to observe the process of refining silver and report back. She went to a silversmith to watch him at work....

The silversmith held a piece of silver over the fire and let it heat up. He explained that in refining silver, one needed to hold the silver in the middle of the fire where the flames were hottest as to burn away all the impurities. The woman thought about God holding us in such a hot spot as in the above verse. The silversmith further said that in the process he had not only to sit in front of the fire the whole time holding the silver being refined, but he had to keep his eyes on the silver the entire time it was in the fire. If the silver was left even a moment too long in the flames, it would be destroyed.
After a moment's pause, the woman asked the silversmith how he knew when the silver was fully refined? He smiled at her and answered, "Oh, that's easy – when I see my image in it."

I will give you a new heart
and a new mind. Ez 36.26

Suggestions

What efforts do you make to collaborate with God's love so as to live up to God's image in which you have been created? Do you realise that while you are struggling to overcome your 'sins' or when you are in the process of repentance, God does not take his eyes of you?

Read meditatively **Heb 12.1-11**. Or, **Ez 36.33-36**.

Ask for the grace to grow in the awareness of God's saving power in Christ that constantly purifies you of your sinfulness.

7/4 Using God's resources

A friend once asked Samuel B. Morse, the inventor of the telegraph: "Professor, while you were at your experiments, did you ever come to a stage when you did not know what to do next?"
Oh, yes, more than once," answered Morse.
"And at such times, what did you do next?"

"I must answer you in confidence," replied the inventor modestly, "but it is a matter of which the public knows nothing. Whenever I could not see my way clearly I knelt down and prayed to God for light and understanding."
"And did the light and understanding come?" asked the friend.

"Yes," declared Morse. "And may I tell you that when flattering honours came to me from America and Europe on account of my invention which bears my name, I never felt I deserved them. I had made a valuable application of electricity, not because I was superior to other men, but solely because God, who meant it for making, must reveal it to someone, and was pleased to reveal it to me."

Each one,... must use for the good of others the special gift he has received from God. 1Pet 4.10

Suggestions

What are your God-given talents?
Take each of your talents and ask yourself: What am I doing with it? Are you using it constructively in keeping with God's plan, or for destructive purposes.

Read meditatively **1Pet 4.7-11**.

Ask for the grace to use your talents entirely for the building up of God's image in you, for serving others, for bringing God glory.

7/5 Optimising your limitations

There once was an oyster, whose story I tell,
Who found that some sand, had got into his shell.
It was only a grain, but it gave him great pain.
For oysters have feelings, although they're so plain.

Now, did he berate, the harsh workings of fate
That had brought him, to such a deplorable state?
Did he curse at the government, cry for election,
And claim that the sea should've given him protection?

No; he said to himself, as he lay on a shell,
Since I cannot remove it, I shall try to improve it.
Now the years have rolled around, as the years always do,
And he came to his ultimate destiny – in the stew.

And the small grain of sand, that had bothered him so
Was a beautiful pearl, all richly aglow.
Now the tale has a moral, for isn't it grand
What an oyster can do, with a morsel of sand?

What couldn't we do, if we'd only begin
With some of the things, that get under our skin.

... trouble produces endurance...

Rom 5.3

Suggestions

How do you tackle such "permanent" limitations or irritants in your life? Do you waste energy trying to fight them? Do you become discouraged, distracted, frustrated? Or do you, with God's grace. work around them, or even use them to optimise your goals? Does the oyster's approach offer you inspiration?

Read meditatively **2Cor 12.7-10**.

Ask for the grace never to succumb to any human limitation in your involvements as co-creator.

Transforming troubles

Eileen Egan, a lay person who worked with the Missionaries of Charity for 30 years, describes her experiences with Mother Teresa in her book *Such a Vision of the Street*.

One day, Eileen was reciting to Mother Teresa a 'litany' of problems she had been faced with. Mother suggested that Eileen change her attitude: "Everything is a 'problem'. Why not use the word *gift*?" From then on, there was a shift in vocabulary. Eileen describes one occasion when she was accompanying the nun on a trip, and had to face a long delay at an airport. She was about to inform Mother of the 'problem', when she remembered Mother's advice and turning to the saintly woman, said, "Mother, I have to tell you about a gift." As soon as Mother Teresa heard of the delay, she settled down calmly to read her favourite book of meditations.

Eileen concluded that after she had learnt the lesson, whenever disappointments or difficulties cropped up, they would be introduced with "We have a small gift here" or "Today we have an especially big gift." This attitude changed the mood and the approach to the mishaps.

Be joyful always, pray at all times, be thankful in all circumstances. 1Thes 5.16

Suggestions

Are you broad-minded so as to accept 'problems' as gifts? Do you generally have recourse to God in times of darkness, doubts, sadness, difficulties...? What motivates you to do so? Are you thankful to God in *all circumstances*?

Read meditatively **Hosea 11.1-9**. Pray **Ps 89.1-18**.

Ask for the grace of complete confidence in God and a positive attitude to life, so that you be an effective co-creator.

Overcoming failures

Word got around that the well-known scientist Thomas A. Edison was seeking a substitute for lead in the manufacture of storage batteries. A newspaper reporter called on the genius for an interview. In the course of their conversation, Edison informed the interviewer that he had made 20,000 experiments but none of them had worked so far. "But aren't you discouraged by all the waste of effort?" asked the astonished reporter.

"Waste!" exclaimed Edison. "There's nothing wasted. I have discovered 20,000 things that won't work."

I am content with weakness... For when I am weak, then I am strong. 2Cor 12.10

Suggestions

How have you reacted/responded to your failures?

Read meditatively **2Cor 4. 7-12**.
Pray **Ps 40**.

Ask to be faithful to God's will even in the face of seeming failures, and let them not stall your work as co-creator.

Instead of wasting energy
in being disgusted with yourself,
accept your own failure,
and just say to God,
"Well, in spite of all I may
say or fancy, this is what I
really like –
so help my weakness."
This, not self-disgust
is the real and fruitful humility.

Evelyn Underhill

PHASE EIGHT

EMPOWERED BY GRACE

Amazing Grace! (How sweet the sound)
That saved a wretch like me!
I once was lost, but now am found,
Was blind, but now I see.
'Twas grace that taught my heart to fear,
And grace my fears reliev'd;
How precious did that grace appear
The hour I first believ'd!

Through many dangers, toils and snares,
I have already come;
'Tis grace hath brought me safe thus far,
And grace will lead me home.

And when we've been there ten thousand years,
Bright shining as the sun,
We'll have no less days to sing God's praise
Than when we first begun. John Newton

Fr David Wilkerson documented his work with New York delinquents in his book *The Cross and the Switchblade*, through anecdotes of young people who gave up sinful living and turned to God. One of his delinquents said: "When I heard about Jesus, it kind of shocked me that he loved people in spite of their sins." Once, when in trouble, the young man prayed to God for help, and experienced a radical change. "That's when He came around. He took over my lips and my tongue and I was speaking a new language. At first I thought I was crazy, but all of a sudden I knew I couldn't be... I didn't want any more drugs. I loved everybody. For the first time in my life I felt clean."

As a disciple of Jesus you are sent forth to 'bring the good news to the poor'. The 'good news' is that JESUS HEALS. This healing takes place in the context of love: a love that "washes the feet" of and "breaks bread" with the 'least of our brothers and sisters'; a love that entails the laying down of one's life so that others may be 'saved', healed! It is a love that fills the lacunae created by 'sin'. It is God's love operative in the world through willing human instrumentation. "No one has seen God, but if we love one another, God lives in union with us, and his love is made perfect in us." (1Jn 4.12)

During the past few weeks you have been asking yourself:
What have I done for Christ?
What am I doing for Christ?
What more must I do for Christ?

At this phase of your prayer-periods you will answer in very concrete terms:
What have I done for my neighbour?
What am I doing for my neighbour?
What more must I do for my neighbour?

At this phase you will focus on how God's fore-given love, and how God's Grace overpowers the evil in the world. "Where sin increased, God's grace increased much more." (Rom 5.20) Once again you will place your reflections in the context of our Crucified Saviour and renew your commitment to follow his command and be at his service.

Ask for the grace to understand that: "Love is made perfect in us in order that we may have courage on Judgment Day, and we will have it because our life in this world is the same as Christ's. There is no fear in love, perfect love drives out all fear." (1Jn 4.18)

Christ's assurance

Here's a true story reported by Don Morales as coming straight from the lips of Cardinal Jaime Sin of the Philippines.

A woman claimed to have not only visions but even conversations with the Virgin Mary. Since Cardinal Sin did not respond favourably to her persistently phone calls, she went to his residence and sought an audience. Cardinal Sin thought that he had better put an end to this foolishness and told her, "When you see the Virgin Mary again tonight, tell her to ask her Son Jesus what my gravest sin was."

And so the woman left, happy that finally Cardinal Sin believed her. And Cardinal Sin was sure that now she would stop telling him about her visions. But the next day she came back and asked to see the Cardinal again.The Cardinal asked her, "Well, did you talk to the Virgin Mary last night?"

And she said, "Yes, but..."

"But what?" Cardinal Sin insisted. "Did the Lady ask Jesus about my sin?"

"Yes, she did ask Him," was the reply.

"What did Jesus tell her then?"

The woman reluctantly answered, "She said Jesus said that He had forgotten."

The Lord says... I will not hold your sins against you. Is 43.25

Suggestions

Are you convinced that God, who is all-merciful, does not only forgive your sins, but also does not hold your sins against you?

Read meditatively **Is 43.18-25**; or, **Is 55.1-8**. Pray **Ps 25**.

Ask for deeper faith in God's forgiving love and for the spirit of forgiveness bequeathed to us by our Saviour Jesus Christ.

Christlike forgiveness

Julian Motheral was shot in the spine by a robber at a petrol pump (filling station) in the U.S. He was totally paralysed. He suffered mental and physical agony, and even contemplated suicide. Then Julian began reading the Gospels, and he was touched by the sufferings of Jesus. He gradually experienced a transformation of mind and heart.

A decade later he wrote an article entitled "Letter to a Stranger" in *Guideposts* magazine, addressed to "Someone Out There". He wrote: "Until that night, I could walk on moonlit nights with my wife. Until that night, I could run and play with my young son. I have not been able to do any of these things now for almost ten years – ever since you put a bullet in my spine.... I do not know your name and may never know it.... Do I forgive you? By myself I couldn't do it.... But when I remembered Jesus on the cross, I found I could pray.... 'Father, forgive the boy who shot me, for he didn't realise what he was doing.'"

Love your enemies. Lk 6.27

Suggestions

Do you keep grudges, even in small matters, and behave in a prejudice manner toward those who have done you harm in word or deed? How strong is your desire to follow Jesus' teachings in this respect?

Read meditatively **Mt 5.38-48**.

Ask from your loving Saviour for a heart that overflows with mercy and forgiveness.

Love is never lost; if not reciprocated, it will flow back and soften and purify the heart.

8/3 Serving your opponents

Mother Teresa, a teacher in an elite school in Calcutta received her 'new' call from God – to reach out to the poorest of the poor. She obtained the necessary permission for her release from the Congregation, the "stepped out with a few rupees in her pocket, made her way to the poorest, wretchedest quarter of the city, found her lodging there, gathered together a few abandoned children... and began her ministry of love." (Muggeridge)

Nirmal Hriday, her home, was lodged next to a Hindu temple, and she met with much opposition from both the Hindus and their priests. It so happened that one of the Hindu priests who suffered from terminal tuberculosis, was refused admission to the city hospital, and found himself homeless. Mother took him to her home and lovingly tended to his needs. When he died, she delivered his body to the temple for the Hindu rites and cremation. News of her ecumenical compassion soon spread throughout the city – and won her the acceptance and love of the people.

The Lord says:"You are stained red with sin, but I will wash you as clean as snow." Is 1.18

Suggestions

Do you look for occasions to do some good, to be of some service, to show compassion, to those who 'hate' you?

Read meditatively **Jn 15.18-25**.

Ask for the grace to counter hate with love, in keeping with the teaching of Jesus.

Forgiveness is the fragrance that the trampled flower casts upon the heel that crushed it.

8/4 Overwhelming reconciliation

The short story called *Somebody's Son* by Richard Pindell, opens with David, a boy who has run away from home, sitting by the side of a road and writing a letter to his mother, in which he expresses the hope that his old-fashioned father will forgive him and accept him again as his son. Then he informs his mother: "In a few days I'll be passing our property. If dad will take me back, ask him to tie a white cloth on the apple tree in the field next to our home."

Days later David is on a train that will go past his house. He is nervous with suspense, wondering whether the white cloth will be there or not. As the train is about to arrive at the spot from which his house will be visible, David can't bring himself to look at it, so he turns to the man sitting next to him and says: "Mister, will you do me a favour? Around this bend on the right, you'll see a tree. Tell me if there's a white cloth tied to it."

As the train rumbles past the tree, David stares straight ahead. Then, in a shaky voice he asks the man, "Mister, is a white cloth tied to one of the branches of the tree?"

The man answers in a surprised tone of voice: "Why, son, there's a white cloth tied to practically *every* branch."

> **Repent, then and turn to God, so that he will forgive your sins.** Acts 3.19

Suggestions

Do you believe that God's love is truly unconditional and that he welcomes back sinners with open arms?

Read meditatively the parable of the prodigal in **Lk 15.11-32**.

Gaze at Christ on the cross, who embraced sinners and loved them back to life. Ask for the grace of even greater trust and confidence in God's fore-giving love.

Taking the initiative

I quarrelled with my brother
I don't know what about.
One thing led to another
And somehow we fell out.
The start of it was slight,
The end of it was strong,
He said he was right,
I knew he was wrong!
We hated one another.
That afternoon turned black.
Then suddenly my brother
Thumped me on the back,
And said, "O *come* along!
We can't go on all night –
I was in the wrong."
So he was in the right. H. Ferris

The Son of Man came to seek and to save who was lost. Lk 19.10

Suggestions

How often have you felt God's gentle voice calling you to greater intimacy with him? Isn't it God who takes the first step in leading you back to him? Do you feel inspired to take the initiative in reaching out to others to restore broken relationships?

Read meditatively **Lk 19.1-10** and **Mt 18.15-17**.

Ask for the courage to reach out to your 'enemies' and those you have offended, so to bring about love through reconciliation.

Forgiveness is the economy of the heart:
forgiveness saves the expense of anger,
the cost of hatred, the waste of spirits. Hannah More

Accepting responsibility

One cold day a trembling old man was brought into the court. He was accused of stealing a loaf of bread. When questioned, the man explained to the Judge that he resorted to the crime because his family was starving.

"The law demands that you be punished," declared the Judge. "I have to fine you Rs 51." At the same time he reached into his pocket and said, "Well, here's your money to pay your fine. And now I remit the fine."

"Furthermore," went on the Judge, "I'm going to fine everybody in the courtroom 50 paisa for living in a town where a man has to steal bread in order to survive." A tray was passed around and the astonished old man left the courtroom with at least Rs 80 in his pocket.

Stop all this evil that I see you doing .... See that justice is done.... help those who are oppressed. Is 1.16-17

Suggestions

Are you sensitive to the evils of society which cause suffering and deprivation among the poor? Do you hold yourself partially responsible for such evils? What do you do by way of restitution?

Read meditatively **Mt 25.31-40**.

Ask for the grace to accept the commandment of love laid down by Christ.

The real problem is in the hearts of men. It is not a problem of physics but of ethics. It is easier to denature plutonium than to denature the evil spirit of man.
Albert Einstein

8/7 Being God's instrument

At a church Group Prayer session, a man prayed aloud for a friend: "Dear Lord, you know Andrew Fernandes. He lives in Three, Union Quarters. He's leaving his wife and kids. Please do something to bring the family together." It so happened that the man prayed again, repeating "Three, Union Quarters." Tony, who was present there, was annoyed, and almost burst out, "Enough! Do you think God's asking, 'What's that address again?" After the session Tony was returning home on his motorbike. At a crossroads he felt an urge to ask a man standing there if he wanted a ride. The man said yes and hopped onto the bike.

As Tony introduced himself and asked the stranger who he was. "Andrew Fernandes," replied the pillion-rider. Tony was dumbfounded. It was the young man for whom the prayer had been offered. Silently, Tony made a left turn at the next crossing.

"Hey, where are you taking me?" asked Andrew.

"Home," said Tony.

Andrew stared in amazement at Tony when they arrived at Union Quarters. How did Tony know where he was staying, he wondered. Before he could ask, Tony shot away without looking back. Andrew, deep in thought, with deliberate steps entered his 'home' – never to leave it again.

> **Praise the Lord... he alone does these wonderful things.** Ps 72.18

Suggestions

How disposed are you to co-operate with God when he needs your services? Hasn't God used people to help you in times of distress?

Read meditatively **Acts 9.10-20**.

Ask for the grace to be sensitive to the 'disguised' messages God sends when he needs your co-operation.

GOD BE MY VISION

Be thou my vision, O Lord of my heart;
Naught is all else to me save that thou art.
Thou my best thought by day and by night;
Waking or sleeping, thy presence my light.

Be thou my Wisdom, thou my true word;
I ever with thee, thou with me, Lord.
Thou my great Father, I thy dear son;
Thou in me dwelling, I with thee one.

Be thou my battle shield, sword for the fight.
Be thou my dignity, thou my delight.
Thou my soul's shelter, thou my high tower,
Raise thou me heavenward, pow'r of my pow'r.

Riches I need not, nor man's empty praise;
Thou my inheritance, now and always.
Thou and thou only, first in my heart,
High King of Heaven, my treasure thou art.

Heart of my own heart, whatever befall,
Still be my vision, O Ruler of all.
Be thou my vision, O Lord of my heart,
Naught is all else to me save that thou art.

H. Dearooquettes

PHASE NINE

ALLEGIANCE TO THE KING

A preacher once compared the 52 Sundays of the liturgical year to a full deck of playing cards, which has been shuffled and dealt out, each with its own particular message. On the last Sunday, Feast of Christ the King, we hold up the last card: the king of hearts.

Jesus is not the king of clubs – they symbolise violence, oppression, and power. Jesus is not the king of spades; the spade is used to dig up dirt, or fill graves. Jesus is not the king of diamonds – symbol of wealth. Jesus is the king of hearts – the symbol of love.

Jesus' life was heart-centred: his heart overflowed with love to the extent that he "emptied" himself for the salvation of humankind. He chose a lifestyle of poverty and befriended the poor. He lived through example his "commandment of love".

Hours before he was crucified, he was dressed like a king and publicly asked in mock solemnity: "Are you a King?" He answered, "Yes! I am a king...but my kingship is not of this world." He was not a king with political, military or monetary power...He was a King of Justice, Love and Peace.

Christ was condemned to death because the values of his kingdom conflicted with those of the world. Jesus warned his disciples that they should be prepared to face this clash of values – till the end of time!

> "If the world hates you, just remember that it has hated me first. If you belonged to the world, then the world would love you as its own. But I chose you from this world, and you do not belong to it; that is why the world hates you." (Jn 15.18-19) "The world will make you suffer. But be brave! I have defeated the world! (Jn 16.33)

The early Christians had to face the wrath of the world: "They are all breaking the laws of the Emperor, saying that there is another king, whose name is Jesus." (Acts 17.7) For this they were persecuted.

Christ instructs us to walk with Him even in pain - carrying our crosses, while the 'world' teaches us to escape pain at all costs, and seek pleasure by all means. Christ tells us to take the last places, to give half of our possessions...to feed, clothe, visit.... On the contrary, the 'world' pressurises us to be first among the cut-throat competitors, to amass wealth so as to gain status and honours.

By worldly standards one is justified in taking "an eye for an eye...a tooth for a tooth"; the gospel-values inspire us to "forgive seventy times seven times, to turn the other cheek..." The 'good thief' on the cross, saw and heard the crucified Christ forgiving his enemies and he realized that this was something 'out of the world'. Christ was, indeed, a unique kind of King.... "Remember me when you are in your kingdom", said the thief, confident that Christ would listen to a 'repentant sinner' and oblige!

You must remember that as a forgiven sinner, you need Christ's power to overcome the world. In the past few weeks you have been asking, *What more can I do for Christ?* Now is the time to respond to his challenges, in completing the work the Father has given him.

Christ invites you not merely to 'follow his example' – like the way people imitate their heroes, but to 'cooperate' with him, hand-in-hand, heart-to-heart, as you would with a friend, because he is not a historical figure but a *living* leader. "I do not call you servants...I call you friends." (Jn 15.15). You must cooperate in the full measure of your generosity.

> There are always two of us at work. At study two, in the pulpit two, in suffering two, in temptations two, in sickness two. Woe to him who is alone! But together a generous soul will have no difficulty in walking in the part of sacrifice or that of labour, or in climbing with his King even to the height of Calvary. Paul Ginhac

Spreading the Kingdom must be your primary concern in life, that for which you must be willing to surrender everything (Mt 6.25-34; 13.44ff) The Kingdom consists of justice, peace and joy (1Cor 4.20).

In this part you will focus on Christ as your King and Leader, and reflect on the manner in which his committed followers down the ages have collaborated with him in making his Kingdom a reality. You must open your heart to God's grace that enables you to make a total surrender of yourself in the service of Faith and Justice.

Eternal Lord and King of all creation, humbly I come before you. Knowing the support of Mary, your mother, and all your saints, I am moved by your grace to offer myself to you and to your work. I deeply desire to be with you in accepting all wrongs and all rejections and all poverty, both actual and spiritual — and I deliberately choose this, if it is for your greater services and praise. If you, my Lord and King, would so call and choose me, then take and receive me into such a way of life. (David Fleming, S.J.)

The Lord's Prayer: An Adaptation

OUR GOD WHO IS IN HEAVEN
and in all of us here on earth; the hungry, the oppressed, the excluded. Holy is your name.
MAY YOUR REIGN COME.

May your reign come and you will be done:
in our choice to struggle with the complexities of this world and to confront greed and the desire for power in ourselves, in our nation and in the global community.
MAY YOUR REIGN COME.

Give us this day our daily bread:
bread that we are called to share; bread that you have given us abundantly and that we must distribute fairly, ensuring security for all. *MAY YOUR REIGN COME.*

Forgive us our trespasses:
times we have turned away from the struggles of other people and countries, times we have thought only of our own security. *MAY YOUR REIGN COME.*

Lead us not into temptation:
the temptation to close our minds, ears, and eyes to the unfair global systems that create larger and larger gaps between the rich and the poor; the temptation to think it is too difficult to bring about more just alternatives.
MAY YOUR REIGN COME.

Deliver us from evil:
the evil of a world where violence happens in your name, where wealth for a few is more important than economic rights for all, where gates and barriers between people are so hard to bring down. *MAY YOUR REIGN COME.*

May your reign come, for yours is the kingdom, the power and the glory forever and ever. Amen.

Adapted by the Center of Concern, USA (*The Rally*, May 2002)

Accepting the challenge

Sir Ernest Shackleton's expedition to the South Pole in 1915 is a story of adventurous pioneering. A voyage of such magnitude, uncertainty and risk required a special crew of tough and self-sacrificing persons. To recruit his men, Shackleton placed a tiny advertisement in the *London Times*:

> **Wanted**: Persons for dangerous journey. Small wages, bitter cold, long months of complete darkness, constant danger, safe return doubtful, honour and recognition if successful.

There was an overwhelming response. Sir Ernest had to select twenty-eight out of over five thousand applicants. They sailed in his ship called Endurance, which was caught in drifting pack ice during the coldest season in memory. On November 21, 1915, after 10 months locked in the ice, the Endurance sank. On short rations, eating penguins and the last of the dogs, the officers and men dragged the ship's three boats, loaded with gear, northward on thin, drifting ice. When the ice cracked, the boats were launched. Seven numbing, soaking days later they landed on an uninhabited island expanse of rock called Elephant Island. By now the men were exhausted, frostbitten and all but defeated. Subsequently, the entire crew was rescued, without a single death. They all received due honour and recognition.

> **Anyone who leaves home... for me and for the gospel, will receive much more.**
> Mk 10.29-30

Suggestions

Are you prepared to 'volunteer' for Christ's 'mission': "Go, then, to all peoples everywhere and make them my disciples?" Do you understand that discipleship means following Christ and sharing in his sufferings?

Read meditatively **Heb 1.5-10** and **Lk 9.1-6**.

Ask for the courage to accept Christ's leadership and challenges.

Remaining united with Christ

Jesus was a man who worked with his hands. For thirty of his thirty-three years of life he was connected with the carpenter's shop in Nazareth. There is an old legend which tells how Jesus was the best maker of ox-yokes in the whole of Galilee, and how people from far and wide came to Nazareth to buy the ox-yokes that Jesus of Nazareth made, for they were the best of all. One of the most famous and beautiful things that Jesus ever said goes back to the days when he was a carpenter. "My yoke is easy," said Jesus, "and my burden is light"
In Palestine ox-yokes were made of wood. The ox would be brought to the carpenter's shop and its measurements taken. The yoke would be blocked out, and then the ox would be brought back for a fit on. This curve would be deepened, that rough place would be smoothed until the yoke fitted so exactly that it would never gall the backs of the patient beasts.

In those days, shops had their signs over them just as they have now; and it has been suggested that the sign above the shop of Jesus was a wooden ox-yoke, with the words painted upon it: "My yokes fit well." Anon

Anyone who ... keeps looking back is of no use to the kingdom of God. Lk 9.61

Suggestions

How prepared are you to put on the 'yoke' that Christ bears so as to collaborate with him in establishing his kingdom – a kingdom of justice, love, peace?

Read meditatively **Mt 11.28-30**. Take to heart Jesus' invitation and the consequences of bearing his yoke? Read **Jn 14.1-10**.

Ask for the grace to surrender yourself totally to Christ and his mission.

Teaming up with Christ

The kingdom of heaven is like a Talent Scout who went round the schools and colleges to spot and train athletes to make the team. "I want the best," he said, "give me your best." And they were afraid, and hesitant and unsure of themselves, and so stood on the side-lines.

"You are the best," the Talent Scout shouted, "whenever you do your best. I don't give a damn for medals, for you have a goldmine within you that I will tap. We'll give you practice, more practice, and still more practice. You will have to train hard to surpass your own previous best performance. But you will also have fun and enjoy yourselves: Better fitness, better health!"

And one put to him this question: "Supposing I stand 4th in the race?" And he became very angry and said, "I don't care if you stand last. As long as you have trained properly and done your best, you are a winner! Are there any here who really want to join the team?"

And they all took that giant step forward on to the tracks that make them members of the team! Bruno D'Souza, S.J.

Whoever remains in me, and I in him, will bear much fruit. Jn 15.5

Suggestions

Do you belong to any group of committed Christians who serve the needs of the Christian community and society at large? If not, why?

Read meditatively **1Cor 12.12-29**.

Ask for the grace to be more and more intimately united with Christ so that you may be more effective in collaborating with him on his mission of salvation.

Identifying with Christ

Vincent Van Gogh, the famous artist, was a Pastor who served the Belgian mining community of Borinage in 1879. The miners suffered appalling injustices: miserable working conditions, extremely low wages. Van Gogh received a small stipend from the Church, and lived moderately. Yet, every time he watched the poor miners, he used to feel guilty that he was better off than they.

One wintry evening, as the scantily clad miners were returning from work through the fields around the Church, he saw an old man trudge along, clutching tightly at a sack-cloth wrap to keep him warm. Van Gogh felt so deeply moved that he immediately pulled out all his clothing from the closet, kept aside just enough for one change and gave the old man a suit, a pregnant woman his overcoat... From that day on, he lived on a meagre diet, almost to starvation. He spent the money thus saved in purchasing rations for the miners.

Once, a wealthy parishioner offered him lodging-boarding for free. Van Gogh declined the offer. He was determined to reject such temptations as would slacken his service to the poor. It was the only proof he could give that God cared for them and loved them through him.

Christ himself... left you an example,
so that you would follow in his steps.
1Pet 2.21

Suggestions

Does the kingdom of God within you radiate outwards? Do you strive – in your own way, with your own talents – to overcome selfishness so as to reach out to Christ in the poor?

Read meditatively **Mt 11.2-6**.

Ask for the grace that you will be a perfect instrument in the hands of the Master so as to make his kingdom a reality.

9/5 Responding to Christ's mission

"You Catholics are useless. You are all for religion, but you can do nothing for the poor." This accusation was directed to a 20-year-old Frenchman, Frederick Ozanam, at a Paris street-corner in 1833. Fred, a student at the School of Law, felt stung by the remark and decided to respond effectively. Fred collected five of his committed Catholic friends and went for guidance to Sr Rosalie, a Daughter of Charity, who worked for the poor. Sr Rosalie was wise enough to give the six young elitists, jobs that would challenge them but not sicken them.

As time went by, the group began meeting Sr Rosalie every week, to share their experiences. One thing they were completely agreed on was, that they were getting much more from poor people than the poor were getting from them.... The rest, as they say, is history. Frederick formed the *St Vincent de Paul Society* to provide the young members (Catholic laity) with an opportunity of visiting and helping the poor both materially and spiritually, and thus deepen their own Faith. Today there are 'Vincentians' in over 130 countries, including India. Pope John Paul II declared Frederick Ozanam 'Venerable' in 1993, and 'Blessed' in 1997.

> **This service you perform... meets the needs of God's people... produces an outpouring of grateful thanks to God.** 2Cor 9.12

Suggestions

How sensitive are you to the demands of Christianity? In what way do you put religion into practice – besides prayers and devotions?

Read meditatively **Mk 10.35-45**.

Pray for the grace to make your love for and commitment to Christ the King, fruitful in service.

9/6 Com-passionate with Christ

Two Spanish artistes, the singer Gayarre and the violinist Sarasate, had performed at the Royal theatre. As they were leaving after the show, a poor blind man with a violin in hand, cried out: "For the love of heaven, please help me."
"What's the matter?" they asked him.
"Some charity, sirs," he replied. "I've been starving for days and have nowhere to go this cold winter's night."

The artistes were moved to pity. Sarasate took the poor man's violin and started to play it masterfully while Gayarre sang. Soon a crowd of theatre-goers gathered and applauded frantically at the end of the piece. Gayarre then passed a hat around saying, "Gentleman and ladies, for the love of heaven, please give a little something to this poor blind man who is hungry and has nowhere to go for the night."

A sizeable collection was made and placed in the hands of the beggar. He was overjoyed as he made for an inn. His benefactors left in joyful silence.

Bow down your ear cheerfully to the poor.
Ecclus 4.8

Suggestions

Does your heart vibrate with the compassion that Christ expressed to one and all? Do you reach out spontaneously to the 'least' members of society?

Read meditatively **Lk 4. 38-43**.

Ask for the grace of compassion – love and service to those in need, for the spread of the kingdom of Christ.

**I am only one: but I *am* one. I cannot do everything, but I can do *something*.
What I *can* do, I *ought* to do. What I ought to do, by the grace of God, I *will* do.**

9/7 Bearing witness to Christ

Few countries on earth have experienced such unrelenting horror as the African nation of Uganda. In the 1970s, the small country was savagely ruled by the tyrant Idi Amin; since then, civil war, oppression and famine have impoverished the East African country.

Janani Luwum was the Anglican Archbishop of Uganda. He steered away from politics, but maintained friendly relations with the Dictator so that he could look after the affair of the church without harassment. When Luwum was challenged about his "friendship" with the dictator, he replied: "The best way to show a stick is crooked is not to argue about it or spend time denouncing it, but to lay a straight stick alongside it." By 1977 Luwum could keep up pretences no longer. When Amin accused the bishops of plotting against him, Luwum strongly demanded for proof. Amin summoned the bishops to his presidential palace and showed them a cache of weapons confiscated from the archbishop. All bishops, except Luwum were asked to return home. Next day it was announced that Luwum had died in a car accident. Only after some weeks was his bullet-riddled body returned to his family. He was shot by Amin himself.

I am sending you as lambs among wolves.
Lk 10.3

Suggestions

Do you realise the various, sometimes strange, situations in which you have to bear witness to Christ? Are you strong enough not merely to stand the pressures of evil elements but even be a source of inspiration to them?

Read meditatively **Mt 13.24-30**.

Ask for the grace to remain strong in your convictions in the midst of evil that surrounds you and to stand out as a disciple of Christ.

Lord Jesus,
in this day of multi-copy and mass-production,
we are caught in the dilemma
of conformity versus nonconformity.
Lord, I don't want to be a conformist.
There are enough carbon-copyishness in the establishment today.
There's room for fresh thinking, need for originality.
But Lord, I don't want to be a nonconformist either
- that is, a deliberate nonconformist
who takes delight in being different
just for the sake of being different.
There is enough madness already in this world...
just another mindless mass with a new look.

Lord, show me how to be myself,
to do my own thinking.
When this calls for being different -
well, then, let me be different.
When not, let me not be embarrassed
for being like others.
Help me to conform to your pattern.
You stood alone, Lord Jesus,
so different from the rest. But dress or
appearance had nothing to do with it.
Such inconsequentials as styles and fads never
do. The difference lay in who you were,
in your purpose in life, in your unyielding truth.
You never ceased being your true self,
though many hated you for it.
You never swerved from your mission
of reconciling man to God, though both
world and church threw obstacles in your way.

Lord Jesus, make me more like you!
Yes, I have the same desire as everyone else -
to be accepted, to be "in" with the group.
But, Lord, I want above all to be "in" with you.
If there be conformity, let it be to your mind and
your ways.

Ray G. Gesch

SECTION THREE

CHOICES AND CHALLENGES

CHOICES AND CHALLENGES

During World War II, a certain Christian gentleman wanted to communicate to the soldiers at a base camp the message of God's great love for them. According to army regulations, he was not permitted to proclaim 'religion' at the camp. But he was so strongly determined to carry out his mission, that he devised a unique way of doing it. He bought several thousand hand-mirrors and had them delivered to the soldiers through the army chaplains. On each mirror's back he had printed the message from the Gospel of John: "For God loved the world so much that He gave His only Son, so that everyone who believes in him may not die but have eternal life" (Jn 3.16). Below this text he had inscribed: "If you wish to see whom God loves, turn to the other side."

In this section your main focus will be on the "mysteries" of God's love as embodied in Christ's, followed by Christ's challenges to his way of life in God. You will begin with the Christ's Incarnation, through Christ's "hidden life" in Nazareth, to his public ministry of teaching and healing.

Jesus is my "normative model": the *Way*, the *Truth* and the *Life*. Christ is my life. Every stage of his life serves as a challenge to me as I attempt to understand him better so as to love him more intimately, to personalise his attitudes and values, to find inspiration in his actions and motivation in fulfilling the mission entrusted to me.

"The proof of *love is imitation*. We wish to be like our Beloved; this is a demand of human nature. As soon as we love one who is better than we, especially one who commands our admiration, we make him our model. We should like to have but one life with him, at least we would have a life like his." St Augustine

In order to understand the full meaning of being a disciple of Christ, you must contemplate Jesus' earthly life, teaching and example, as presented in the Gospels, not as an exercise but in the spirit of genuine search. You must seek gradually to transform your attitudes into his BEATITUDES so that you become more and more sensitive to his call to love, and more truly Christ's co-worker in establishing the Kingdom of God.

> "We must enter into the Heart of the Lord Jesus, so as to form our hearts upon His, to penetrate by an attentive consideration into the heart of the Master, the holiest and the purest of all hearts, to try by our aspirations in prayer, by our efforts in action, to have a heart like His." Alvarez de Paz, S.J.

> "His heart and His will must be applied to our heart and to our will, so that our heart live through His heart and share in His virtue, His joys, His delights, that our will pass into His will, that we become with Him and in Him one single heart." Le Gaudier, S.J.

For the next few weeks the grace you will seek is to know Jesus Christ in a deeply personal way, through an intimate knowledge of his life and his values. You will pray for a greater understanding of the mystery of God embracing your humanity so that God can be present in you, as he was in a human way in his Son Jesus. You will ask God to set your heart aflame with love for Jesus, and to create in you a burning desire to follow him in all things, even unto death.

Please note: St Ignatius instructs that one use "Contemplation" during prayer, as well as the "Application of the Senses" Please read the NOTES at the end of this book to learn how to proceed.

PHASE TEN

GOD'S MISSION OF LOVE

Into a world oppressed and torn,
Of boundless hate and forces wild,
Where men were hungry, lost, forlorn,
God sent a child.

Into a world maimed and dead,
Of nations each with selfish plan,
Where men were leaderless, or mislead,
God sent a man.

And when an age has lost its way,
And power is valued more than men.
In lives where He has voice and sway,
God comes again. John Morrison

If everyone were holy and handsome, with *'alter Christus'* ('reflections of Christ') shining in neon lighting from them, it would be easy to see Christ in everyone. If Mary had appeared in Bethlehem clothed, as St John says, with the sun, a crown of twelve stars on her head, and the moon under her feet, then people would have fought to make room for her. But that was not God's way for her, nor is it Christ's way for himself, now when he is disguised under every type of humanity that treads the earth. Dorothy Day

In this unit you must "contemplate" the events, the atmosphere and the people involved in the circumstances surrounding Jesus' birth – but most particularly, contemplate the Christ-child in the manger. In the "suggestions" below you will be asked to 'contemplate' persons, scenes, events.

Ask for the grace: to grow in your enthusiasm for Jesus, and in your eagerness to 'know' him better, with a knowledge that springs from love and leads to love; to love him more, so as to follow him more closely.

He was born in a stable, in an obscure village the child of a peasant woman. He grew up in still another village, where he worked in a carpenter shop until he was thirty. Then for three years he was an itinerant preacher.

He never wrote a book. He never held an office. He never had a family or owned a house. He didn't go to college. He never travelled 200 miles from the place where he was born. He did none of the things one usually associates with greatness. He had no credentials but himself.

He was only thirty-three when the tide of public opinion turned against him. He was betrayed by a close friend, and his other friends ran away. He was turned over to his enemies and went through the mockery of a trial. He was unjustly condemned to death. He was nailed to a cross between two thieves, on a hill overlooking the town dump. While he was dying his executioners gambled for his clothing, the only property he had on earth. When he was dead, he was laid in a borrowed grave through the pity of a friend.

Twenty centuries have come and gone, all the armies that ever marched, all the navies that ever sailed, all the parliaments that ever sat, all the kings that ever reigned, put together, have not affected the life of man on earth as much as that One Solitary Life.

He is the central figure of the human race the leader of mankind's progress. He is the Messiah, the Son of God, JESUS CHRIST. Author Unknown

Love from heaven

It was a historic occasion in Space Technology. On July 21, 1969, Astronaut Neil A. Armstrong, setting foot on Tranquillity Base of the Moon exclaimed: "That's one small step for man, one giant leap for mankind." Since then scientists have probed deeper into *outer* space, and the exploration goes on. Satellite pictures have provided 'close-ups' of the earth, helping us predict cyclones, earthquakes, floods.... However, the most state-of-act technology can capture only physical dimensions. Only the human eye and mind that can comprehend the depths of the human heart, and to a finite level, the length-breadth-height-depth of God's unconditional love.

About two thousand years ago, God 'looked' at the 'chaotic' state of the world and of man's heart, and sent his Son to redeem it. Jesus was born in Bethlehem: *one tiny Child, one gigantic revolution for humankind!* His birth open infinite possibilities for probing *"inner space"* – and the exploration goes on.

God's love for us was revealed when he sent his only son into the world, so that we could have life through him. 1Jn 4.9

Suggestions

Do you realise the goodness and largesse of God in sending his only Son into the world? Do you believe Jesus Christ has made an impact on our planet for the better?

Read Meditatively **Phil 2.5-11**.

Ask for the grace to become an effective instrument of God's saving mission in the world today by letting God take flesh in you.

One day, feeling overwhelmed by the "excessive graces of His love," St Margaret Mary Alacoque told Christ that she wanted to make an adequate response. He told her: "You could make me no greater return than to do what I have so often asked of you," she wrote. "And showing me His divine heart: 'Behold the heart which has loved men so much ... I ask that the first Friday after the octave of Corpus Christi be dedicated as a special feast to honour My heart...'."
"But dear Lord," Margaret answered, "to whom are you applying? To a wretched creature, a poor sinner whose very unworthiness would be capable even of preventing the accomplishment of Your plan? You have so many generous souls to carry out your purpose?"
"Ah, poor innocent that you are, [Christ replied], don't you know that I make use of the weakest subjects to confound the strong, that it is ordinarily the smallest and the poor in spirit in whom I make my power visible with greater brilliance, so that they will not attribute anything to themselves?"
"Give me then," I said to Him, "the means of doing what you command."

How I love to do your will,
my God! Ps 40.8

Suggestions

Have you experienced a struggle in understanding God's will for you? Have you accepted it unconditionally?

Contemplate Mary, to whom God communicates his desire that she become the mother of the Saviour: **Lk 1.26-38**.

Ask the Blessed Virgin to intercede for you, that you may experience her deep faith and trust in God, and her willingness to give Christ to the world.

Love-filled service

A twelve-year-old girl was asked to write an essay about a missionary she knew. A few personages came to mind, including Mother Teresa. Then it occurred to her that she had only second-hand knowledge of these people, but did not know what they were like. The one person who was a missionary, she realised, and a good one, was her own mother.

She wrote: "My mum's mission is to be a housewife and a mother to me and my family. My mum has never been selfish and put herself first before her family. I have never been starved or been without her endless love.

"Just like the famous missionaries my mother has needed a lot of courage. She could easily have gone off to parties and left me, but she didn't. She made the supreme sacrifice of thinking about me before herself. I am very lucky to have a missionary mother."

Mary stayed about three months with Elizabeth. Lk 1.56

Suggestions

Do you realise how Mary's instinctive feeling on hearing about her aged cousin's pregnancy is one of concern and care? How she rushes to her cousin's aid instead of basking in her own glory?

Contemplate Mary as she journeys over the hills, and her meeting with Elizabeth: **Lk 1.39-45**.

Ask Mary to intercede for you so that through God's grace you may feel a greater desire and urgency to share your joy with others in service, as a preparation for being fully open to God's coming into your heart.

Love incarnate

The torching of a bogey of the Ahmedabad-bound Sabarmati Express at Godhra (Gujarat State) by miscreants on February 27, 2002, in which 58 passengers were charred to death, was followed by unprecedented looting and carnage in Gujarat. Zubeda Biwi lived with her husband Mehmood Ali in a chawl (residence for poor people) in Narodia Patiya which was attacked by a mob on February 28. Ali managed to move Zubeda in the nick of time, just before his chawl went up in flames. "I took Zubeda to the fields behind the chawl. We huddled there for almost eight hours and it was nothing less than a miracle that we were rescued," said Mehmood Ali with tears in his eyes.

A police team took them to the relief camp in Shah Alam at around 11 pm. The turmoil proved to be too much for Zubeda, who was nine months pregnant and she went into labour... "Initially, almost everyone was tense as the camp did not have a doctor or even a midwife. But the women over here were very helpful and together we managed to deliver my baby," said Zubeda. "It's God's will that my child came into this world in these circumstances. He is very special to us."

The Word became a human being. Jn 1.14

Suggestions

What were the circumstances at your birth? How indebted do you feel toward your parents and others who helped bring you into this world?

Contemplate the scene of the Nativity: **Lk 2.1-21**.

Ask for grace to understand why God chose to be born in poverty. Pray that you become more sensitive to the homeless, the 'least' of Christ's brothers and sisters.

Love and suffering

Some high school students were decorating their school auditorium in preparation for a Christmas celebration. Since the Crucifix did not seem appropriate for the season, they were thinking of removing it from the wall when one of their teachers, a priest, walked in. The priest urged them to allow the crucifix to remain. "After all," he explained, "that is why Jesus was born – to die on the Cross!"

God sent his Son into the world...
so that the world might be saved
through him. Jn 3.17

Suggestions

Do you understand the true meaning of Christ's birth? Can you relate it to the cross?

Contemplate the scene of the Presentation: **Lk 2.22-38**.

Prostrate yourself before the fragile King of kings and offer him yourself. Pray that you may understand the challenges and the courage to stay faithful to him as his Mother Mary did.

The whole life of Christ was a continual
Passion; others die martyrs but Christ
was born a martyr. He found a Golgotha,
where he was crucified, even in Bethlehem,
where he was born; for to his tenderness
then the straws were almost as sharp as
the thorns after, and the manger as uneasy
at first as the cross at last. His birth
and his death were but one continual act,
and his Christmas Day and Good Friday are
but the evening and morning of the same day.
John Donne

Love that shines

The Magi seek the Wisdom of God. By the light of the star, they go in search of the Light – a beautiful symbol of the response of faith. It was through nature that God revealed himself to the Gentiles (Rom 1.19-20; 2.14.15). The star indicates something more wonderful than itself: the Child. He is the one to be worshipped, not the stars. The Magi thus echo the very heart of the gospel message: the good news is for everyone, even for the star-gazing peoples. It knows no barriers of space or race. Jesus is the Saviour of all.

The star is an imperfect revelation. While it tells them of the birth, it does not tell them where they can find the new born child. The ultimate secret of his whereabouts is to be found in the special revelation of the Scriptures (Mt 2.2-6). Matthew highlights the paradox: those who have the Scriptures reject Jesus, while the Gentiles come and, with the hope of the Scriptures, find and adore Him. (Clarentian Bible Diary)

Jesus is the visible likeness of the invisible God. Col 1.15

Suggestions

Does the star shine in your own heart? What is your response to the birth of Jesus Christ 'today'?

Contemplate Jesus in the manger. Read meditatively **Is 9.2-7**.

Ask for the grace and courage to follow the 'star' – your inner light, till you find Christ.

We must not see the child Jesus only in the pretty figures of our Christmas cribs and children's plays. We must seek him among the undernourished who have gone to bed tonight without eating... Archbishop Oscar Romero

Love dislodged

Lebanon's population of three million includes a hidden population of 150,000 illegal migrants and refugees from Africa and Asia. The Pastoral Committee for Afro-Asian Migrants (PCAAM) offers them pastoral support, legal aid and medical assistance. PCAAM helps those from Ethiopia and Sri Lanka who have the greatest difficulties with the language, visits those in prison, broadcasts radio programmes and publishes a bulletin. Iraqis and Sudanese are the majority of political refugees, but the Sudanese (usually Christians from the south who have fled from the war) are rarely granted asylum. The migrant labourers are mostly women, hired by upper-middle class Lebanese for domestic work, and they are often terribly exploited by their agencies and employers and harassed by the police.

The Son of Man has nowhere to lie down and rest. Lk 9.58

Suggestions

How often have you experience uncertainty, fear, anxiety, harassment from public officials....? Can you empathise with the plight of refugees, migrants..., the homelessness of victims of natural calamities or human exploitation?

Contemplate the Holy Family on its flight to Egypt: **Mt 2.13-23**.

Ask for the grace of a heart that goes out to displaced and oppressed people.

This is the secret of joy. We shall no longer strive for our way; but commit ourselves, easily and simply, to God's way, acquiesce in his will and in so doing find our peace.
Evelyn Underhill

The Will of God

The will of God will never take you,
Where the grace of God cannot keep you.
Where the arms of God cannot support you,
Where the riches of God cannot supply your needs,
Where the power of God cannot endow you.

The will of God will never take you,
Where the spirit of God cannot work through you,
Where the wisdom of God cannot teach you,
Where the army of God cannot protect you,
Where the hands of God cannot mould you.

The will of God will never take you,
Where the love of God cannot enfold you,
Where the mercies of God cannot sustain you,
Where the peace of God cannot calm your fears,
Where the authority of God cannot overrule for you.

The will of God will never take you
Where the comfort of God cannot dry your tears,
Where the Word of God cannot feed you,
Where the miracles of God cannot be done for you,
Where the omnipresence of God cannot find you.

The will of God will never take you....

Anon

PHASE ELEVEN

FINDING GOD'S WILL

In the past unit you have been contemplating the events surrounding Christ's birth. You have realised that God chose poverty as a way of life for his Son. Jesus was not born into royalty – as a prince in some magnificent palace, but as an ordinary, village craftsman's child, in a nondescript dwelling.

However incredible it may appear, Jesus, when he became man "of his own free will gave up all he had, and took the nature of a servant" (Phil 2.7). Jesus was a human being in every sense of the word. He had, like anyone else, to learn, to grow, to make choices, to be tested... The life of Jesus, till the age of thirty, is 'hidden', unknown. It is presumed that he worked with his father – who was a carpenter, till he left home to become an itinerant preacher and teacher.

Of the first twelve years of his life no words of his survive. About the time of his twelfth birthday a bare score are reported: "Why are you looking for me? Did you not know that I must be busy with my Father's affair?" After that, for a further eighteen years he retires to his original silence. The history of those thirty years is dismissed in the gospels in a single sentence: "He went down to Nazareth and was subject to his parents."

In an attempt to describe those 'hidden years', reputed theologian Fr J. Neuner says: "In this world of striking contrasts – rural beauty and peace, human poverty, oppression, helplessness and messianic hope – Jesus' vision of God's reign develops. He becomes himself. We have no records of this time of his growth, his prayer, his waiting and patience. The only thing we know is his anonymous identity with the world into which he is born and his obedient acceptance of it."

Jesus' childhood and adolescence appear uneventful – in the eyes of the world he did nothing worth remembering. But at the end of those "hidden years" his Heavenly Father was so pleased with his life that he declared: "You are my beloved child; in you I find delight!" (Mk 1.11) Fact is, Jesus had made a radical choice in life – to live by the 'greatest of all commandments' (see Mk 12.29-31), and ultimately to surrender his whole life to God, even unto death. You are now challenged to check the choices, the vital decisions you made in life, especially those related to your 'vocation' as a Christian, and your career in life.

> "Vocation", is described by James W. Fowler (in *Becoming Adult, Becoming Christian*), as "the response a person makes with his or her total self to the address of God and to the calling to partnership. The shaping of vocation as total response of the self to the address of God involves the orchestration of our leisure, our relationships, our work, our private life, our public life, and of the resources we steward, so as to put it all at the disposal of God's purposes in the services of God and the neighbour."

Ask Jesus to help you "increase in wisdom and understanding" of the mystery of his life so that you may love him more intimately and follow him more closely.

Growing in wisdom

Hermann Hesse, winner of the Nobel Prize for his writings, describes his childhood evolution in *Autobiographical Writings*: In my twelfth year, when the question of my taking Greek arose, I answered yes without hesitation, for to become in time as learned as my father, and if possible my grandfather, seemed essential. But from that day on, a life plan was laid out for me, I was to study and become either a preacher or a philologist, for there were scholarships for these professions. My grandfather too had once followed this path.

On the surface there was nothing wrong with it. Only now all of a sudden I had a future, signposts lined my road, and every day and every moment brought me closer to the prescribed goal, everything pointed towards it, everything led away, away from the playfulness and awareness that had filled my days hitherto, qualities that had not been without meaning but without a goal and without a future.

> **"Where did he get such wisdom?" they asked. "And what about the miracles? Isn't he the carpenter's son?"** Mt 13.55

Suggestions

Was your childhood eventful? What were the things, or who were the people that influenced or motivated you to "grow in wisdom and knowledge"?

Read meditatively **Jas 3.13-18**.

Ask for the grace to 'grow in wisdom and knowledge' just as Jesus did.

> **To know others is to be learned;**
> **to know yourself is to be wise.**

Responding to God's call

Ben Kingsley, the versatile film-star, realised his dream to become an actor, thanks to the encouragement he received from his parents.

When he was young, Ben, inspired by his father who was a doctor, wanted to go to medical school. However, the summer after he graduated from high school, he attended a Shakespearean play, *Richard III*, and got totally absorbed in it. During the performance Ben began to imagine himself in the role with such intensity that, drained of energy, he fainted.

After the show his parents picked him up at the auditorium and informed him that he had been given an appointment for an interview at medical school. But Ben said to them, "This is where I want to be. This is what I want to do." His father looked at him thoughtfully, then said, to the future star of *Gandhi:* "All right. I will encourage you." And thus Ben got started on his illustrious acting career.

> **My food, Jesus said to them, is to obey the will of the one who sent me and to finish the work he gave me to do.** Jn 4.34

Suggestions

When did you discover your 'call' to be a co-creator with God? How faithful have you been to your 'vocation'?

Read meditatively **Lk 2.41-52**. The Temple incident indicates a distinct awakening in the heart of Jesus to the call of God. He 'discovers' his 'vocation' as it were.

Ask for the grace to understand more clearly that God has called you to grow into the image of his Son, through your particular calling in life.

Obeying God's will

Jesus was a carpenter's son, so he grew up amidst the sawdust and the shavings of a carpenter's workshop and picked up his father's trade. His work involved craftsmanship: Jesus learned to make ploughs and yokes for the local farmers. "Take my yoke..." (Mt 11.29) is an image that comes from his own trade. He must have made boats for the local fishermen, fashioned furniture, and built houses.

It was God's will that Jesus spend a major part of his life in obscurity. Of course, Jesus must have had a great longing to launch out on his mission: "I came to set the earth on fire, and how I wish it were already kindled" (Lk 12.49). So at some stage in his life, having discovered – through a period of doubt, anxiety, searching – where God was really leading him, Jesus must have made the decision to leave his trade and begin his ministry of teaching and preaching.

Here I am to do your will,
O God. Heb 10.7

Suggestions

Are you fully aware of God's personal design or plan for your life? Have you responded to it with inner freedom, in shaping your life accordingly? Are you living out God's design today, faithfully and generously, whatever your career or occupation?

Read meditatively **Mk 12.28-34**.

Ask for light to understand God's will for you even more clearly so as to follow close in the footsteps of Jesus.

What we usually pray to God is not that his will be done, but that he approve ours. Anon

11/4 Choosing one's vocation

Edith Stein was born in Breslau, Germany (now in Poland), in 1891, of Jewish parents. At 14, Edith began to profess herself as an atheist. However, while studying Philosophy at the university of Breslau she came to know the philosopher Max Scheler, and had her first contact with Catholic thinking. During World War I, Edith felt it her duty to discontinue her studies and work as a nurse for the Red Cross.... In 1921, she read the autobiography of St Teresa of Avila at one sitting — through the night. It transformed her mind and heart....

She was baptised on January 1, 1922 and chose the name of Teresa-Hedwig. Edith abandoned her university studies and began to teach in a Dominican school in Speir. She spoke publicly on the vocation of women and their inclusion in modern society. After she lost her job because of measures taken against Jews, she gave in to her heart's desire and entered the cloistered Discalced Carmel monastery in Cologne-Lindenthal in 1933. In1942 she was arrested by SS Officers, taken to Auschwitz and to her death in the gas chambers. She was canonised by Pope John Paul II on October 11, 1998.

The. call of God is irrevocable. Rom 11.29

Suggestions

Do you believe that in the twists and turns of life God reveals his plan for you? How sensitive have you been to God's intervention?

Pray in the words of **Ps 40**.

Thank God for his goodness to you, for his grace which helped in the development of your personality. Offer your entire being to God, and ask for the grace to be always God-oriented.

11/5 Fulfilling one's desires

"Rose, you will either become a saint or a devil," the teacher had chided. "Me? I am going to be a nun," was the bold reply of the youngster. Sorrow and misfortune challenged her early in life. She lost her father and her three sisters in succession. At fourteen, she was sent to a boarding school in Tours, where she had to endure excessive strictness. At 17, her mother died unexpectedly. Rose's heart was weighed down by unbearable sorrow.

Rose wondered what life was all about. Kneeling before the Tabernacle one day, she found the answer in God. Remembering her early desire, she entered a convent, and years later at her profession took the name of St Mary Euphrasia. She was assigned to work for girls who needed protection from an unhappy and unwholesome environment. Having experienced pain and suffering, she was filled with compassion for the poor, sick and lonely. Eventually she founded a congregation – Contemplatives of the Good Shepherd. She was declared a Saint by Pope Pius XII in 1940. Today there are over 7000 Good Shepherd sisters working in 67 countries.

He defended the cause of the poor and the needy.... Jer 22.16

Suggestions

How convinced are you of the real challenge of Jesus to his disciples: to live a life of Poverty, Dishonour and Humility, by shunning Riches, Honour and Pride?

Read meditatively **1Tim 6.3-19**.
Pray in the words of **Ps 119.25-32**.

Ask for the grace to understand the value of poverty and do all in your power to identify with Christ poor.

Attaining one's goal

Ignace Jan Paderewski (1860-1941) was a Polish pianist, composer and statesman. At an early age, while studying at the Warsaw Conservatory, several teachers attempted to dissuade him from taking up a career as a pianist; they said his fingers were stubby; they urged him to try the cornet. Paderewski, however, was convinced that his vocation was to be a pianist.

Then he met the great pianist Anton Rubenstein who said, "Young man, you might be able to play the piano... if you practice seven hours a day." Given his self-confidence and determination, Paderewski practised for long hours. Even the remark of the great musician Theodor Leschetizky, under whom he later studied, that "You might have been a great pianist if you had started earlier; it is too late now!" – did not deter him.

He made his debut in Vienna in 1887 and Paris 1888. In 1891 he made the first of many concert tours in the United States. He amassed a large fortune, most of which he donated to the service of Poland and the benefits of needy musicians and Jewish refugees.

> **I do not judge as man judges. Man looks at the outward appearances, but I look at the heart.** 1Sam 17.7

Suggestions

Do you realise that whatever your 'status' in life – or your profession, you can always make room in your heart for the poor?

Praying the words of **Ps 119.33-40**.

Ask for the gift of understanding God's goodness inspite of obstacles faced in life, so as to always remain faithful to him, and be compassionate to the needy.

Taking sound decisions

A young woman once confided to her friend that she was facing a rather tricky problem. She had three boyfriends who were madly in love with her, and each wanted to marry her. After considerable reflection she had come to the conclusion that it would be easy for her to live with *any* of them. So the big question was: which one should she finally select.

Her friend thought a while, then came up with a striking suggestion in order for her to make the best decision. "You have been thinking all along on how you would be able to *live with* each of the three as his future wife. Why don't you change your perspective? Decide which man you will not be able to *live without* for the rest of your life!"

You are all I want, O Lord. Ps 119.57

Suggestions

Does God still have the topmost priority in your life? Are all your choices God-centred?

Pray in the words of **Ps 119.41-48**.

Ask for the grace to have God involved in all the choices you make in life, so that you will always have God's greater glory at heart.

A student, visiting his popular classmate, saw a homemade plaque in his room with the words "I Am Third" on it. When asked to explain it the lad said: "That's my motto for life. It means God is first, Others are second, and I am Third."

I Will

Sometimes the hardest thing
Is simply to decide
To make the choice to change your life
To change it from inside.
The journey's uneventful
With waters calm and still
Never clear destinations
Until you say – I Will.
The power of decision
Is the greatest force on earth
Opening the hidden doors
To all the universe.
The second you discover
The strength that stirs in you
You'll feel your dream within your grasp
Because you said – I'll Do.

The promise of tomorrow
Is the vow I make today
New horizons will appear
The moment that I say
I Will because I can
I'll Do cause I believe
The strength I need to make the change
Is deep inside of me.
I'll Walk where I have crawled
I'll Run till I can fly
My wings will fill with winds of change
The moment I decide. Anon

PHASE TWELVE

MASTER AGAINST ENEMY

Literature and legend present the devil in varying forms. Artists have treated him with fun. Hieronymous Bosch portrays him as the ape of God, supreme master of disorder. Durer depicts him as the pig waiting to snatch a human soul. Goya shows him as a goat. Sometimes he is shown as a flamboyant figure with magnificence and power allied with low cunning – a Mephistopheles offering wealth in exchange for souls!

To many people the devil is not a reality. He is simply a fictional figure – a mixed-up kid with horns, hoofs and a tail, a product of ignorance and superstition.

They may say that the devil has never lived.
They may say the devil has gone.
But simple folk would like to know
Who carries the business on.

The power of evil in the world may overwhelm us. There is too much disorder for comfort. Some helplessly believe that Evil has vanquished Good, and it now dominates the globe. The reason why we turn from Christ the Light to the "powers of darkness" is because we are often deceived by the devil. "Satan can disguise himself to look like an angel of light" (2Cor 11.14). He is a skilful schemer. He does not drag us into sin all at once. It would be almost impossible for him to do so to one who is genuinely committed to Christ. So he uses subtle tactics and camouflaged baits.

What makes the battle against Satan and his army even more difficult is the evil drive within our human nature that often clashes with our motivation to do good, and often get the upper hand in the end. We feel bound, powerless, freedomless. "For I do not do the good I want, but the evil I do not want is what I do" (Rom 7.19). We inadvertently land up in situations where we are caught between two serving "two masters" – one of whom is God/Christ, the other the Evil One. And we can only serve one. (Mt 6.24)

Those with Faith, however, have a very different perspective of reality. Satan is, for all his influence, only a tiny creature before God Almighty – a glow-worm before the Sun. The Universe is God's, after all. It is God's love that dominates the whole of Creation and sustains it. Christ is Lord and King through the power of the Resurrection. Love conquers all.

Alone, we are powerless against Satan and his army. With Christ, by our side, nothing can destroy us or tamper with out freedom. "So put on God's armour now! Then, when the evil day comes, you will be able to resist the enemy's attacks, and after fighting to the end, you will hold your guard." (Eph 6.13)

So far, through prayer, you have committed yourself to being a co-creator with God, to collaborate with Christ the King at all costs. In the last couple of weeks you have felt inspired by the early life of Christ, and have taken him as your model for a life of *Poverty*, *Dishonour*, and *Humility*. Now you must go a step further and learn what this commitment and collaboration mean in practical terms.

In this unit, you will seek the grace of perceiving the wicked designs of Satan and his followers, so as not to be victimised but remain faithful to Christ. You will deepen your quest for the true Christ by identifying with his characteristic traits: Poverty, Dishonour, Humility – as your priorities in life. You will take up the challenges of Christ and ensure that "the powers of darkness" have no place in Christ's kingdom of light.

Note: St. Ignatius recommends in the *Spiritual Exercises* at this point, to close your prayer periods with the "three-fold Conversation". (63) as follows:

"*The First Colloquy* will be with our Lady, that she may obtain for me from her Son and Lord grace for three things:

First, that I may feel an interior knowledge of my sins and also an abhorrence of them;

Second, that I may perceive the disorder in my actions, in order to detest them, amend myself, and put myself in order;

Third, that I may have a knowledge of the world, in order to detest it and rid myself of all that is worldly and vain. Then I will say a Hail Mary.

The Second Colloquy, I will make the same request to the Son asking him to obtain these graces for me from the Father. Then I will say the prayer 'Soul of Christ'.

The Third Colloquy, I will address these same request to the Father, asking that he himself, the eternal Lord, may grant me these graces. Then I will say an Our Father."

> ...the Triple Colloquy always indicates a significant phase of the Exercise journey... This instrument of growing enlightenment and freedom is a way for the directee to exercise oneself so that one will become free enough to receive the gifts which God desires to give one. The Triple Colloquy can help a directee to remove blockages and to detect the below-the-surface, disordered tendencies in ones heart which could undermine one's decision-making process later in the journey. John Veltri, S.J.

12/1 The enemy at large

An elderly woman was well known for her kindness; she never had a bad thing to say about anyone. She had the uncanny ability of finding at least one good quality even in the worst of people, including those unkind to her.

One day two men saw this kind-hearted woman walking down the street. One of them said, "I'll bet you can't name a single soul whom Mrs Sosebee can't say a good word about."

"I'll take you on that," said the other man. They greeted her as she passed them, and this man said, "Hello, Mrs Sosebee. May I ask you a question? What do you think about the devil?"

"Well", said the woman with a smile, "You'll have to admit he's always on the job!"

Your enemy the Devil roams like a roaring lion looking for someone to devour. 1Pet 5.8

Suggestions

Do you believe that there are many 'sources' of evil in the world? Are there in your life?

Read meditatively **2Tim 3.1-5**.

Ask for the grace of staying alert so as not to succumb to evil, by living in the light of Christ.

Satan is never too busy to rock the cradle of a sleeping Christian.

The enemy disguised

When a mother learned that her young son had told a lie she was shocked and decided it was necessary to put the fear of the devil into him in order to convince him to change his ways. When all was quiet that evening, she sat him beside her on the sofa and asked him to pay close attention to her.

"An ugly-looking monster, with sharp horns on his head and fire streaming out of his eyes snatches all children who tell lies and carries them away. He takes them to a distant planet and makes them do hard work day and night, beating them if they disobey his commands. Only when they get very old does he bring them back to his family."
Feeling satisfied that she had made an impression on the lad, she concluded, "You will not tell lies any more, will you?"
"I guess not, mum," said the boy, "You tell better ones."

Even Satan disguises himself to look like an angel of light. 2Cor 11.14

Suggestions

Do you realise the various 'disguises' through which evil enters the human heart? Are you sensitive enough to resist evil in every way so as to remain faithful to Christ?

Read meditatively **1Pet 5.8-11**.

Ask for the grace to be alert to the devil's ways so that you may never succumb to evil but courageously fight against it to spread Christ's kingdom on earth.

Wherever God erects a house of prayer,
The Devil always builds a chapel there,
And 'twill be found upon examination,
The latter has the largest congregation.

Daniel Defoe

Self-made fetters

"Prisoner, tell me, who was it that bound you?"
"It was my master," said the prisoner. "I thought I could outdo everybody in the world in wealth and power, and I amassed in my own treasure-house the money due to the king. When sleep overcame me I lay upon the bed that was for my lord, and on waking up I found I was a prisoner in my own treasure-house."
"Prisoner, tell me, who was it that wrought this unbreakable chain?"
"It was I," said the prisoner, "who forged this chain very carefully. I thought my invincible power would hold the world captive leaving me in a freedom undisturbed. That night and day I worked at the chain with huge fires and cruel hard strokes. When at last the work was done and the links were complete and unbreakable, I found that it held me in its grip." Tagore

Why did you let Satan take control of you? Acts 5.3

Suggestions

Do you find yourself trapped by your unchecked tendencies and attitudes? Can you recall to mind people you know who have broken their bonds with wickedness and now experience true freedom in Christ?

Read **Mt 12.22-29, 43-45**.

Ask for the grace to be freed from the chains of evil influences that besiege you everywhere, so that you may follow Christ in freedom of heart.

If man is not rising upwards to be an angel, depend on it, he is sinking downwards to be a devil. G.K.Chesterton

Riding the tiger

In 1981, Anupam Kher came to Bombay like hundred of young people do, hoping to hit the big time in Bollywood.He was twenty-six, bald, divorced. No one would have given the boy from Simla a second look. He rented a ramshackle room in a slum where eight others like him shared his dreams. Kher went from door to door begging for a break.That break came two years later when Mahesh Bhatt, a famous but struggling director, decided to cast him in the role of a 70-year-old in *Saaransh*.The film made Bhatt into a legend and Kher became an instant draw.

While Anupan was riding the waves of success, Mahesh once queried him: "Is this what you had asked for, Anupam?"

Anupam paused, smiled and then replied: "No, I am tired. I feel like running away from it all.... But I know I cannot. It is like riding a tiger. If I try to get down the tiger will gobble me up."

Will a person gain anything if he wins the whole world but is himself lost or defeated? Lk 9.25

Suggestions

Do you realise that ambitions can lead you to a point of no return? Do you understand that greed can gobble you up in the end?

Read meditatively **Rom 7.14-25**.

Ask for the grace to understand the allurements of the world so that they may not draw you away from your commitment to Christ.

The devil has three children: Pride, Falsehood and Envy. A Welsh proverb

The web of deceit

William Barclay tells the story of three devils who were being sent to earth for the first time to begin their work of deceiving people. Before their departure, they were each called for an interview with their Chief, Satan. Satan puts each of them this simple question: "What plan do you have to deceive people and destroy them?"

The first answered: "I plan to convince them that there is no God."

The second said: "I plan to convince people that there is no hell."

The third said his approach was going to be less intellectual: "I simply plan to convince people that they have plenty of time to prepare for death and for the Second Coming of Jesus."

Satan was pleased with the third answer. He said, "Do that, my son, and you will deceive many."

The enemy who sowed the weeds is the devil. Mt 13.39

Suggestions

Are you aware of the subtle ways in which you can get trapped into a life of laxity, even evil – through false rationalisations?

Read meditatively **Eph 6.10-18**.

Ask for the grace of such a deep love and loyalty to Christ and evil will have no foothold in you.

The devil's cleverest wile is to convince us that he does not exist. Baudelaire

I could be defined as a rebel,... always defying tradition, orthodoxy and the need to fit into mould, cast by a society of stereotypes. I enjoyed creating chaos in disciplined atmosphere. Why did I do this? A need to be my own unique person, with my own creativity and individuality. Very often my attitude was influenced by the books I read, movies I saw and behaviour I disliked.... I came to believe I had all the answers and that man was at par with God.... I did without God, gave up the Church for quite a while, explored alternate religions and dined with the devil quite often. I was ecstatic with the way things were going. I was on a 'high' that showed no signs of coming down....

But like every drug or stimulant, the feeling of euphoria wears off after a while and depression sets in and no matter how closely I surrounded myself with friends, I was still lonely... As the lights went off one by one, I crouched in the darkness, afraid... I started to pray... working with a prayer group... Down he road, I knew exactly what I wanted to do with the rest of my life.... I wanted to love the unloved and reach out to those who haven't been touched yet with the amazing Grace of a most wonderful God. Fr E. Fernandes

Give in to God, then; resist the devil, and he will run away from you. Jas 4.7

Suggestions

Have you felt trapped by unchecked tendencies and attitudes? How did you get out of them? How attracted are you by the attitudes of Christ?

Read meditatively **1Jn 3.7-18**.

Ask for grace to be freed from the chains of evil influences that besiege us everywhere, so that you may follow Christ in freedom of heart.

Standing up for Christ

The government of El Salvador has been abusing its people for many years. Rebellion has led to mass murder. Those who dared to speak out for the poor have been tortured, threatened, and in many instances, killed. A striking example is that of Archbishop Romero.

In the face of incredible odds, the archbishop spoke for justice, criticising the government for oppressing the poor. "I am an optimist... What sustains me in the struggle is my love for God, my desire to be faithful to the Gospels and my love for the Salvadorean people, especially the poor." By his leadership, his care, and his love, he reminded the people of El Salvador of their true heritage as God's children. He called the poor to solidarity with one another.

On March 25, 1980, Archbishop Romero was assassinated while celebrating the Eucharist. On the day of his internment there was a large banner above the cathedral altar which said: *Monsignor Romero, you did not die. You live in the struggle of the people.*

> **The dragon was furious... and went off to fight against... all those who obey God's commandments and are faithful to the truth revealed by Jesus.** Rev 12.17

Suggestions

To what extent are you prepared to give full witness of the values of Christ to the world?

Read meditatively **Jn 8.31-44**.

Ask for the grace to understand the real meaning of commitment to the values of the Kingdom and for courage to fight bravely under the banner of Christ.

PHASE THIRTEEN

QUALITY CHOICES

Richard, Rose, and Ronald are three persons each of whom had unexpectedly received a large sum of money. They were, of course, thrilled. But after the initial excitement died down, all three being God-fearing people, were concerned about what the wealth would do to them and their relationship with God. So each in his or her own way made certain decisions about his/her riches.

Richard enjoyed the prestige, power, comfort and security that wealth brought him. He invested his money carefully. Once settled, he began to realise that his attachment to riches and his lifestyle were making him progressively self-centred. He felt that he should do something to reach out to the less fortunate in society. However, whenever the opportunities came, it was hard for him to let go of his riches, so he would hesitate and say 'next time'. He landed up doing nothing till the day he died.

Rose, too, is, quite content with the status her newly-acquired fortune brought her. She realised that it would be too selfish to keep for herself all this God-given wealth. She decided to do something that could make God happy. One Sunday at Mass the Parish priest made an appeal for funds for a Social Works centre. Rose approached him after Mass and pledged a large amount of money. Months later, Rose was invited to the inauguration of the new building. She was shown a brass plate at the entrance with her name proudly displayed on it – for she was the biggest donor! Rose silently thanked God for the honour.

Ronald was a very religious-minded person. At first he was attracted to his newly acquired wealth, but eventually turned his attention to God. He realised that all good things come from God, and his unexpected riches were but an added gift of God. What would God want him to do with it, he asked himself. He did not want to take any rash decisions but wait for an answer from God. He put the money in a Trust, so as to surrender it completely. Should God demand that he give the money away to the poor, he would be ready for it. Or for anything else – provided it was God's will.

What would you have done if you had been given a large amount of money? Would you be a Procrastinator – like Richard, a Compromiser – like Rose, or a Surrenderer – like Ronald? In this unit you will spend your prayer periods checking out your attitudes and actions. You will examine how deep your commitment to Christ is and the steps you take to surrender yourself unconditionally to the will of the Father even at the cost of giving up all you have, or of losing your life.

Note that in cases where selfish interests are in conflict with some higher value, when making a choice between two good things, or when you show a tendency of shying away from some greater good simply because it is difficult or unpleasant, it would be important to swing toward the higher value, even if it goes against the grain, so that the choice for the better may be ensured. You must reinforce your choices with prayer.

To be a fully committed Christian, you have realised so far in this book of *spiritual exercises*, is to *praise*, *reverence*, and *serve* God, to take responsibility as a 'co-creator', and – if you have decided to follow Christ the King in a deeply spiritual way, – then to make choices that include *poverty*, *dishonour*, and *humility*. In this unit you will examine what attitude guides you in making your choices for greater or lesser commitment to Christ.

Making choices

Let us imagine a party of tourists who have set out to climb a difficult peak, and let us take a look at them some hours after they have started. By this time, we may suppose the party to be divided into three subgroups. Some are regretting having left the inn. The fatigue and risks involved seem out of all proportion to the value of a successful climb. The decide to turn back.

Others are not sorry that they set out. The sun is shining, and there is a beautiful view. But what is the point of climbing any higher? Surely it is better to enjoy the mountain from here – in the open meadow or deep in the wood. And so they stretch out on the grass or explore the neighbourhood until it is time for a picnic meal.

Lastly there are the others – the real mountaineers – who keep their eyes fixed on the peaks they have sworn to climb. So they set out again.

The tired – the hedonists – the enthusiasts. Three types of men: and deep within our own selves, we hold the germ of all three. Pierre Teilhard de Chardin, S.J.

Wise people walk the road that leads upwards to life. Prov 15.24

Suggestions

Which of the above three attitudes dominates your life generally? How does it effect the choices you make daily?

Read meditatively **Lk 18.18-32**.

Ask for the grace to make proper choices in life and then live them out responsibly and deliberately.

Deciding priorities

Sylvia Plath, the American poet, describing a person unable to risk commitment, in *The Bell Jar*, captures the attitude very precisely: I saw my life branching out before me like the green fig tree in the story. From the tip of the branch, like a fat purple fig, a wonderful future beckoned and winked. One fig was a husband and a happy home and children, and another fig was a famous poet and another was a brilliant professor, and another was EE Gee, the amazing editor, and another fig was Europe and Africa and South America, and another fig... and beyond and above these figs were many more figs I couldn't quite make out.

I saw myself sitting in the crotch of this fig tree, starving to death, just because I couldn't make up my mind which of the figs I would choose. I wanted each and every one of them, but choosing meant losing all the rest, and, one by one, they plopped to the ground at my feet.

None of you can be my disciple unless he gives up everything he has. Lk 14.33

Suggestions

Are you torn between many choices? Do you find it difficult to make a commitment? Is it because of your weak will?

Read meditatively **Lk 19.12-27**.

Ask for the grace not to dilly-dally with the choices before you but to be firm in making a commitment to God.

The heart is rich when it is content, and it is always content when its desires are fixed on God. Nothing can bring greater happiness than doing God's will for the love of God.

Bld Cordero-Munoz

Compromising ideals

When Colleen McCullough worked on *The Thorn Birds* she was a struggling medical researcher in Australia, badly in need of funds. On completing her manuscript she submitted it to a publisher. Then she thought of writing a novel based on hospitals, and in order to get some background McCullough went to England to enter nurse's training. "I didn't tell them I wrote books, of course," she said. "I was looking forward to some really hard physical labour because I am a workaholic."

The training was scheduled to begin in April, 1977. However, in February of that year, *The Thorn Birds* made a record sale. "I hit the headlines everywhere," McCullough recalled. "I could no longer go on nursing. Can you imagine a millionairess author carrying a bedpan!"

It is harder for a rich person to enter the kingdom of God than for a camel to go through the eye of a needle. Mt 19.24

Suggestions

Have you had to compromise with your ideals because of some material attachments or unexpected successes? How sincere have you been in fulfilling the mission of Christ?

Read meditatively **Lk 12.16-21**.

Ask for the grace to deepen your conviction of and to strive to live by the values of the Gospel and to be so detached from wealth and status as to be free to serve Christ in the needy.

You don't make decisions because they are cheap, or easy, or popular; you make them because they're right.

Faith choices

A young dare-devil acrobat would show-off his skills by crossing a 240-foot span over a strong cable which linked two banks of an exceedingly deep canyon. He even walk blindfolded over the cable, and without supports. One evening he added an extra-special feat. He pushed a wheelbarrow from one bank to the other, across the chasm, to the cheers of an admiring crowd. Then he filled the wheelbarrow with sand, and made the return trip. The moment his steady feet touched solid ground, the terrified people went wild with applause for his bravery. "You can do anything on the high wire," one young man shouted, hugging the courageous acrobat. "You're the greatest I've ever seen." Picking up a shovel, the performer began to remove the sand. "So you really believe in my ability?" he said to his admirer.
"Oh yes, I do believe in you, I certainly do. You are the best there is."
"Well then," countered the daredevil, "I'll cross the chasm once more and this time you get in the wheelbarrow."
Suddenly the young enthusiast lost all his faith – and quickly disappeared from the scene.

Courage! It is I... Don't be afraid! Mt 14.27

Suggestions

Have you had the experiences of taking 'risky' decisions that involved total trust in God? Were you able to do so with courage and faith? Are you ready and willing to take the plunge now? The desire and the call to a life identical with that of Christ is God's gift. You must be attentive to his voice and have an open mind to accept his challenge.

Read meditatively **Mt 14.22-33**.

Ask for the grace to be determined enough to throw in your lot with Christ, spontaneously, trustingly.

Option to be like Christ

Clarence and Robert McClendon were two brothers, very prominent in their careers and very good Christians, too. Robert was a prominent lawyer, while Clarence had published a "Cotton Patch Version of the New Testament", and had become very much involved in the interracial work in Georgia, in the '50's and '60's. At one particular time, Clarence asked Robert for legal help. Clarence was shocked, when his lawyer (and politician!) brother refused to help him. What shocked Clarence most was the fact that both were "committed" to Christ, and he let Robert know about it.

"I follow Jesus, Clarence, up to a point... I follow him to the Cross, but not on the cross. I'm not getting myself crucified."

Clarence looked at his brother and said, "Robert, you're not a follower of Jesus, you're only an admirer of his."

None of you can be my disciple unless he gives up everything he has. Lk 14.33

Suggestions

Total commitment to Christ may call for a deliberate choice to be poor, humble, isolated or thought little of by rich, powerful and influential people. How prepared are you for such a lifestyle?

Read meditatively **Gen 22.1-17**.

Ask for the grace to have at least the desire to be poor and humble, like Christ, and to always choose the tougher option should it be more conducive for the spread of the Kingdom.

Two roads diverged in a wood, and I –
I took the one less traveled by,
And that has made all the difference. R. Frost

Lofty decisions

The Nobel Peace Prize winner (1952) Albert Schweitzer, has been acclaimed the world over as a multiple genius. It was his remarkably deep Christian faith which influenced even the smallest details of his life. It motivated him to turn his back on worldly fame and wealth and serve the poorest of the poor in Africa. At 21, Schweitzer decided he would enjoy art and science until he was 30, and devote the rest of his life for the needy. So, when he turned 30, he joined the university for a degree in medicine, in order to work in Africa as a missionary doctor.

"My relatives and friends all joined in expostulating with me on the folly of my enterprise. I was a man, they said, who was burying the talent entrusted to him... A lady who was filled with the modern spirit proved to me that I could do much more by lecturing on behalf of medical help for the natives than I could by the action I contemplated," he says in his book *Out of My Life and Thought*. At 43, he left for Africa as a full-fledged medical doctor. With the proceeds from his books, organ recitals and lectures given on visits to Europe, he established a hospital at Lambarene in Gabon, on the edge of the jungle in Equatorial Africa. He died there in 1965 at the age of 90.

I keep striving to win the prize for which Christ Jesus has already won me to himself.

Phil 3.12

Suggestions

At what stage/s in your life did you make crucial decisions? Were you responding to 'the will of God' in each of those choices? Is there anything that needs to be done to set things right now?

Read meditatively **Lk 9.57-62** and **Phil 3.12-16**.

Ask for the grace to surrender your whole being to God, for him to do with you what he pleases.

A sign of contradiction

One of the character traits possessed by exceptional people is their ability to live their lives in terms of what the Gospel called "a sign of contradiction" to the world – which brings out their uniqueness. Mother Teresa was one such person. As one of the weekly magazines reported after her death on September 6, 1997: Her humility was burdened by celebrity. She raised millions for her work but lived simply, befriending the rich and famous to aid the poor and anonymous. She was a woman of power in a church run by men. Although a missionary of Christ, she insisted that God wanted Hindus to be good Hindus, Muslims good Muslims.

One of the editorials in *The Examiner*, Mumbai, said: It is a world, starved of heroes, who put her on a pedestal so high that she was forced to feel the cold winds of controversy and hostility. In death, she would wish to be completely effaced, letting nothing remain but the good work she did.

The scars that I have on my body
show that I am the slave of Jesus. Gal 6.17

Suggestions

How determined are you to live by Christ's value-system – against all odds, objections, opposition or criticism?

Read meditatively **Lk 14.25-33**.

Ask for the strength to choose a life of 'contradictions' – in keeping with the symbol of the Cross of Christ.

In order to arrive at having pleasure in everything, desire to have pleasure in nothing. In order to arrive at possessing everything, desire to possess nothing. In order to arrive at being everything, be nothing. In order to arrive at knowing everything, desire to know nothing. St John of the Cross

SURRENDER WITHOUR FEAR

I am afraid of saying "yes", Lord.
Where will you take me? ...
I am afraid of the "yes" that entails other "yeses".
And yet I am not at peace
You pursue me, Lord, you besiege me.
I run after noise for fear of hearing you,
but in a moment of silence you slip through.
I turn from the road, for I have caught sight of
you, but at the end of the path
you are there awaiting me.
Where shall I hide? I meet you everywhere.
Is it then impossible to escape you?
But I'm afraid to say "yes" Lord
I am afraid of putting my hand in your hand,
for you hold on to it.
I am afraid of meeting your eyes, for you can
win me. I am afraid of your demands,
for you are a jealous God....
When I stretch out my hand to catch hold of
people and things, they vanish before me.
It's no fun, Lord, I can't keep anything for myself.
The flower I pick fades in my hands.
My laugh freezes on my lips....
I am hungry and thirsty,
And the whole world cannot satisfy me.
And yet I loved you, Lord; what have I done to
you? I worked for you; I gave myself for you.
O great and terrible God,
What more do you want? .....
O Lord, I am afraid of your demands,
but who can resist you?
That your Kingdom may come and not mine,
That your will may be done and not mine,
Help me to say yes.

Michel Quoist

SECTION FOUR

THE MISSION OF CHRIST

THE MISSION OF CHRIST

Jesus Christ will continue to be your focus – "the Way, the Truth and the Life" (Jn 14.6). He will no more be the "hidden" Jesus of Nazareth, for he steps out of the threshold of his home to become a wandering teacher, preacher, and miracle-worker.

In Jesus – the "Word" – God reveals the plan of salvation for the world. To be a true disciple of Jesus does not mean *compliance* to a set of 'commandments' but *union* to the Person of Jesus through practising them.

> "I reckon everything as complete loss for the sake of what is so much more valuable, the knowledge of Jesus Christ my Lord. For his sake I have thrown everything away; I consider it all as refuse, so that I may gain Christ and be completely united with him... All I want is to know Christ and to experience the power of his resurrection" (Phil 3.8-10).

To *know* Christ, in the sense that St Paul uses the term, means a person-to-person encounter – rather than book-knowledge. Christ is not merely a historical person you study about, but a life that you imbibe, a *living friend* who wants you to get intimate with him.

You have been taught about him in class and church, you have come heart-to-heart with him in prayer. You must deepen this contact, so that you can answer with conviction the question he poses you: "Who do you say I am? Do you love me more than these others do?" (Jn 21.15)

In the coming units you must contemplate the human life of Jesus as found in the Gospels so as to transform your attitudes and behaviour according to that of Jesus. You must take up more seriously the challenges of God's mission – to collaborate with Christ in the establishment of his Kingdom. In turn, you must become more passionately in love with the Person of Jesus, and feel strongly drawn to follow him and serve him to the end.

Father, I abandon myself into your hands; do with me what you will. Whatever you may do, I thank you; I am ready for all, I accept all. Let only your will be done in me and in all creatures. I wish no more than this, O Lord.

Into your hand, O Lord, I commend my soul. I offer it to you with all the love of my heart, for I love you, Lord, and so must give myself, surrender myself into your hands, without reserve and with boundless confidence, for you are my Father. Charles de Foucald

Oh, they can take away our right to pray
And even throw us all in jail;
But they can't take away the life he gave
They can't send my soul to hell.

Oh they can take my Blessed Bible
Tear the pages all apart;
But they'll never, never take my Jesus
Out of my heart.

Oh they can take my life and bury me
In a grave so cold, cold and dark;
But they'll never take my Jesus
Out of my heart
NEVER GET HIM OUT OF MY HEART! Roy Moore

PHASE FOURTEEN

JESUS: FULLY HUMAN

Mahatma Gandhi was a fond admirer of Jesus. He was deeply touched by the principles of the Sermon on the Mount – which he heroically put into practice in his life. "...If then I had to face only the Sermon on the Mount and my own interpretation of it, I should say, 'Oh, yes, I am a Christian.'" On his own confession, though, he did not accept Jesus as the Son of God. Once his good friend and great admirer, the Rev Stanley Jones, a Protestant, wrote him the following letter:

> You know my love for you and how I've tried to interpret you and your non-violent movement to the West.... I thought you had grasped the centre of the Christian faith, but I'm afraid... you have grasped the principles, but you have missed the Person. You said in Calcutta to the missionaries that you did not turn to the *Sermon on the Mount* for consolation, but the *Bhagavad Gita*. Neither do I turn to the Sermon on the Mount for consolation, but to this Person who embodies and illustrates the Sermon on the Mount; but is much more. Here is where I think you are weakest in your grasp. May I suggest that you penetrate through the principles to the Person and then come back and tell us what you have found....

Gandhiji replied immediately:

> I appreciate the love underlying the letter and kind thought for my welfare, but my difficulty is of long standing. Other friends have pointed it out to me before now. I cannot grasp the position by the intellect; the heart must be touched. Saul became Paul not by an intellectual effort but by something in his heart. All I can say is that my heart is absolutely open; I have no axes to grind. I want to find the truth, to see God face to face.

In your prayer, "penetrate through to principles to the person" of Jesus Christ. Let yourself be touched to the core as you reach for the core of the Way, the Truth and the Life, as you meditate on the human side of Jesus in this unit. Experience the struggles he went through and the radical options he made in life so as to be totally faithful to the Mission entrusted to him by the Father.

Pray for grace to have a heart that is 'absolutely open' so that you can find the truth, and be able to see the image of God in the face of Christ his Son. Ask that you may know Christ more intimately, love him more deeply and follow him more faithfully.

O loving Father, make me like Jesus:
The Jesus who could spend nights in prayer.
The Jesus who went about doing good.
The Jesus who could not bear to see
the mother cry at Nain.
The Jesus who took a towel and knelt
and washed the feet of the men
who were going to deny, betray and forsake him.
The Jesus who could give a patient word
when smitten on the face.
The Jesus who could pray for the men
who nailed him to the Cross.
The Jesus who was strong enough
not to answer back when accused unjustly.
The Jesus who could sleep peacefully
in a gale and storm.
The Jesus who would not let the marriage
at Cana be spoilt by lack of wine.
The Jesus who would not condemn
the woman taken in an act of sin.
The Jesus who could shrink from the cup
of suffering yet drunk it to the last dregs.
O loving Father, make me like the Jesus
who came to the world to show what you were like.

Bishop Jacob of Travancore

The man from Galilee

What exactly was Jesus like to meet? If one had been a fellow-guest when he asked himself to dinner with Zacchaeus, or when he was eating with the Pharisee, what sort of a man would one in fact have seen and spoken to? What was his conversation like? Having asked this question, I looked at the Gospel again, and quite suddenly a new portrait seemed to stare at me out of the pages. I had never previously thought of a laughing, joking Jesus, physically strong and active, fond of good company and a glass of wine, telling funny stories, using, as every good teacher does, paradox and exaggeration as among the most effective aids to instruction, applying nicknames to his friends, and holding his companions spellbound with his talk... the first thing we must learn about him is that we should have been absolutely entranced by his company.

Lord Hailsham of St Marylebone

Isn't he the carpenter's son...?

Mt 14.55

Suggestions

How often have you visualised Jesus as a charming person – very human, very loving and lovable?

Read meditatively **Mt 16.1-4**.

Ask for the grace to understand the 'human qualities' of Jesus so as to follow him more closely.

There are three miracles of our Brother Jesus not yet recorded in the Book: the first that He was a man like you and me; the second that He had a sense of humour; and the third that He knew He was a conqueror though conquered.

Kahlil Gibran

One of us

A scene not recorded in the Gospels is that of Jesus bidding farewell to his family at about age 30. Unlike the lad of twelve who slipped out of his mother's grasp to stay back at the Temple, this time Jesus must surely have explained why he had to go: to be about his 'Father's business'. But the parting nonetheless must have been a sorrowful one, for Jesus was human after all.

One must not overlook the fact that Jesus was, indeed, a 'real man'. His contemporaries recognised him as an ordinary 'carpenter's son'. As a normal human being, he ate and drank (Mk 7.33, 8.23, Mt 9.10); he experienced hunger (Mk 4.2) and thirst (Jn 19.28); he felt tired (Jn 4.5, Mk 4.38). Jesus also expressed a wide range of human emotions. He was filled with joy (Lk 10.21), surprise (Mk 6.6), anger (Mk 8.21), pity (Lk 7.13), compassion (Lk 15.20), disappointment (Lk 17.17). He was surrounded by female friends (Lk 8.2, Jn 11.5). He embraced children (Mk 9.36, 10.16). He wept for his friend Lazarus and people exclaimed, "See how much he loved him!" (Jn 11.35). And he suffers at his Passion.

He became like man and appeared in human likeness. Phil 2.7

Suggestions

Do you believe that the phrase 'fully human fully alive' applies to Jesus in his earthly life? To what degree?

Read meditatively **Phil 2.1-11**.

Ask for the grace that like Jesus, you too may be 'fully human fully alive.'

All that I am I owe to Jesus Christ, revealed to me in His Divine Book. David Livingstone

Jesus does not set out from Nazareth as a majestic messiah, but as a man on a mission. His first step towards fulfilling his Father's plan was to associate himself as closely as possible with *sinful humanity*. So he joined the queue of 'sinners' who were receiving from his cousin John the 'baptism of repentance'. John was reluctant to baptise Jesus, since he recognised him as the one who is much greater than he. Only on Jesus's insistence does John agree.

As soon as Jesus came out of the water, a voice came from heaven, "You are my own dear Son. I am pleased with you." This was a moment of truth for Jesus, when he realised more clearly than ever before who he was and what he was supposed to do with his life. It was like a moment of revelation, of encouragement and affirmation. It was a moment of divine confirmation of his mission.

And he who sent me is with me....;
because I always do what pleases him.
Jn 8.29

Suggestions

Has there been a time in your life when the affirmation and encouragement of God, others, has made you feel supported, important, loved?

Read meditatively about the humility of John, the people's approach to his baptism, and the attitude of Jesus in **Mt 3.1-16**.
Apply the words of **Is 42.1-7** to Jesus.

Ask for the grace to understand Jesus' obedience to his Father's will, so that you may feel inspired to follow him more closely.

He was meek, benevolent, patient, firm, disinterested, and of the sublimest eloquence. Thomas Jefferson

Led by the Spirit

The Spirit of God took possession of Jesus in a very special way to direct his energies towards his allotted task, his messianic mission. After he was baptised by John, the Spirit that had hovered over the chaos at the dawn of creation hovered over Jesus, thus ushering in the "new creation" – the new Adam.

The entire life and work of Jesus is guided by the Spirit. First the Spirit leads Jesus into the desert to face in solitude the issues that are implied in his mission. Then, in his first public appearance in the synagogue at Nazareth, Jesus realised, as he read from a scroll, that "the Spirit of the lord is upon me, because he has chosen me to bring good news to the poor." As Jesus moved among the people, the Spirit continued to show him that he could teach with his own authority about God's Kingdom. The Spirit helped Jesus see everything from God's point of view. The Spirit gave Jesus the power to work miracles, to heal the sick and those possessed by evil spirits.

The Spirit of the Lord is upon me.
Lk 3.18

Suggestions

Would you be able to confidently declare that the Spirit of God is guiding you in your life? What evidence do you have?

Read meditatively **Lk 3.16-21** and **31-37**.

Ask for the grace to be filled with the Spirit so that your knowledge and love of Jesus increase, and your desire to follow him closely grow.

Everyone has his own specific vocation or mission in life; everyone must carry out a concrete assignment that demands fulfilment. Therein he cannot be replaced, nor can life be repeated. Thus, everyone's task is as unique as is his specific opportunity to implement it.
Viktor Frankl

Tempted by the devil

Years ago, a British television team went to the Holy Land to make a movie of the life of Jesus. They ran into trouble when it came to filming the temptations of Jesus. The big problem was how to portray the devil. Many ancient artists portrayed the devil in an incredible way....

The British television team eventually decided to portray the devil by simply showing a shadow on the sand. The solution seemed to work. It avoided useless argument about how Jesus experienced the devil. Was the devil present in the mind of Jesus? Or was the devil present in a physical way? That is, did the devil approach Jesus the way I'd approach you on the street? The British television team decided to place the focus on Jesus, not on the devil. Mark Link

When the Devil finished tempting Jesus in every way, he left him for a while.
Lk 4.13

Suggestions

Are you aware of the ways in which you are led into and yield to temptations? What are the nature of your 'temptations'? Who are your 'tempters', generally?

Read meditatively **Mt 4.1-11**. Contemplate Jesus as he argues with the Evil One. Notice that Jesus was tempted to choose Riches – Honour – Pride, and he responded with conviction that his mission demanded Poverty – Dishonour – Humility.

Ask for the grace to be always faithful to Jesus and his Mission which you have undertaken, under all circumstances.

I too am visited by angels and devils but I get rid of them. When it is an angel I pray an old prayer, and he is bored; when it is a devil I commit an old sin and he passes by. Kahlil Gibran

Tackling the tempter

At a main shopping thoroughfare, a woman asked a passerby: "Isn't there a shop near here that sells imported perfume?"

"Yes, there is," replied the passerby. "Go straight ahead, and it's the first shop after the intersection."

Thanking him, she started off in the opposite direction. "Excuse me," he called after her, "didn't you understand my explanation?"

"Oh, did," she replied. "It's just that I don't want to go past the shop and be tempted."

Jesus was tempted in every way that we are, but did not sin. Heb 4.15

Suggestions

How do you deal with temptations? Do you understand the implications and consequences of the temptations you face?

Read meditatively **Jas 1.12-18**.

Ask for strength to fight the 'enemy' and the grace of total dedication to Christ: to love him and follow him passionately.

**You cannot play with the animal in you without becoming wholly animal...
He who wants to keep his garden tidy doesn't reserve a plot for weeds.**
Dag Hammarskjold

14/7 Jesus' powerful weapon

The Secret is a film rich in symbols. A stranger, who seems to represent Christ, is shown as coming down a mountain. He is tall, walks with dignity and holds his head high. The people he mingles with are aware that he has a great vision which enables him to lift his sights above the petty squabbling and silly preoccupations that surround him. He will not share his vision lightly. To catch it a man has to climb the hill for himself.

In the Gospels there are seventeen recorded instances of Jesus praying. He made time and space for prayer by climbing mountains or by walking into the desert. We know that sometimes he got up early to spend time with his heavenly Father. On occasions he would give a whole night to prayer. Always we see him favouring lonely places and the quiet times.

> **The Sovereign Lord has taught me what to say, so that I can strengthen the weary.**
>
> Is 50.4

Suggestions

How often do you feel the urge to be alone with God? Are you convinced that prayer is a powerful 'weapon' against evil temptations?

Read meditatively **Mk 1.35-37**; **Lk 4.42**; **11.1-4**.

Ask for the grace to be a person of prayer with a deep longing to be united with God through intense moments of prayer.

> **When I was crossing into Gaza, I was asked at the checkpost whether I was carrying any weapons. I replied, "Oh yes: my prayer books."** Mother Teresa

Lord Jesus Christ, the things that hold us back from you are so varied: all those sterile worries, futile pleasures and vain preoccupations. So many things tend to distract or frighten us and make us hold back; pride which makes us too cowardly to accept help from others; timidity which draws us back to self-destruction; remorse for past sins, which flees before the purity of what is holy, as sickness flees from the doctor's remedy. And yet in spite of all, you are stronger than all. Draw us to you ever more strongly. Amen.

Soren Kierkegaard

Lord, you seized me, and I could not resist you.
I ran for a long time, but you followed me.
I took by-paths, but you knew them.
You overtook me. I struggled. You won.
Here I am, Lord, out of breath,
no fight left in me, and I've said "yes"
almost unwillingly.
When I stood there trembling like one defeated
before his captor, Your look of love fell on me.

The die is cast, Lord, I can no longer forget you.
In a moment you seized me.
In a moment you conquered me.
My doubts were swept away, My fears dispelled.
For I recognized you without seeing you.
I felt you without touching you.
I understood you without hearing you.
Marked by your fire of love,
I can no longer forget you....
Thank you, Lord, thank you!
Why me, why did you choose me?
Joy, joy, tears of joy.

Michel Quoist

PHASE FIFTEEN

THE CALL TO DISCIPLESHIP

When Dr David Livingstone was working in Africa, a group of friends wrote to him: "We would like to send other men to you. Have you found a good road into your area yet?"

According to a member of his family, Dr Livingstone sent this message in reply: "If you have men who will only come if they know there is a good road, I don't want them. I want men who will come if there is no road at all."

In Jesus' day, young jews who wanted to study religion at depth would select a wise and holy Rabbi and enrol themselves as his disciples. They would have regular meetings with the Rabbi at his residence to be tutored, and as 'payment' be of service to the Rabbi.

Jesus turned the system upside down. He himself chose his disciples – from the waterfront, the marketplace, and the tax office. He wanted young men who were suited to his kind of ministry. It is amazing how at his simple bidding – *"Come, follow me"*, – they would give up everything and become his disciple.

There was no set place where the disciples met for instruction. Because Jesus was always on the move. He preached to the multitudes in the open or to believers in the synagogues, and the disciples as well listened to him eagerly; later they would ask questions and seek clarifications in quiet moments with him.

"What gives life is God's Spirit; man's power is of no use at all. The words I have spoken to you bring God's life-giving Spirit."(Jn 6.63) Sometimes the ideas of Jesus were so challenging that some of his disciples could not take them in and left him (Jn 6.66).

Jesus chose twelve men as his 'inner circle' of disciples. They remained his constant companions throughout the three years of his ministry. "I do not call you servants any longer," Jesus assured them, "because a servant does not know what his master is doing. Instead, I call you friends, because I have told you everything I have heard from my Father. You did not choose me, but I chose you and appointed you to go and bear much fruit..." (Jn 15.15-16).

Jesus taught his disciples primarily through example. His life of loving service to them and others was to be the model for their own lives: "Love one another just as I love you," (Jn 16.12). At one point during his last meal with them, Jesus dramatised this point by actually serving them, and washing their feet. "I have set an example for you, so that you will do just what I have done for you." (Jn 13.15).

As a Christian, you are called to be a follower of Jesus. Some have a specific "vocation" as Priest, Brothers, Sisters... but every Christian is called to give witness to God's love by living a life pattern and principles Jesus has given.

Spend the next few days examining prayerfully what it really means to be a follower of Jesus – a 'Christian' in the fullest sense of the word.

Jesus Christ is the same yesterday,
today, and for ever. Heb 13.8

The personal call

Fr Edouard Le Joly was born in Liege, Belgium. His father, a jeweller, hoped that his only son would succeed him in the family business. Edouard studied arts and law and qualified to be a barrister. He did a year's military service and became a lieutenant.

"I toyed for some time with a plan to earn much money, so that I could send a large sum to build a church for new Christians in a poor area. But deep down in my heart the Lord God was saying: 'I do not need your church and your money, I want you'"

I countered: "Myself, Lord, my whole life? – no, that is too much, it is beyond me, and I am not able to give...." Finally the Lord won: he took me by force. I left everything and went to join the religious life," says Fr Le Joly in his autobiography, *The Call of Jesus*. At 24, he joined the Jesuit Order. He later came to India, became a prolific writer and a confidante of Mother Teresa. His Life of Christ was translated into a dozen Indian languages.
"God never let me down," said Fr Le Joly, who died in Kolkata in May 2002, at age 93!

"Where do you live, Rabbi?"
"Come and see," Jesus answered. Jn 1.39

Suggestions

Do you understand that discipleship in Christ means giving up your plans to follow his? In what ways do you feel challenged to do this?

Read meditatively **Mt 9.9-13**.

Ask for the grace to be attentive to the call of Christ and the courage to follow it.

Called by name

Grimm's *Rumpelstiltskin* is a fascinating tale. The Dwarf will keep the Princess as payment unless the Queen discovers his name. Fortunately for her, she hears him singing out his name, and thus wins back the Princess.

Like many fairy tales, this one is much more than entertainment for children. It contains something of the ancient idea among many peoples that the name of something – a man or a god or a devil – has almost a life of its own.

Your name is symbolic of all that you are as a person. When you reveal your name to someone, you establish a relationship. You are no longer a stranger. Now your name can be used – or abused. You can also be summoned, and controlled. You can be enrolled and commissioned.

At your Baptism as you were anointed with the sign of the cross, your name was pronounced; it was stamped onto your personality as a Christian – a disciple of Christ.

Your names are written in heaven.
Lk 10.20

Suggestions

To what extent have you understood your 'person' call to discipleship through your baptism?

Read meditatively **Jn 1.35-42**.

Ask for the grace to bring glory to the name of Jesus by following faithfully in his footsteps.

God does not call us to be successful;
he calls us to be faithful.

God's mysterious ways

After writing my B.A. exam, I was staying with my very religious-minded doctor uncle in his clinic. One evening... most unexpectedly my uncle shot this question at me: "Why don't you become a priest?" My spontaneous reply was, "I can't even pray for five minutes. How will I ever become a priest?" It was perfectly clear to me that I had no such vocation. I meant what I said, and dismissed the idea from my mind. I didn't think any further deliberation was needed.

Days later, we were paying a visit to the parish church, when suddenly, unexpectedly, I had a flash of inspiration. I must become a priest. I understood that God was calling me. If He wanted it, any obstacles I had imagined, like my distrust of myself and fear of the exalted job, could be overcome. After I received my call, it was clear to me that I must learn to pray. In the school library I discovered the volume, The *Spiritual Exercises* of St Ignatius.... For the first time I was beginning to understand what human life is all about. I went through the whole volume with great zeal. A friend... came to the clinic. He told me about the Jesuits and their work. Here was a new opening. In my impatience about making a decision, I wrote a long letter to the Jesuit Provincial in Madurai.... I received a reply of welcome by return of post. Fr C. M. Cherian, S. J.

I chose you and appointed you to go and bear much fruit. Jn 15.16

Suggestions

Have you experienced the 'call' of God in the depths of your heart?

Read meditatively **Mk 1.16-20**.

As for the grace to be generous and courageous in answering Christ's call.

15/4 The transforming voice

The Mexican Jesuit martyr, Michael Augustine Pro, who was beatified in 1998, recalls his vocation:

Does God speak to the soul?... Yes, indeed, he does and his words are sweet. He does speak, and the soul understands his voice, understands his language. I know this from experience and assure you that I did not have the dispositions you have in order to understand his call. Rather, I had all the opposite dispositions, all the obstacles, and these were not due to factors independent of myself but to my own actions and conduct, which were entirely contrary.

But God in his infinite mercy cast his eyes on the dry and barren tree-trunk of my life and saw the statue he could carve with his most holy grace; he called me out, in spite of my opposition, from the corrupt world where I lived, so that the beautiful words of the psalmist might come true: "I raised you from the dunghill to place you among the princes of my people."

My Beloved lifts up his voice and says to me: Come then, my lovely one, come. Songs 2.10

Suggestions

How do you feel about Christ's call to you? What is your response?

Read meditatively **Jn 10.1-5**.

Ask for the grace to be attentive to the call of Christ and to respond to it with your whole heart.

***Joan of Arc*: I hear voices telling me what to do. They come from God.**
***Robert* : They come from your imagination.**
***Joan* : Of course. That is how the messages of God come to me.** G.B.Shaw

Call within a call

Every Christian has to be Christ where Christ wishes to be in him. The apostolate is independent of outward circumstances and additional vocations of work or service imposed upon it. The vocation to be Christ, the 'channel of his grace' precedes and supersedes all other vocations, making them always secondary....

It was the summons of the personal Christ, personally known and personally loved that led me into his Church. He said to me, a person, by name Barbara, as she said to Philip, Peter, James, John, and he rest, "Come follow me." And just as they responded without the least hesitation because their hearts knew he was the Lord, so did I. It was impossible to do anything else. His influence is hypnotic, when you meet him person to person. "Deep calls unto deep," and the spontaneous reply is, "Yes, Lord, I'm coming. Right now." Barbara Dent

Before I was born, the Lord chose me and appointed me to be his servant. Is 49.1

Suggestions

Have you discovered your 'vocation' to be Christ – 'the channel of his grace'?

Read meditatively **Lk 10.1-12**.

Ask the Lord to enable you to discover your inner calling and to respond to it with full generosity so as to grow more and more into the likeness of Christ.

When I have learned to do the Father's will,
I shall have fully realised my vocation.

Carlo Carretto

15/6 Following Jesus' example

New York Bishop Egan travelled to one of the poorest areas of Brooklyn to ordain five young men as deacons for the congregation of priests and brothers founded by Mother Teresa. Mother Teresa herself and many of the Sisters of Charity were there. After the rite of ordination, Bishop Egan proceeded to the altar for the Eucharistic Prayer. Suddenly, shouts were heard from the rear of the church. A young man was lunging up the aisle, his face covered with blood; he waved a bloody T-shirt in the air, begging for help amid his shouts and sobs. Mother Teresa led two of her sisters and two ushers in gently carrying the man to the sacristy. Eventually, the Mass was able to continue.

At the end of the Mass, a young man came up to Bishop Egan and said: "I was in the sacristy when the bloodied man was carried in. He had been beaten badly and his language was terrible. But never in my life had I seen anything like the way he was treated. Mother and her two sisters and the pastor and the two laymen were wonderful. They calmed the man. They washed the blood off him. They found him a clean shirt and they arranged a place for him for the night. It was everything that Jesus Christ had ever taught. *It was everything, Father, that Jesus Christ had ever taught."* [*The New York Times*, June 19, 2000]

> **Jesus began to wash the disciples' feet and dry them with the towel round his waist.** Jn 13.6

Suggestions

Are you fully aware of the implications of being 'Christian'? To what degree do you live out your commitment.

Read meditatively **Lk 5.1-11**.

Ask for the grace to follow the "commandment of love" and the example that Christ gave his disciples.

The cost of discipleship

Padre Pio of Pietrelcina (1887-1968), the Stigmatist, was canonized a saint by Pope John Paul II on June 16, 2002. Following is an excerpt of the pontiff's homily delivered during the ceremony:

"But may I never boast except in the cross of our Lord Jesus Christ" (Gal 6:14). Is it not, precisely, the "glory of the Cross" that shines above all in Padre Pio? How timely is the spirituality of the Cross lived by the humble Capuchin of Pietrelcina! Our times have need of rediscovering its value in order to open the heart to hope.

Throughout his life, he always sought greater conformity with the Crucified, being very conscious of having been called to collaborate in a special way in the work of redemption. His holiness cannot be understood without this constant reference to the Cross.

In God's plan, the Cross constitutes the true instrument of salvation for the whole of humanity and the way explicitly proposed by the Lord to all those who wish to follow him (see Mt 16:24)."

Whoever does not carry his own cross and come after me cannot be my disciple. Lk 14.27

Suggestions

Do you gladly accept the crosses you have to endure in your following of Christ – as a Christian?

Read meditatively **Mt 16.24-28**.

Ask for the grace to follow Christ through thick and thin, bearing joyfully your crosses in life.

We become what our conception of Jesus Christ is.... In the degree of the truth of our conception of him,
our minds grow broader, deeper and warmer;
our hearts grow wiser and kinder;
our humour deeper and more tender;
we become more aware of the wonder of life,
our senses become more sensitive;
our sympathies stronger;
our capacity for giving and for receiving greater;
our minds are more radiant with the burning light,
and the light is the life of Christ. Caryll Houselander

Love and Peace will become real and attainable:

- if we believe that a smile is stronger than arms;
- if we believe in the power of an out-stretched hand;
- if we prefer hope over suspicion;
- if we choose to take the first step to get closer to our adversaries;
- if we can rejoice when our neighbours succeed;
- if we believe that forgiveness goes further than revenge;
- if we accept criticism without defence;
- if the Gospel does not scandalize us;
- if we restrain from always blaming someone else;
- if we choose to feel wounded rather than hurting others;
- if we look at the poor and oppressed without feeling "superior";
- if we accept that Love is stronger than Force.

PHASE SIXTEEN

THE GURU'S PRINCIPLES

Jesus was an itinerant preacher. He taught in the synagogues occasionally, but most of his teaching was done on the move. His classroom was the roadside, the seashore, the hillside, the streets and homes of villages.

These open-air settings attracted a great mixture of listeners: young, old, believers and non-believers, Jews, Greeks, Romans, the literate and illiterate, labourers and teachers. To ensure that he captured the attention of his motley audience and make an impression on them so that they remember his message, Jesus used several teaching techniques: Debates, Parables, Figures of speech, one-liners... The Sermon on the Mount (Mt 5) is said to contain the essence of Jesus' teaching. It describes the qualities required of a true follower of Jesus – which are a complete reversal of conventional values and standards.

> "Of all the things I have read what remained with me forever," said Gandhi, the champion of non-violence, "was that Jesus came almost to give a new law – not an eye for an eye but to receive two blows when only one was given, and to go two miles when they were asked to go one. I came to see that the Sermon on the Mount was the whole of Christianity for him who wanted to live a Christian life. It is that sermon that has endeared Jesus to me." Mahatma Gandhi

In this phase you will focus on attention on the core of Jesus' message – his basic principles for the realisation of the kingdom of God. Ask for the grace of total openness to the challenges that Jesus' teaching evoke and to respond with a generous heart.

Happy those who trust in themselves
 – they experience no need of others.
Happy are the aggressive
 – they shall enjoy walking on people.
Happy are they who are unwilling
 to forego any comfort
 – they shall never know what sacrifice is.
Happy are those for whom money comes first
 – money shall be their consolation.
Happy are those who have no pity
 – their hearts are not vulnerable.
Happy are the sex consumers
 – they shall never know what tenderness is.
Happy are the violent
 – Satan shall call them his sons.
Happy are those who get away
 with doing wrong
 – theirs is the kingdom of the world.

What a contrast from Jesus' Beatitudes!

Mark Tierney, O.S.B.

Heaven and earth will pass away,
but my words will never pass away.

Mt 24.35

Suggestions

Do the 'modern beatitudes' quoted above find an echo in your life?

Read reflectively **Mt 5.1-12**.

Ask for greater understanding of the teachings of Jesus and the courage to walk in his footsteps.

16/2 Make existence palatable

In 1988, the popular American movie star Michael J. Fox, shared the story of his seven-year battle with Parkinson's disease – the details of his diagnosis and the prognosis, his brain surgery and the effects his illness had had on his family, friends and coworkers – in *People* Magazine on the ABC News programme 20/20.

Parkinson's disease is a progressive degeneration of the central nervous system, that ultimately renders some patients unable to walk, take or care for themselves. At present, its cause is unknown and, worse, there is no cure.

"I was scared a lot at the beginning and still am. I'm also optimistic. To sit in a chair and feel pain in every muscle and say, 'Oh, no, I'm going to get worse' – why do that?" he says. Instead he focuses on the good things in life. "I'm not crying, 'What a tragedy,' because it's not. It's a reality. It's a fact." He concludes: "I think I can help people by talking," Fox said.

You are the salt for all mankind.
Mt 5.13

Suggestions

Do you realise that through his frank sharing, Fox became "salt" for families experiencing the same trauma – giving the victims hope and courage, and the others compassion?

Read meditatively **Mt 5.13**.

Ask that you may realise your vocation to be 'salt' for the earth – to make God's presence and grace realities in your own time and place.

Radiate your light

The sun had already set when the young monk was departing from the Master's house to his monastery in a remote area. He was somewhat apprehensive, and the Master sensing the youth's fear, asked, "Are you afraid of the dark?"

"Yes, I am," confessed the monk, "but I was feeling ashamed to say so."

"Don't be afraid," said the Master, reaching out for a candle. He lighted it and handed it over to the young man. "Take this, and go in peace."

The Master accompanied the monk to the gate, and there, in the same breath in which he said 'goodbye' he blew out the candle. The young man's eyes popped out with astonishment.

"Master," he said after a thoughtful pause, "it was out of great compassion that you gave me this light for the way. Why have you blown it out?"

The Master smiled. "The candle will not be of much use to you. Be a light unto yourself."

I am the light of the world. Jn 8.12

Suggestions

If you fail to recognise the light shining in you, how can you take away the darkness around you?

Read meditatively **Mt 5.14-16** and **Eph 5.6-14**.

Ask for the grace to be Christlike so as to let his light shine through you.

16/4 Live the spirit of the law

At an army headquarters, a Duty Officer summoned the Regimental Sergeant Major (RSM) and asked him to find out how high the guard-room flagpole was. The RSM went to the guard-room and ordered the sentry to take one end of the measuring tape he held out, climb the pole, and hold the tape-end at the top.

The sentry suggested that it would be simpler to take the pins out of the bottom of the pole, lay it to the ground, and then measure it. The RSM snapped: "The officer wants to know how high it is, not how long it is, so get up that pole."

We know that the law is good if it is used as it should be used. 1Tim 1.8

Suggestions

Do you make out the difference between the 'letter' and the 'spirit' of the law? What are your 'attitudes' regarding the laws of the Church?

Read meditatively **Mt 5.17-20** and **Mt 12.1-4**.

Ask for the grace of an understanding heart, like that of Jesus', and to be free and courageous to 'transcend' the law whenever necessary for the greater good.

I will do more than belong- I will participate.
I will do more than care- I will help.
I will do more than believe- I will practice.
I will do more than be fair- I will be kind.
I will do more than forgive- I will love.
I will do more than earn- I will enrich.
I will do more than teach- I will serve.
I will do more than live- I will grow.
I will do more than be friendly-I will BE a friend.

Respond positively

An officer who had some urgent business to transact reluctantly dialled his assistant at six o'clock in the morning. After several rings a sleepy female voice answered and told him he had the wrong number. He apologised, hung up, and scouted in vain for his telephone diary to re-check the number.

Some time later he risked dialling again, and was embarrassed to hear the same voice. Expecting a rebuff, he started to apologise profusely. But the woman interrupted him.

"There's no need to be sorry," she said assuringly. "I'm sitting by my window enjoying a truly beautiful sunrise. I would have missed it if it hadn't been for you. Thanks!"

Do not let your anger lead you into sin, and do not stay angry all day.
Eph 4.26-27

Suggestions

How do you normally express your anger or hurt feelings?

Read meditatively **Mt 5.21-26**.
Review some of your recent 'conflict situations'. How would Jesus have behaved were he in your place?

Ask for the grace to be large-hearted and to always preserve your respect for people, even when they hurt and need to be reprimanded.

Things turn out best for the people who make the best out of the way things turn out.

16/6 Preserve your integrity

There is a story told of two monks, Tanzan and Ekido, in Japan who were making their way through a heavy downpour when they reached a flooded junction. They saw a lovely young girl, dressed in a flashy silk kimono and sash, looking helpless and stranded as she struggled to cross the road. Tanzan spontaneously went to her rescue. Sweeping her up in his arms, he carried her over the much and deposited her safely on the other side.

The monks then proceeded in silence. When the reached the gate of their monastery, Ekido suddenly burst out: "Monks are not expected to go near females," he said reprimanding Tanzan, "especially if they are young and beautiful. It can be dangerous. Why did you carry that lady?"

The remark took Tanzan by surprise. He had not so much as given a second thought to the incident. So, gauging Ekido's mind, he replied: "I dropped the lady at the crossroad. Are you still carrying her?"

**Your bodies are parts of the body of Christ.
Shall I take a part of Christ's body and
make it part of the body of a prostitute?**

1 Cor 6.15

Suggestions

How sincere are your efforts to preserve the purity of your heart and mind, the integrity of your whole self?

Read meditatively: **Mt 5.27-30**; **1Cor 6.12-20**; **1Cor 12.12-30**.

Ask for the grace to love the Lord, your God, with your whole heart, soul, mind and strength.

**Many are prone to judge themselves
by their ideals and others by their acts.**

16/7 Pray for your persecutors

Louis B. Mayer, founder of Metro-Goldwyn-Mayer, once told about an experience in his childhood. Louis had a fight with another boy and returned home with bruises on his face. While his mother was attending to his injuries, he explained that the other boy was completely to blame for starting the fight.

His mother did not say anything, but when she finished, she took Louis by the hand out the back door of their home. Facing them were several hills that created distinct echoes. She told him to imagine that the hills were the boy who had beaten him up, and instructed him to shout out, at the top of his voice, all the nasty names he would like to call his 'enemy'.

Louis did so, and the bad names were all echoed back to him. That done, his mother said, "Now shout, 'God bless you'."
He did so and back came "God bless you". Mayer never forgot that lesson.

Pray for those who persecute you.
Mt 5.43

Suggestions

Do you follow Christ's dictate of "praying for your enemies"?

Read meditatively on each of the passages dealing with Jesus' teaching on revenge in **Mt 5.38-48**, and his practice of it in **Mt 26.47-56**.

Ask for the grace and strength to treat your enemies with love, after the example of Jesus.

Love your crooked neighbour
with all your crooked heart.

PHASE SEVENTEEN

THE MASTER'S MESSAGES

"Jesus told stories to jolt the conventional thinking of his listeners. The Kingdom of God was such a radical dream for new possibilities of relating to each other and Abba, that it required the surprise of a parable story to tease our imaginations. Parables were like magic carpets to take us beyond our stereotype boundaries. The symbols of story cannot be exhausted, they lead us to other places where we can re-examine our values and actions in the light dawning of the Kingdom. Somehow, the opening 'Once upon a time...' or 'The Kingdom of God is like...' suggests another realm of thinking about someone or something.

Matthew records that 'the people all stood on the beach and Jesus told them many things in parables' (Mt 13.3). "As a story teller Jesus used everyday incidents of travellers being ambushed, shepherds, servants, labourers in the field, bakers and sleepy wedding attendants." Keven Treston

At this Phase you will enjoy as well as draw inspiration from some of the stories that Jesus told his listeners.

Ask for the grace to let Jesus' words sink into your heart and transform it by their power, so that you may be moved to love Jesus more intimately and follow him more closely.

After reading the doctrines of Plato, Socrates or Aristotle, we feel the specific difference between their words and Christ's is the difference between a inquiry and a revelation. Joseph Parker

Listen to his voice

At a family reunion, a famous Shakespearean actor was persuaded to demonstrate his skills at eloquence. In consenting, he insisted that someone suggest a passage for recitation. A clergyman suggested the Psalm of the Good Shepherd. The actor agreed on one condition, that the priest recite the same psalm after he had finished. "I'm no orator," protested the preacher taken aback, "but if that's what you want, I will."

The actor rendered the Psalm excellently. His voice and diction were perfect. Everybody hung on his lips. At the end of his 'performance' the applause was deafening.

Then came the pastor's turn to declaim the Psalm. As he began his voice sounded somewhat hoarse, and the diction was shaky. But the words came alive and the atmosphere seemed pervaded with a mysterious spirit. When he finished there were a few moments of reverential silence; not a few of those present had tears in their eyes.

The actor stood up and in a quivering voice said, "I reached your eyes and ears; but our priest here has reached your hearts. The reason is simple: I know the *Psalm* – but he knows the *Shepherd*!"

My sheep listen to my voice; I know them, and they follow me. Jn 10.27

Suggestions

How would you rate your personal relationship with Christ?

Read meditatively **Jn 10.1-16/Lk 15.1-7** (The Good Shepherd).

Ask for the grace to always follow Jesus, and to be a 'shepherd' in your own way, after his example.

17/2 Be a 'good samaritan'

A German philanthropist, Oberlin, was journeying through a snowstorm, near Strasbourgh, and lost his way. Overcome with fatigue, he lay helpless in the snow, almost sure of death. A wagoner happened to pass that way after Oberlin had sunk in the drifts. The kind wagoner immediately rescued him, wrapped a thick blanket around the frozen body and brought him home. Oberlin was deeply touched by the man's charity and timely help, and expressed his desire to offer his rescuer a reward. It was refused pointblank. "Tell me your name at least," pleaded Oberlin, before the man could leave.
"Tell me," replied the man, "the name of the Good Samaritan."
"His name isn't recorded," said Oberlin wondering.
"Then allow me to withhold mine, too," said the 'good Samaritan' as he left.

Be careful not to parade your good deeds before men to attract their notice. Mt 6.1

Suggestions

Is your life full of 'good deeds'? Do you generally take the attitude of 'your left hand not knowing what your right hand is doing' (cfr Mt 6.1.3)?

Read meditatively **Lk 10.25-37** (The Good Samaritan).

Ask for the spirit of selfless service. You may pray in the words of St Ignatius Loyola:

Dearest Lord, teach me to be generous. Teach me to serve you as you deserve; to give and not to count the cost; to fight and not to heed the wounds; to toil and not to seek for rest; to labour and not to ask for any reward, save that of knowing that I do your will, O God.

Look beyond self

A knock was heard at the kitchen door of a little house in a run-down section of a city. A six-year-old opened the door.

"I was frightened. Standing there was a man dressed in shabby clothes. He had no raincoat and was badly in need of a shave. I ran to get my father. 'Daddy, there's a scary man at the kitchen door,' I said. Daddy immediately went to investigate. He asked the sorry-looking man what he wanted. 'I'm hungry,' the man said, 'I need something to eat.' I looked at my daddy to see what he would do. We barely had enough food to keep ourselves going.

'Come in and wait here,' daddy said to the man. Then he went to the refrigerator and took out a few slices of bologna. He made a bologna sandwich and handed it to the man. Then he took the last little cookie out of the cookie jar and slipped it into the man's torn coat pocket. My sisters and I then watched our daddy put his arm around the man and walk a few steps with him before sending him on his way. It was the saddest sight my eyes had ever seen. We continued to watch until the man was out of sight. Daddy was very quiet. I broke the silence: 'Who do you think it was, daddy?'
'I don't know,' he replied. 'Maybe he was an angel.'"

R.L. Bailey

God fills the hungry with good things.

Ps 107.10

Suggestions

What lessons have you learned from the above story?

Read meditatively **Lk 16.19-31** (The Rich Man and Lazarus).

Ask for the grace to be sensitive to the needs of others, especially the poor and needy, after the example of Jesus.

17/4 Discard possessiveness

A king had everything the world had to offer – anything money could buy, absolute power... yet, he was not happy. He summoned the wise men of his kingdom and commanded them to find out the best means by which he could attain true and lasting happiness. After elaborate consultations and discussions, the wisest of them came up with this solution: "Your majesty must find a truly happy man in your kingdom," he told the king, "take his shirt from him and wear it yourself for a day. That will bring you lasting happy."

The king immediately dispatched his courtiers to different parts of the kingdom to look for a truly happy man. It was no easy task, but one such man was eventually found. He happened to be a lean, bare-chested, old beggar in a street corner. "Rush home," said the courtier, "and bring me your shirt. The king has need of it."

The poor fellow, totally confused, muttered: "But I have no shirt."

> **Jesus said... true life is not made up of the things one owns, no matter how rich one may be.** (cfr Lk 12.15)

Suggestions

Are you convinced material possessions are not the criteria by which to measure the quality of your life? What is the proportion of your dependance on them and your trust in God?

Read meditatively **Lk 12.13-21** (The Rich Fool).

Ask for the grace to be free of greed and to trust fully in God's Providence rather than on perishable goods, after the example of Jesus.

17/5 Worship without compromising

One day the saintly Pope Leo XIII went to visit a convent church which he had been told was very much neglected. He entered the church without being seen and knelt down in a pew, and then went to the convent and spoke affably to all. When leaving, the father superior begged him, "Holy Father, do you wish to leave us a remembrance of the high honour you have bestowed on us?"

"A remembrance?" said the Pope smiling. "Go to the church and look at the pew in which I was kneeling and you will find a remembrance there."

As soon as the Pope left, everybody went to the church to see the 'remembrance', and on the layer of dust covering the pew they say this name written in large letters: LEO XIII.

My devotion to your Temple burns in me like a fire. Ps 69.9

Suggestions

Do you experience God's presence in places reserved for worship? Do you give God your undivided attention?

Read meditatively **Jn 2.13-22**. (Jesus drives out money-changers)

Ask for the grace to have single-minded devotion to God and to have a great desire to follow Christ with single-mindedness of purpose.

We must stop giving the impression that the church is surrounded by a wall fighting for its existence againsta a world that is trying to destroy it; instead, we must realise that the church is a force pushing out into the world. Isaasc K. Becker

Take the plunge

I stood in the warm Mexican sunshine in Acapulco and watched the divers hurling themselves off the high, rocky point to plummet into the foaming sea far below. How daring those divers are! They hurl themselves out into the air on faith, literally, for when they leave the cliff there isn't enough water below to break the dive. The wave that will bring the necessary swell of water into the cove is still out in the ocean. Those divers have to have faith that the wave will be there when they need it.

Isn't that the kind of faith I need? The feeling of assurance that God – like the wave – will be there when I hurl myself into the unknown. Barbara Hudson Dudley

"Courage!" Jesus said. "It is I. Don't be afraid!" Mt 14.27

Suggestions

Do you place your hand in the hand of God and walk wherever he leads you with confidence? How deep is your faith, how total your surrender?

Read meditatively **Mt 14.22-32**.

Ask for courage to take risks whenever demanded in service to the Kingdom.

Give me the love that leads the way,
The faith that nothing can dismay,
The hope no disappointments tire;
The passion that will burn like fire.
Let me not sink to be a clod:
Make me thy fuel, flame of God.
Amy Carmichael

Spread the Good News

A woman once attended a Mission conducted in her parish. She was so inspired, that she approached the preacher and said, "I feel that God is calling me to preach the Gospel. The problem, however, is that I have nine children. What should I do?"

The preacher replied, "Praise the Lord for giving you this inspiration, for calling you to preach his Word. Don't you see, he has already provided you with a congregation?"

* * *

A professor was once asked by a stranger, "What's your occupation?"
"I'm a Christian," he answered.
"That's not what I mean. What is your job?"
"I told you," replied the professor, "I'm a Christian"
"Maybe I should put it another way," said the stranger. "What do you do for a living?"
"Well, the fact is that I have a full-time job as a Christian To maintain my house and family, however, I teach at the university for a salary."

Go and preach. Mt 10.7

Suggestions

Do you realise that there are very many concrete ways in which you can be the "good news" to those around?

Read meditatively **Mt 10.5-15**.

Ask for enlightenment on ways of spreading the Gospel of Christ and for power to work 'miracles' in Christ's name.

PHASE EIGHTEEN

COMMITMENT TO THE MASTER

Fr J. Veltri, S.J. outlines three important "moments" in the growth of a continuing relationship that "manifest the attitude of loving response. First come *moments of fidelity* which consists of a 'steadfast love' in the basic commitment between lover and beloved. The second are moments of *loving concern*, when the lover lives his commitment for better, for worse, for richer, for poorer, in sickness and in health, until death... and is in such complete detachment from his own selfishness that even in the smallest ways he is faithful to his beloved. The third are moments of the *heart*; these are deep-felt moments, "when the lover desires and chooses to share even the suffering and hardship, the poverty and rejection of the loved one."

You must focus in this phase on the degree and depth of your commitment to God, Christ. At which of the "moments" is your way of life at present?

> The first "moments" – those of fidelity, spring from a strong sense of duty and loyalty – which are commendable. The lover assures the beloved: "You are an *important* person in my life; I will never do anything to displease you." You will keep your fidelity going even if circumstances happen of change – like, for instance, if you age given the highest position in life.
>
> Those at this level avoid anything that leads them to committing sins, at least grave ones, especially regarding the

commandments. Moreover, they let God's Spirit rule over their consciences, and constantly obey the Spirit's voice. But they do not necessarily seek positive means to enhance their relationship with God.

The second "moments" advances a step further, with the beloved saying to the lover: "You are the *dominant* person in my life; my only desire in life is to foster your happiness." There is direct commitment here.

Those at the second level take a deliberatively more positive attitude towards their role as co-creators. They are devout souls, with their sights on God alone. They avoid sin, of course. They stay away even from legitimate, permissible things if they sense some danger to their relationship with God. Their greater concern is finding God's will and seeking to serve God in even relatively unimportant matters. They have become so sensitive to their attachment to God that they are very careful about their activities and use of things. Hence they will deal with persons and things only in so far as they help them get closer to God.

The third "moments" however, demands a radical commitment that far surpasses the other two. It is a gift of God, and you must pray for it if you desire to practice it. This state entails a growth in Christlikeness, com-passion with Christ, a love for the Cross, a readiness to become a "fool for Christ". "You are *everything* in my life," says the beloved. "Even if you become a leper or an outcast, I will be with you." It means dying with Christ – while you are still in this world.

Those at the third level have learnt to see all reality through the eyes of Jesus. They follow in his footsteps and try to identify totally with his life-style. Jesus chose to be born poor and to live poor; he mingled with sinners, outcasts, and victims of injustice. He chose to serve rather than to be served. He was humiliated, persecuted, tortured, and condemned to a shameful death.

Jesus has said: "He who wants to save his life, will lose it, and he who spends it for me, will gain eternal life." But we feel frightened for ourselves. A very powerful instinct of preservation leads to egotism, and enslaves us when we want to give out our life. Everywhere we find hooks and pegs to prevent losing it. Above all, we are downright cowards.

Lord Jesus, we feel frightened to spend out life. But you have given it to us in order to spend it. We cannot keep it save in sterile egoism.

To spend one's life means to work for others, even if they do not pay us back; to do a favour to him who will not reciprocate. To spend one's life is to expose oneself to failure, if necessary, without any false prudence. It is to burn one's boats for the sake of the neighbour.

We are torches meant to be burnt. Only then we give our light. Free us from the cowardly prudence that makes us avoid the sacrifice and seek for security.

We can spend our life without fanfare and false popularity. One gives one's life most simply, without any publicity, like the water in the spring, like the mother who gives her breast to the baby, like the plain sweat of the farmer.

Teach us, Lord, to plunge ourselves into the impossible, because behind the impossible lies your grace and your perseverance. We shall not fall into a vacuum.

The future is mystery, our path gets lost in the mist. But we want to continue giving ourselves, because you are awaiting in the night, with a thousand eyes, shedding tears.

Luis Espinal, S.J. (Bolivian martyr, 1980)

At this phase of prayer you must check at which level of commitment to God you find yourself. Then, if you feel inspired to surrender yourself completely to Jesus and identify yourself with him as closely as you can, pray God to grant you this desire. Only the grace of God can make it possible. It would entail a deeply 'personal commitment' – to the Person of Jesus. You will have to throw in your lot with him. You will have to take up your cross daily – the cross of misunderstandings, dishonour, rejection, insults, betrayals and the like, after the experience of Jesus himself.

You will find it helpful to use the *Threefold Conversation* method in prayer. Speak first to Mary our Mother requesting her to ask Jesus to call you wherever he wants you. Then speak to Jesus, begging him to make your self-surrender to him genuine, and for courage to follow him wherever he leads you. Finally, speak to the Heavenly Father, repeating the above requests, entreating him to give you the grace you need to respond with all your heart.

Ask for the grace to follow Christ in the highest degree of commitment.

I ask for daily bread, but not for wealth
lest I forget the poor;
I ask for strength, but not for power,
lest I despise the meek;
I ask for wisdom, but not for learning,
lest I condemn the simple;
I ask for a clean name, but not for fame,
lest I condemn the lowly;
I ask for peace of mind, but not for idle hours,
lest I fail to harken to the call of duty.

Inazo Nitore

18/1 Keeping the rules

During Traffic Safety Week, a recently recruited traffic policeman on duty at a busy crossroads, apprehended a driver for violating a traffic signal. He pulled out his entry book and politely asked to see the driver's licence. The driver, who happened to be a high-ranking officer in the Police Department, flashed his credentials. The traffic cop glanced at it, then continued making the entry. Visibly annoyed, the officer said sternly: "Remember, lad, that one day when your name comes up for a promotion, I may be the one in charge of approving it."

Without the slightest hesitation, the policeman offered the senior officer his ticket, and said with a smile: "When it comes to that, sir, please remember that you have one honest policeman in your employ."

I have not come to do away with the Law... Mt 5.15

Suggestions

How conscientious are you in following the Laws of the Church and Gospel principles? Do you tend to compromise or yield to social pressure?

Read meditatively **Mk 3.31-35** regarding the priority Jesus gives to doing God's will.

Ask for the strength to do God's will, not only with your mind and lips, but with your whole heart.

Where there's a will, there's a way;
Where there's a way, there's a law;
Where there's a law, there's a loophole;
Where there's a loophole, there's me.
WALK IN. Sign outside a lawyer's office

18/2 Beyond selfish considerations

In *Adventures in Two Worlds*, A. J. Cronin describes his experiences as a medical officer to a Welsh Mining Company. There was a middle-aged nurse there "who for more than twenty years, with fortitude and patience, calmness and cheerfulness, served the people of Tregenny.... Although she was much loved by the people, her salary was most inadequate." Cronin, impressed by her "unconscious selflessness," thought she deserved a better remuneration.

"Nurse," Cronin said, "why don't you make them pay you more? It's ridiculous that you should work for so little." She raised her eyebrows slightly. But she smiled. "I have enough to get along."

"No, really," he persisted, "you ought to have an extra pound a week at least. God knows you're worth it."

There was a pause. Her smile remained, but her gaze held a gravity, an intensity which startled me. "Doctor," she said, "If God knows I'm worth it, that's all that matters to me."

You cannot serve both God and money. Mt 6.24

Suggestions

Have you discovered your 'personal vocation' – which goes beyond human considerations?

Read meditatively **Mt 13.44-46**.

Ask for the grace that enables you to drain your heart of all egoism and fills it with a deep personal love for Jesus thus making you totally free for God.

Developing compassion

Jim Towey is director of President Bush's Office of Faith-Based and Community Initiatives since February 1, 2002. Towey had been the legal counsel for Mother Teresa for 12 years; he had lived for one year as a full-time volunteer in her home for people with AIDS in Washington.

Years ago, when Towey was visiting the home for the dying in Calcutta, the sister, who assumed he was there to help, handed him some cloths and antiseptic and asked him to clean a man with scabies who was dying. "I was too proud to say I couldn't do it," Towey said, but he acknowledges that "not the tiniest bit of me wanted to be with the poor."

That encounter and subsequent volunteer experiences with these nuns ended up changing his life, making his faith come alive and showing him for the first time that he "had the capacity to love people". Being with the poor, he said: "Either your heart grows cold or compassionate. It can't be indifferent."

I am happy about my sufferings for you.
Col 1.24

Suggestions

Are there concrete expressions of your love for Christ? Are these limited to thoughts and words, or found in your actions?

Read meditatively **Col 1.2-29**.

Ask for the grace to be totally committed to the mission of Christ in the world.

Compassion is the ultimate and most meaningful embodiment of emotional maturity. It is through compassion that a person achieves the hightest peak and deepest reach in his or her search of self-fulfilment. Arthur Jersild

Seeking Christ poor

In *Mother Teresa, Her People and Her Work*, Desmond Doig describes his first memory of her in Nirmal Hriday, her first home for dying destitutes in Calcutta. Mother was kneeling beside a dying man whom she had just admitted. "Stripped of his rags, he was one appalling wound alive with maggots.... With quiet efficiency she began to clean him as she talked to him caressingly in Bengali."

Some years ago, Billy Graham, the American evangelist, visited Mother Teresa in Calcutta. He was impressed by the holy nun's religious attitude toward people. "Mother Teresa looks past the physical features of every man, woman, and child," he observed, "and sees the face of Jesus staring up at her through them. In every starving child she feeds, she sees Jesus. Around every sick and frightened woman she cares for she sees Jesus. Surrounding every lonely, dying man she cradles in her arms is Jesus. When she ministers to anyone, she is ministering to her Saviour and Lord."

I was sick and you took care of me.
Mt 25.36

Suggestions

Are you ever-ready to assist others in their needs – with dignity, even if you have to suffer inconvenience or pain?

Read meditatively **Gal 6.1-10**.

Ask for the strength to humble yourself in service to others.

In the face of suffering, one has no right to turn away, not to see. In the face of injustice, one may not look the other way. When someone suffers, and it is not you, he comes first. His very suffering gives him priority. Elia Wiesel

Radical self-surrender

Shortly after his priestly ordination, Francis Xavier was assigned to work in a hospital in Venice, crowded with patients suffering from incurable sicknesses.

One day a syphilis patient whom Francis was tending asked the saint to scratch his back – which was covered with pus-filled sores and emitted a nauseating stench. Suddenly, a crippling fear seized Francis. What if he caught this contagious disease? Then, in a flash, he remembered his commitment to Jesus. Francis plucked up courage. He not merely scratched the patient's back, but when the task was done, he put his fingers into his own mouth and sucked them. That night, he dreamed that he had been infected with the sickness in his throat and kept coughing and spitting the whole night. The following day he realised that there was no sign of any sickness. From then on he lost his sense of repugnance and fear of contagion and freely served people suffering from the worst diseases.

If anyone wants to come with me,
he must forget self. Mt 16.24

Suggestions

Do you understand what it really means to 'forget self' in order to follow Christ?

Read reflectively **Mt 16.21-28**.

Ask for the grace of total surrender to Christ in complete 'self-forgetfulness'.

Jesus wants us to be headlong enthusiasts in our exercise of discipleship. It has been a very long time since there was much throbbing, panting enthusiasm in most Christians. Andrew Greeley

18/6 Complete identification

Fr Damien deVuester had committed himself fully to the lepers on the Molokai island. The leper colony was in a dreadful state; the lepers were left alone to die amid dirt and hunger and thirst. Worst of all, they were deprived of the sacraments, their only source of consolation. He nursed them, built houses for them, counselled them, and made their coffins.

Fr Damien knew only too well that he would probably catch the disease himself, but he in no way compromised his service. After twelve years of total involvement, he came to the altar one Sunday morning in June 1885 for his regular Mass. At the homily, instead of his usual greeting of "My dear brethren," he said, very slowly, "We lepers..." It was Fr Damien's way of informing the lepers that finally he was one of them in every way in their affliction. There was joy in his voice!

The world is crucified to me,
and I to the world. Gal 6.14

Suggestions

Do you follow the example of Jesus, who though God, became man in order that we might truly live as children of God? Are you prepared to identify yourself with Christ poor and suffering?

Read meditatively **Phil 2.6-8**.

Ask for genuine humility so that you can bear up with anything in order to stand up for your commitment to Christ.

Are you willing to be sponged out, erased, cancelled, made nothing? Are you willing to be made nothing? dipped into oblivion? If not, you will never really change. D.H. Lawrence

Total commitment

From their hideouts in the jungle, fully armed guerillas stormed into a chapel in Columbia, one Sunday when Mass was about to begin. Some soldiers dragged the priest out. A fierce-looking chieftain then challenged the congregation: "Those committed to the Christian creed, stand up."

One man stood up and said simply, "I love and follow Jesus." Immediately the soldiers pounced on him and dragged him out. Several others took courage, stood up, and were driven out. Then came the sound of machine-gun fire. The Guerilla chieftain ordered those that remained sitting, petrified by fear, to leave the chapel. "You have no right to be here!" he shouted.

Outside, these "deserters" were astonished to see their pastor and the others, quite safe. Strangely, the commander instructed the priest to lead his 'faithful' back into the chapel for the service. He turned to the 'unfaithful' and admonished them in a piercing tone: "Stay out of this chapel until you have the courage to stand up to your beliefs and convictions." Then he and his men returned to the jungle.

All I want is to know Christ... and to share his sufferings. Phil 3.10

Suggestions

Are you so committed to Christ as to suffer insults, persecution, and even death for his sake?

Read meditatively **Phil 3.8-12**.

Ask for the grace of total surrender to Christ, to the point of giving your life if needed.

CHRIST: The Epitome of All Races

Since I have learnt to know Christ afresh in the Eastern setting, it has been easy for me to point out the weakness of the portraiture when his character has been depicted with only Western ideals to draw form , as though these comprehended "the fullness of Christ". For in such pictures the true proportion has not been kept. Some of the marked traits of his character have not appeared at all. Much has been lost. Someday I would like to draw His likeness anew with the colour of the Eastern sky added to the scene.

In the same way, no doubt, the proportion would have been lost in due time, if Christianity had spread only in Asia in the first century, instead of passing in into Europe. Then, after many generations of Christian culture, we would have had an Oriental Christ, whom the West would rightly recognize as inadequate, and wish to draw over again.

For the supreme miracle of Christ's character lies in this that he combined within Himself, as no other figure in human history has ever done, the qualities of every race. His very birthplace and home in Childhood were near the concourse of the two great streams of human life in the ancient world, that flowed east and West. Time and space conspired, but the divine spark came down from above to mould for all time the human character of the Christ, the son of Man.

For those who, through intimate contact with other races, have gained the right to be heard, have borne witness that each race and region of the earth respond to his appeal, finding in the Gospel record that which applies specially to themselves. His Sovereign character has become the one golden thread running through mankind, binding the ages and the races together.

C.F. Andrews

PHASE NINETEEN

CHRIST'S PRESENCE AND POWER

This is the final phase of a major section of your progress in the *Spiritual Exercises*. We have so far been deepening your FAITH – the Faith which is the basis of all your attitudes and activities whether internal or external, personal or social, during or outside your time of prayer. You have grown deeper in the knowledge "that a person is put right with God only through faith in Jesus Christ" (Gal 2.16). "He has brought us by faith into the experience of God's grace, in which we now life" (Rom 5.2).

At this phase you must renew your confidence in Jesus Christ by understanding further his divine power, his radical service to the Father's mission, his unconditional love, his authority as a Master, and his affable nature.

Ask for the grace of greater interior knowledge of Jesus Christ, so as to love him more intimately and follow him more closely.

Make the Threefold Conversation whenever you feel moved to do so.

I praise him most, I love him best,
all praise and love is his;
While him I love, in him I live,
Love's sweetest mark, laud's highest theme,
man's most desired light,
To love him life, to leave him death,
to live in him delight. St Robert Southwell

Christ – for all time

Jesus had the most open and all - encompassing mind that this world has ever seen. His won inner conviction was so strong, so firm, so unswerving that He could afford to mingle with any group secure in the knowledge that he would not be contaminated. It is fear that makes us unwilling to Listen to another's point of view, fear that our own ideas may be attacked. Jesus had no such fear, no such pettiness of view point, no need to fence himself off for his own protection. He knew the difference between graciousness and compromise and we would do well to learn from him. He set for us the most magnificent and glowing example of truth combined with mercy of all time, and in departing said : "Go ye and do likewise" (Lk 10:37) Billy Graham

Christ is the visible likeness of the invisible God. Col 1.15

Suggestions

How often have you admired Jesus Christ as a Person with extraordinary, attractive, inspiring human qualities?

Read meditatively **Col 1.15-23**.

Ask for the grace to deepen your faith in Jesus Christ, and to grow strong in your desire to follow him and serve him.

Jesus Christ teaches men that there is something in them which lifts them above this life with its hurries, its pleasures and fears. He who understands Christ's teaching feels like a bird that did not know it has wings and now suddenly realises that it can fly, can be free and no longer needs to fear. Leo Tolstoy

Christ – 'miracle-worker'

Go into the great art museums of the world and walk through the classics and you will inevitably come upon a painting of the wedding feast of Cana. It's a favourite subject of artists who like to picture rich biblical scenes.

Cana has all the ingredients of a good story: plot, personalities, place, a problem – a solution. It has all the ingredients of a good metaphor: something easy to picture and something with rich emotional undertones and overtones....

The story of the wedding feast of Cana... not only offers painters a great possibility for a rich picture, it also offers viewers an invitation to a wedding of theology and everyday moments, emptiness and fullness, Christ human and Christ divine, Christ and Mary, life and eternal life. It's a banquet of images and grace. One has to sit here like a viewer in an art museum, ... in prayer, using the imagination to picture what Christ can bring into the picture frame of one's life.

Andrew Costello, CSSR

Jesus revealed his glory... and his disciples believed in him. Jn 2.12

Suggestions

Do you recognise the presence and power of Jesus in your life? What 'miracles' do you seek from him?

Read meditatively **Jn 2.1-12**.

Ask for the grace of an increase in your confidence in Christ and a great depth in your relationship with him.

Every believer is God's miracle. Philip J. Bailey

Christ – anchor of faith

Commenting on that Gospel incident where Jesus is asleep in the boat during a storm, Fr John L. McKenzie notes: This episode is often erroneously called a "miracle story". There is nothing clearly miraculous about it. It is true that the Sea of Galilee, situated close to surrounding mountains, often has squalls which rise and fall with equal suddenness. The men in the boat, experienced sailors, knew this. They also recognised the danger. They could have said to Jesus, "If it had not been for you, we would have stayed where we were." To his question, "Why are you afraid?", they might have answered impolitely, "Because the boat is sinking." ...

The story tells us that the disciples were frightened, not without reason, that Jesus slept when the others were terrified, that he told them not to be scared, that he spoke to the wind as if it were a demon like those he had recently expelled, that the wind died down, that the disciples said, "He is more than we can figure out." One who does not fear nature is himself somewhat frightening.

"Who is this man?" Mk 4.41

Suggestions

Does the power of Jesus evoke fear or confidence in you?

Read meditatively **Mk 4.35-41**.

Ask for the grace of deeper understanding of the power and presence of Jesus in your life.

If anyone could prove to me that Christ is outside the truth, and if the truth really did exclude Christ, I should prefer to stay with Christ and not with truth. There is in the world only one figure of absolute beauty: Christ, that infinitely lovely figure is a matter of course, an infinite marvel.

Fyodor Dostoyevsky

19/4 Christ – love transfigured

In his book, *Something Beautiful For God*, on Mother Teresa, Malcolm Muggeridge describes a miracle. A BBC camera crew wanted to do some shooting inside Nirmal Hriday – the home for the dying and destitute. The hall in which the sisters and their volunteers nurse the patients, has tiny windows high up in the wall. There was not sufficient light in the room – and the crew had not brought portable lights with them. Though they doubted about the usefulness of shooting there, they decided to do it anyway. When the film was developed, however, to the astonishment of everyone, the scenes taken in the ill-lighted dormitories were found to be clearer than those taken in sunlight!

Muggeridge explains the phenomenon thus: Mother Teresa's Home for the Dying is overflowing with love.... This love is luminous, like the haloes artists have seen and made visible round the heads of the saints. I find it not at all surprising that the luminosity should register on photographic film."

His face was shining like the sun.
Mt 17.2

Suggestions

How often have you dwelt on the divinity 'hidden' in Christ?

Read meditatively **Mt 17.1-13**.

Ask for the grace to understand the Christ, though God, lived a fully human life, and accepted suffering as part of God's plan for him.

The One remains, the many change and pass;
Heaven's light forever shines, Earth's shadows fly;
Life, like a dome of many-coloured glass,
Stains the white radiance of Eternity. P.B. Shelley

19/5 Christ – Friend to the end

A few years before his death, Bishop Fulton J. Sheen underwent open-heart surgery. Everyone of his friends was concerned whether the Prelate would survive the ordeal, given his advanced age. The Bishop, however, recovered marvellously from the operation. During his convalescence he was interviewed by a reporter who asked: "Were you at any time gripped by the fear of dying?" Bishop Sheen replied that he had not been at all anxious about or afraid of death. "If I should leave the world, I will be in heaven with Christ and if I remain, Christ will be here with me," he said with childlike simplicity.

I am certain that nothing can separate us from his love: neither death nor life.

Rom 8.38

Suggestions

How deep is your faith, how genuine your surrender to Christ?

Read meditatively **Jn 11.1-45** – The Raising of Lazarus.

You may try out this 'fantasy exercise': Imagine yourself in a cave-tomb. Feel the coldness, the damp, the suffocation. Ask yourself: What is it in me that has given shape to the stones that form my prison? You may place a label on each of the stones (eg. apathy, loneliness, self-centredness, fear, hurts, ...) Then focus your attention on the large stone that blocks the entrance. Hear Jesus' voice piercing that slab as he calls out your name and says, " _____, *come out.*" Let these words resound in your heart. Feel yourself coming out of the tomb, and seeing the face of Jesus -- your Friend!. Allow him to unbind you and set your free.

Ask for the grace to surrender all you are and have in faith to Christ so that you may follow his path to the bitter end.

19/6 Christ – wellspring of joy

There was a grand old man who preserved a few fine bottles of rare old brandy for rare old friends. One day his house caught fire and one fireman, in particular, behaved with great gallantry. The old gentleman could think of no more handsome gesture than to offer him a glass of this oldest and most noble brandy. The fireman, drenched by the hoses, sat down, took off his boots and socks and said, "Thank you kindly, sir. A very happy thought. I'm a teetotaller myself, sir, but I've always found that there's nothing like brandy to stop you getting a cold," and poured the precious fluid over his feet. Cyril Ray

God has poured out his love into our hearts. Rom 5.5

Suggestions

What are your reactions/responses to the gesture of the old gentleman and the behaviour of the fireman?

Read meditatively **Jn 12.1-7**. (The anointing of Jesus' feet)
Exercise based on the above passage: Contrast the attitudes of Jesus and Judas. Which line of reasoning appoeals to you? Why? Then contrast the 'crafty mind' of Judas with the 'loving heart' of Mary who anointed Jesus' feett. Observe Mary's gesture which is so spontaneous and overwhelmingly generous. Her surrender to Jesus is genuine and total. How deep is your faith in and how genuine your surrender to Jesus? Are you a cheerful giver?
What do you have to 'anoint' Jesus' feet with?
There are various ways of showing appreciation and love, and of receiving appreciation amd love. What is generally your way of both giving and receiving love?

Ask for an intimate knowledge of Jesus so as to offer him the best of yourself in service.

Christ – King of hearts

Louis XIV, called the Grand monarch, the "Sun King" – reigned seventy two years – the longest in French history and possibly the world to date. He built the renowned palace of Versailles. Jesus lived to the age of thirty-three with only three years of public service. He had not where to lay his head.

Ivan IV, called "Ivan the Terrible" was the first ruler of Russia to take the title of Czar. He did much for his country, cruel as he was. In his later years, he became violent and fierce. He accidentally killed his son and in repentance became a monk, shortly before he died. God gave His son who did not withdraw from the world but walked among the poor, the downtrodden and the sinful.

The only kingdom Jesus sought to expand was the Kingdom of God within the hearts of his followers. He built no palace to be remembered by. He extended no physical boundary lines. He is building heavenly mansions for us and extending the horizons of our souls. What a loving and gracious potentate! Herbert C. Gabhart

Look, your king... comes triumphant and victorious, but humble and riding on a donkey. Zech 9.9

Suggestions

Which characteristcs of Christ attract you the most?

Read meditatively **Mt 21.1-9 /Mk 11.1-10 /Lk 19.29-48 / Jn 12.12-29**.

Ask for the grace to become like that 'donkey' ready to bear the King of Glory through the streets of everyday life and proclaim his greatness to everyone.

SECTION FIVE

CHRIST'S SACRIFICIAL LOVE

CHRIST'S SACRIFICIAL LOVE

There is a carving of a lamb in the roof of the Cathedral at Werden, Germany, with a story behind it. During the construction of the Cathedral, a man was at work on the roof when a rope holding the scaffolding snapped. The worker was pitched headlong into the air and to the ground.

The yard below was cluttered with huge blocks of stones. But the man escaped unhurt! Between two blocks stood a lamb nibbling grass. The falling man landed smack on the lamb, crushing it to death.

The lamb saved the man from a fatal fall. In gratitude for his deliverance the worker obtained permission to carve a lamb out of stone and place it in the roof at the spot from which he fell.

Jesus Christ is "the Lamb of God Who takes away our sins." Christ brought us freedom from sin and death by laying down his own life for us (1Cor 15.3).

For the past several weeks you have been following closely in the footsteps of Jesus Christ as you contemplated him in action: praying, preaching, performing 'miracles'.... as he lives out the mission given him by his Heavenly Father. For the next few weeks you will accompany Christ in the final stages of his life: as he gives us his Body symbolically at Last Supper or the Paschal Meal, then sacrifices it on the Cross.

The Paschal Meal is the first step towards Calvary. It is full of rituals symbolising God's intervention in the deliverance of the Israelites from slavery.

Jesus, the Saviour of humankind, who rescued us from the slavery of sin, gives this supper a new significance for his followers. He inaugurates the Eucharist. "Do this in memory of me," he says, and to this day we 'remember' his presence in a very real way every time we celebrate the Eucharist.

The "Passion" which follows the Meal, from Gethsemane to Calvary, is Jesus' greatest hour at which he accomplishes the purpose of the incarnation and his mission on earth.

Ask for the grace to be more intimately united with Christ as you absorb with your mind and heart these final phases of his life.

> "Dom Helder, a thief has broken into one of our churches and opened the tabernacle. He threw away the hosts – and threw them into the mud!..."
>
> I said: "Lord, in the name of my brother, the thief, I ask your pardon. He did not know what he was doing. Thou art truly present and living in the Eucharist...
>
> But my friends, my brothers, how blind we all are! We are shocked because our brother, the poor thief, threw the Eucharistic Christ into the mud. But here in the North East, Christ lives in the mud all the time. We must open our eyes!... the best possible outcome of our communion with the Body of Christ in the Eucharist would be if Christ thus received would open our eyes and help us to recognise the Eucharist of the poor, the oppressed, the suffering."
>
> **Dom Helder Camara, Bishop of Recife, Brazil**

PHASE TWENTY EXPRESSIONS OF LOVE

A lively and convincing street-corner preacher was once faced by a hostile crowd. "How", one of them demanded, "is it possible for bread and wine to become the body and blood of Christ?"

The preacher looked calmly at the stout questioner for a moment and answered: "You have certainly grown somewhat since you were a child and have more flesh and blood than you had then. Surely, if the human body can change food and drink into flesh and blood, God can do it, too."

"But how, countered the heckler, "is it possible for Christ to be present in his entirety in a small host?"

The preacher glanced up at the sky and down the city street before them and answered, "This city scene and the sky above it is something immense, while your eye is very small, yet your eye contains in itself the whole picture. When you consider this, it won't seem impossible for God to be present in his entirety in a little piece of bread."

Once more the heckler attacked. "How, then, is it possible for the same body of Christ to be present in all your churches at the same time?"

The preacher's answer was, "In a large mirror you see your image reflected but once. When you break the mirror into a hundred pieces, you see the same image of yourself in each of the hundred fragments. If such things occur in everyday life, why should it be impossible for the Body of Christ to be present in many places at once? And tell me, just what ISN'T possible for God, anyhow?"

The Eucharist was established at the fag end of Jesus' life, as his greatest gift to his followers. Jesus has only a few hours to live. He presides at the Last Supper in solemn consciousness of the fact. They are the last hours of a condemned Man, the last things he did, the last things he said, before the blow fell, before the end.

In this phase you will enter the Upper Room to celebrate the Last Supper with Jesus. Observe and listen with your whole heart and soul to all that happens there. Enter each prayer-period with a seriousness of purpose and with a strong desire to draw the utmost from Jesus' words and actions.

Ask for the grace to understand how Jesus wants to be intimately one with you in the Eucharist (in its complete aspect) so that you experience the fullness of life and are prepared for your 'passion' whenever it should come.

The symbols of God's kingdom
are not the sword and crown,
but bread and wine –
the broken body of the Lord.
The call to the disciples is nothing
less than to follow that way – in
absolute opposition to any reasonable
search for accomplishment and success.
It is not a call to powerlessness,
but to a life that has its source
in the power of the Holy Spirit –
the life-giving, forgiving, healing
and community-building power,
a non-coercive power,
a non-violent power.

Jacques Matthew

Lowly service

Sylvia Hill has been in the shoeshine business at Boston's Logan Airport since her husband death in 1995. From early morning until late afternoon, travellers plop down on one of the leather chairs at her stand, and she engages them in conversation while she shines their shoes with rags, brushes and polish.

With her degree in counselling and managerial experience, Sylvia could have opted for a career in the corporate world. But she considers her job as a special vocation from God. "I didn't want to just come to the airport and shine shoes. I wanted to provide service to people, and I wanted to make a difference...."

Responding to her affable and cheery personality, some customers warm up to her and share something personal. That gives Sylvia an opportunity to use her counselling skills. She tries to offer words of support and even shares how her faith has helped her.

Sylvia notes down the many prayer requests she receives every day – for people facing problems like serious illness, divorce, loss, or financial crisis.

> **I, your Lord and Teacher, have washed your feet.** Jn 13.14

Suggestions

How low are you willing to stoop to make your love for Christ fruitful in service?

Read meditatively **Jn 13.1-20** (Washing of Feet)

Ask for a deeper understanding of Jesus' message in his symbolic action, and for strength to translate it into your life, by following in his footsteps.

Fond remembrances

There was an Italian labourer who used to prepare excellent wine. Once a year his large family which was scattered, used to get together for a celebration and Papa would bring out his homemade wine. The members around the table would sip the wine and compliment him on its superb quality. He would smile to himself, happy that his family appreciated both him and his labours. He died, leaving many of his untapped bottles in the wine-cellar.

"Now," a member of the family stated, "every time we all get together for anniversaries and celebrations, we continue to share a bottle of papa's wine. It helps us to remember the good time of the past. In the wine we sense his presence as still being with us."

Do this in memory of me. Lk 22.19

Suggestions

How sensitive are you to Christ's presence in the Eucharistic species of Bread and Wine?

Read meditatively **Lk 22.14-23**. Let the scene of the Last Supper come alive through your imagination. Gaze at Jesus who is aware of his impending death. Listen to what he says, observe his gestures, feel his emotions... Focus your attention on the bread and wine in his hands... "Do this is memory of me."

Ask for the grace to be sensitive to the symbolism of the Bread of Life and the Cup of Salvation and its significance for you today.

No love that in a family dwells,
No carolling in frosty air.
Nor all the steeple-shaking bells,
Can with this single truth compare,
That God was man in Palestine,
And lives today in Bread and Wine. John Betjeman

20/3 Life-giving nourishment

Fifteen days after the atom bomb destroyed the entire city of Hiroshima in Japan, leaving 80,000 dead and countless wounded, Fr Pedro Arrupe, S.J., who was then a Novice Master in a suburban area there, was making his usual rounds of the streets with medicines, bandages and food for the helpless victims.

He came across a hut of tin and poles where a big house had once stood. In the hut he found a young Christian girl named Nakamura San. Her whole body was one big wound, full of burns and pus oozing out. When Fr Arrupe sought to clean her wounds the flesh just fell off – rotten and swarming with maggots. Fr Arrupe knelt by her side, dumb with horror and compassion.

It was then that Nakamura opened her eyes, and with eager joy she asked him, "Father, have you brought me Holy communion?" Fr. Arrupe nodded. With tears of joy the fervent girl received the Bread of Life. Soon after that she breathed her last.

I am the bread of life. Jn 6.35

Suggestions

How precious and life-giving is the Bread you receive in Holy Communion at the Eucharist?

Read meditatively **Jn 6.25-40**. Place yourself in the scene. Observe the conviction in Jesus' eyes as he speaks, the reactions of Peter, Thomas, Judas... What is going on in the hearts of those present there?

Ask for the grace to become like Christ – "bread broken and shared".

20/4

Genuine fellowship

One Sunday morning the congregation of a ritzy church (with vaulted ceilings, hand-carved oak pews, stained glass windows) had a stir. A man, horribly dressed, came in just minutes before the service was to begin. He had on boots, overalls, a flannel shirt, and a hat. Everyone whispered disapprovingly. At the end of the service the priest greeted the humbly dressed man and asked him if he enjoyed the service. The man exclaimed that he enjoyed it very much. The priest asked him to consider possibly dressing differently, suggesting he could ask Jesus in prayer what would be a fitting dress.

The next week the man returned, dressed the same, and once again the congregation was disturbed. Once again the priest again met the man and asked what he had been told by Jesus concerning his dress for church.

The man exclaimed, "I spoke with Jesus about this but Jesus said he didn't know how I should dress for this church because He has never been here."

Your meetings for worship actually do more harm than good. 1Cor 11.17

Suggestions

Where do you focus your heart when you are present for worship in church?

Read meditatively **1Cor 12.17-34**.

Ask for the grace to make your participation in the Eucharist very meaningful, and to create in your heart a deep feeling of universal fellowship.

Before Mass, speak to God
During Mass, let God speak to you
After Mass, speak to each other.

Do you honour the Body of Christ? Do not despise him when he is naked. Do not humour him here in the church building only to neglect him outside, when he is suffering from cold and nakedness. For he who said, "This is my Body", is the same who said, "You saw Me – a hungry man and you did not give me to eat." Of what use is it to load the Table of Christ?

Feed the hungry and then come and decorate the Table. You are making a golden chalice and you do not give a cup of cold water? The Temple of your afflicted Brother's body is more precious than the altar of stone on which you celebrate the holy Sacrifice. You are able to contemplate the altar everywhere, in the street and in the open square.

St John Chrysostom

We are one body,
in union with Christ. Rom 12.5

Suggestions

Do you realise that when you "take and eat" the body of Christ, the Holy Communion must be made effective in your "giving" back to Christ in the poor?

Read meditatively **Rom 12.1-8**.

Pray that your participation in the Eucharist and Holy Communion changes you radically into the Body of Christ, and gives you the power to serve your 'neighbour' in need.

The Holy Supper is kept indeed,
In whatso we share with another's need,
Not what we give, but what we share,
For the gift without the giver is bare;
Who gives himself with his alms feed three:
Himself, his hungry neighbour, and Me.

James Russell Lowell

Cheerful giving

At the close of the film *Monsieur Vincent*, directed by Jean Anouilh, St Vincent de Paul says to the youngest novice in the Daughters of Charity:

"The street will be long and unfriendly, the stairs steep and the poor often ungrateful. You will soon find charity a heavy burden, Jeanne, heavier than the jug of soup or the full basket. But you will still be pleasant and smile. Distributing soup and bread is not everything. The rich can do that. You are the little servant of the poor and the daughter of Charity, always smiling and good tempered. They are your masters and you will find them terribly exacting masters.

So the more unattractive and dirty they are, the more rude and unfair they are, the more you must lavish your love upon them. It is only by feeling your love that the poor will forgive your gifts of bread."

> **You prepare a banquet for me... you welcome me as an honoured guest and fill my cup to the brim.** Ps 23.5

Suggestions

Do you realise that the Christ who comes to you in Holy Communion, "unworthy" as you are, gives you the spiritual strength you need to reach out to the seemingly 'undeserving' and ungrateful people?

Read meditatively **Lk 14.14-24**.

Ask for the grace to value the 'banquet' God offers you, to be nourished at his table, and to share his gifts by playing host to Christ in the poor.

Giving is the thermometer of your love.

Fr Gerard McGinnity, in *Christmen*, tells of a young art teacher Josie who suffered from chronic multiple sclerosis. She was able to move only her eyes and her head a little. When Josie first learnt about her illness she seethed with anger. Gradually she overcame it, and discovered her vocation – to do God's will as Christ did, with her bed as the cross.

"She lives with the realisation that in every passing now she has all the time there is in the world and only one thing to do with it, his will. Nothing has charged her more than this limitation of herself to each moment that is given to her... God has overturned her plans and revealed to her the preciousness of time as an opportunity to simply give herself to him. It's ten years since I met her and her words have never left me. 'I'm not fit to get up and go up to mass but,' she said, trying to rub her hand on the bed, 'I think I'm suffering my own mass on this altar.'"

Offer yourselves as a living sacrifice to God. Rom 12.1

Suggestions

Are you convinced that the greatest sacrifice you can offer is to be obedient to the will of God for you at all times?

Read meditatively **Heb 10.1-14**.

Ask for a deeper understanding of the "sacrifice" of Christ – which is to do God's will, and to offer yourself completely to God.

Life breaks all of us sometimes,
but some grow strong at broken places.
Ernest Hemmingway

MY LIFE A EUCHARIST

Jesus, let my life a Eucharist be,
offered as holocaust for humanity.
May all I meet throughout the day,
with joy and love go on their way.

Make me your word not by my speech,
but by my life, Lord, let me preach.
Take me up with the bread and wine,
that I may taste our touch divine.

Spirit of God, pray, descend on me,
that like the Lord's body I may be.
Rouse up my being, help me to pray,
"Abba, Father, have thine own way!"

Break my body, serve me like bread,
that your life in me, I may spread.
Make my life a sacrifice of praise,
squandered for others, all my days.

Stay with me from morning to night,
for life to promote, evil to fight.
Give me grace to drink of your cup,
draw me to you, when my time is up.

Fr Francis Gonsalves, S.J.

PHASE TWENTY-ONE

CHALLENGES OF OBEDIENCE

If they answer not to thy call, walk alone,
If they are afraid and cower mutely
facing the wall;
O thou of evil luck,
Open thy mind and speak out alone.

If they turn away, and desert you
when crossing the wilderness
O thou of evil luck,
Trample the thorns under thy tread.
and along the blood-lined track travel alone.

If they do not hold up the light
When the night is troubled with storm
O thou of evil luck,
With the thunder-flame of pain
ignite thine own heart
And let it burn alone. R. Tagore

The Passion is Jesus' greatest 'hour' – at which he accomplishes the purpose of his Incarnation and his mission on earth. And, he faces it alone – with the help of his heavenly Father. All through his Passion Jesus' divine nature hides itself. We do not see any more the calm noble Christ who walked the waters of the lake, whom living nature and death alike obeyed. He who performed miracles will now not raise a finger to save himself. He is reduced to a most miserable situation, "like a leper and one struck by God." He reaches the rock-bottom of pain, misery, agony, ignominy, shame and failure. "A worm and no man."

After the gesture in the Garden when the armed band 'went backward and fell to the ground,' he never again uses his power even remotely on his own behalf, even when rejected, disgraced, dishonoured, despised, anguished, suffering, and dying.

After the Last Supper Jesus goes to the Garden of Gethsemane to prepare himself in prayer, and to mediate for the last time on the bitterness of his sacrifice. Jesus knew what was coming, he knew there was no going back on his mission. In Gethsemane Jesus prayed earnestly that the cup of suffering pass from him. But in the course of his prayer he resolved that his will be so emptied as to become the divine will. And all through his Passion, suffering, loneliness despair... are all indications of the process through which Jesus was letting go in order to let God act. He emptied himself completely in order to be fully human (see Phil 2) in accepting the will of God.

At this Phase you must accompany Jesus in his agony in the Garden. You must constantly keep in the back of your mind the fact that he is going through his sufferings for you, for your sinfulness. Do more than merely meditate over the events of Jesus' last hours, or even simply contemplate him as he undergoes his passion. Live the passion. Experience his sorrow, anguish, tears and interior pain – feeling it in your own heart. Get involved in the scenes, become part of the action, identify with the situation and make the words of Jesus come alive to you. At times, then, you may feel the dryness and desolation that Jesus felt, but not let it discourage you from continuing in prayer.

Love, even Divine Love, Jesus teaches us through his own experience, does not interfere in natural processes. But we can experience love deep within us only if we learn to let go of ourselves and let God be God, and let God act in our lives as he feels it is best for us.

In a letter to her spiritual director, Mother Teresa expressed her "interior darkness": "In my soul, I feel just the terrible pain of loss, of God not wanting me, of God not really existing." In another letter she wrote that she wanted to love God "like he has not been loved," and yet she felt her love was not reciprocated.

Fr Brian Kolodiejchuk, a Missionaries of Charity Father who published these intimate writings, explained that Mother Teresa was convinced God existed and had a plan for her life, even if she did not feel his presence occasionally. He hoped that reading about Mother Teresa's spiritual struggles would help people come to "a fuller and deeper appreciation of holiness, which Mother Teresa lived in a way both simple and profound: she took what Jesus gave with a smile and stayed faithful even in the smallest things."

This explains Mother Teresa's inspiring words to her Sisters: "Without suffering our work would be social work.... All the desolation of poor people must be redeemed and we must share in it."

The sorrow in my heart is so great that it almost crushes me. Mt 26.38

Suggestions

Have you experienced moments of 'spiritual darkness' when you were challenged 'to let go and let God'? What were your responses?

Read prayerfully **Mt 26.36-41**: Agony in the Garden.

Ask for the grace of steadfast faith even in times of trial, so that you may always adhere to the will of God for you.

Martin Luther King was about to retire after a long, tiring day, when the phone rang. King picked it up. A voice on the other end said: "Listen, nigger, we've taken all we want from you. Before next week, you'll be sorry you ever came to Montgomery."

King hung up. Suddenly he felt gripped by fear, as his courage oozed out. He grew restless and started pacing the floor. He went to the kitchen, heated a pot of coffee, poured out a cup, then sat there benumbed. He felt lost and confused. Then he began to pray: "Lord, I am taking a stand for what I believe is right. But now I'm afraid, deeply afraid. People are depending on me for leadership. If I am without strength or courage, they too will grow fearful. I am at the end of my rope. I don't know what to do. I can no longer face this responsibility."

At that moment, recalled King later, "I experienced the presence of the divine as I have never experienced him before."

Father... take this cup of suffering away from me. Yet, not what I want, but what you want. Mk 14.36

Suggestions

In moments of inner struggle, do you remain sensitive to God's power and seek his will?

Read prayerfully **Mk 14. 32-42**: Jesus' agony and surrender.

Kneel silently beside Jesus as he throws himself on the ground. Pray slowly, meaningfully, the words of the Our Father: "Your will be done...", letting the words sink in your heart.

In 1984 Fr Martin Jenco, OSM, an American, was appointed Director of Catholic Relief Services in Beirut. In 1985, he was abducted by Muslim extremists and held hostage for 594 days in Beirut. He endured beatings, illness and heartbreaking periods of loneliness – as he disclosed in his book, *Bound To Forgive* (1995).

Terry Anderson, a journalist, also imprisoned in the same building, persuaded his captors to allow him to go to Fr Jenco for Confession. For months after that, Terry and other hostages joined Fr Jenco daily to offer the Eucharist with bread saved from the morning meal. Through this spiritual union they developed courage to forgive their captors. "Just look at the madness that goes on in the world today," notes Fr Jenco in his book..... We [must] stop and look at each other and say, 'I am so sorry for the hurt I caused you. I ask your forgiveness.' ... We're all bound to forgive.

My God, my God, why did you abandon me? Mt 27.46

Suggestions

Have you experienced the pain of loneliness? What has been your response to it?

Read reflectively **Mt 27.45-50**.

Ask for strength to always find consolation and inspiration in the Cross of Christ and to help others do the same in times of loneliness and despair.

The lonely way that you once walked, has made me sorrow-wise... Your love has turned to brighter light this night-like way of mine.... Stay with me, Jesus, only stay; I shall not fear if, reaching out my hand, I feel that you are near. Fr Jenco

21/3 Open-ended relationships

A Sufi mystic arrived at the outskirts of a town with his disciples. They had travelled far, and were desperately in need of shelter and food. Unfortunately, the townsfolk, being of another religion, refused them hospitality. Without so much as a word of reproof, the Master sought out a large tree, spread his mat under it, and began his meditation.

He prayed in a low voice, "You are great, O God, for you always provide us whatever we need."

Overhearing this, some of the novices who were on their first pilgrimage, turned to him and said, "Master, your prayer is not sincere. Here we are, out in the cold, exposed to wild beasts, tired, famished; we have been insulted and rejected. How can you say God provides?"

"Well," replied the saint with kindly patience, "What we need tonight is poverty, hunger, rejection and danger. If we didn't need it, He would not have given it. So should we not be grateful? He always takes care of our needs. Great is His Name!"

Father... not my will but your will be done. Lk 22.42

Suggestions

Do you always accept the 'sufferings' you have to undergo in carrying out God's mission, as part of God's plan for your?

Read prayerfully **Lk 22.39-46**.

Ask for the grace of courage to do God's will under all circumstances.

Facing rejection

William Barclay tells of a certain artist, Sigismund Goetze, who had a painting hung in the Royal Academy exhibition of 1904, entitled *Despised and Rejected of Men*. The picture depicts Christ on the steps of St Paul's Cathedral in London.

There are crowds about him, but no one pays him any attention. One man is so concentrated while reading the Sports page of the newspaper, that he almost brushes against Christ as he walks by.

A bishop, elegantly dressed, is too self-conscious about his own piety and position, and passes by oblivious to Christ. A radical priest is so fiercely engaged in a theological argument, that he does not notice Christ.

A street-preacher is giving a sermon on human rights to a small crowd of men, but his gaze does not reach Christ. Only a nurse glances at Christ and passes by.

Barclay concludes: "That is the commonest situation of life. If Jesus Christ came again, there are many who would not bother to crucify him; he would not seem sufficiently important for that."

Then all the disciples left him and ran away. Mt 26.56

Suggestions

Do you see Jesus today with the eyes of faith? Do you welcome him or ignore him?

Read meditatively **Mt 26.47-56**.

Speak to Jesus as your heart dictates. Thank him for his unconditional love for you and for all people.

Enduring denial

At the Last Supper an interesting dialogue took place between Jesus and Peter:

Jesus: This very night all of you will leave me and run away.
Peter: I will never leave you, even though the rest do.
Jesus: I tell you that before the cock crows tonight, you will say three times that you do not know me.
Peter: I will never say that, even if I have to die with you.

A couple of hours later, Jesus' prediction comes true. Peter swears that he does not know Jesus, when confronted by different people soon after Jesus' arrest. The cock crows. Jesus turns round and looks at Peter, and Peter remembers. He goes out and weeps bitterly. That look! No hard feelings, Peter knows; just a wee bit of disappointment. But he did not miss that sparkle of reassurance that shone from the Master's eye. The Lord has never failed to understand man's weakness: He forgives freely and fully. Peter is up on his feet once again.

The Lord turned round and looked straight at Peter. Lk 22.61

Suggestions

Do you stick to your promises to Christ in the face of threats and challenges to your commitment?

Read prayerfully **Lk 22.54-65**.

Ask for the grace of courage to be always faithful to your commitment as a Christian.

Christ's look went straight to the heart of Peter. In that moment he was converted. That was the beginning of his reconciliation. And fittingly, the cock crowed, for it was the beginning of dawn for him. William Breault, S.J.

21/6 Compromising convictions

In *The Wife of Pilate*, Gertrude von le Fort has imaginatively recreated the terror and panic that grips Claudia, the wife of Pilate, when she awakens from a dream in which she has seen future generations of people all praying the words of the creed: "suffered under Pontius Pilate". She is so shocked by what the dream seems to forebode that she sends an urgent warning to her husband. "Have nothing to do with that innocent man."

Pilate, after the interrogation, feels convinced that Jesus is innocent and is inclined to set him free. Claudia's warning echoes in his own conviction. Nevertheless, Pilate yields to mob pressure, condemns Jesus to the most brutal form of Roman execution – crucifixion, then attempts to purge himself of guilt by ritual washing of his hands.

They are misled, their malice
makes them blind. Wis 2.21

Suggestions

Are you influenced into compromising your convictions owing to social pressures?

Read meditatively **Mt 27.11-25**.

Feel the shame and loneliness of Jesus. Experience the pain in his heart. Thank him for undertaking his Passion for your sake.

The ruler called for water, and thought his hands were clean
Christ counted less than order, the man than the machine.
The crowd creied, "Crucify him", their malice wouldn't budge.
So Pilate called for water, and history his judge. J. Ferguson

21/7 Exemplary sensitivity

Part of a TV antenna perched on a high pole on a roof was broken. The company sent two repairmen to do the job. Since a ladder was not available, and the antenna was a little out of reach, one of the workmen, a tall, broad-shouldered fellow, offered to stand the other on his shoulders and hand over the melted lead so that he could weld the broken parts together.

The job completed, the welder crawled down from the shoulders of his husky partner and climbed down the roof. Then his partner came down, very slowly. As he reached the ground he toppled over. His shoulders and arms were covered with terrible burns.

What had happened was that while the welder was soldering the antenna, the boiling lead ran drop by drop on the shoulders of the man holding him up. Though the pain was intense, he had not moved an inch. Any movement would have plunged the welder to his death. It took weeks for the painful burns to heal.

> **In order to set us free from this present evil age, Christ gave himself for our sins, in obedience to the will of our God and Father.**
>
> Gal 1.4

Suggestions

How sensitive are you to others? Are you ready to 'suffer' for their benefit?

Read meditatively the above quote. Reflect over the insights and inspirations you have received over the past week of prayer.

Ask for the grace to always feel compassionate toward Christ suffering in the poor.

PHASE TWENTY-TWO

THE ROAD TO CALVARY

One of the most prominent sights on the Andes Mountains between Argentina and Chile is a colossal statue of Christ holding a cross. There is a very inspiring story on how the statue came to be built. Argentina and Chile were preparing for a large-scale war between them, over a dispute regarding a piece of land that each of the countries claimed for itself.

The Church, however, urged people to pray for a solution without bloodshed. On Easter Sunday, the bishops of both countries, Argentina and Chile, began a special appeal for peace. They toured the country asking people to resort to peace in the name of Christ. Their efforts paid. The people prevailed on their respective governments to sort out the problem without going to war, and an amicable settlement was reached.

More, the soldiers decided to melt down the big guns that were stocked up ready for war and make it into the great bronze statue of Christ. That is the symbolic statue that inspires both countries from its vantage point high in the mountains. An inscription on the statue reads: "These mountains shall fall and crumble to dust before the people of Chile and the Argentine shall forget their solemn covenant sworn at the feet of Christ."

You have meditated on the Passion of Jesus at least once a year – during the liturgical season of Lent. You have also retraced step by step the road to Calvary – in the Stations of the Cross. In this phase of the programme of *Spiritual Exercises* you will re-trace those steps.

Passion is a deliberately selected term meaning deep suffering which includes severe physical pain, intense emotional stress and acute depression. As you contemplate the Passion of Jesus, you may feel helpless and confused in understanding the mystery of his suffering. When you empathise deeply with the agony of Jesus, you will feel out of depth, speechless. You may want to respond but words fail you. Perhaps the best response is to remain silent, letting Jesus know that you are around and you care. "Just as in human situations of taking care of the sick or ministering to the dying, our presence is often more important than our faltering words or awkward action, so too to *be with* Christ in His Passion describes our prayer response at this time better than any words or actions.... the dept of feeling, love, compassion, which allows us just to be there." (David Fleming, S.J.)

A spiritual writer suggests another image. In contemplating the Passion, you may feel like a child does in the presence of its parents who cry over a tragic event. The child is too innocent to understand the world of sorrow or adults, but it does take the hands of its parents. Feeling the hands of their child in their own consoles the suffering parents. The experience also does something to the child. It is initiated into the realm of suffering. It's heart is transformed. It looks at the world from a newer perspective. So can you if you know how to share the Passion of Jesus. More. Throughout his Passion, at every stage, Jesus addresses you:
"All this I undergo for you. What are you doing for me?" You must ask yourself: "What ought I to do for Christ? What ought I to suffer for him?"

Ask for the grace to be totally one with Christ in his suffering: to be able to feel sorrow with Christ in sorrow, to be anguished with Christ's anguish, and even to experience tears and a deep grief because of the sufferings which Christ endures for you.

Mockery

What follows the scourging, while Jesus lies exhausted on the ledge, is a shameful baiting, bullying, and beating of a dying man, by irresponsible soldiers. "This great fool claimed to be a king," they mocked, "so let us give him his due!" Stripping Jesus of his clothing, they put on him an old legionary's scarlet cloak; they find a reed that will do for a sceptre.

"Now for something original! For (twenty) centuries he will be known by this crown, which no other crucified had worn. It is something like a basket which they place on his head. They beat down the edges and with a band of twisted rushes they bind it on the head from the nape of the neck to the forehead. The thorns did into the scalp and it bleeds. The top of the head is presently clothed with blood. Long streams have flowed down to the forehead, under the band of rushes, have soaked into the tangled hair and into the beard." Barbet

My kingdom does not belong to this world. Jn 18.36

Suggestions

How faithful have you been to Christ the King and to his Kingdom?

Read reflectively **Jn 18.33-38, 19.1-3**.

Ask for the grace to feel the suffering of Jesus, to experience his shame, and to realise that he suffers because of you. Pray for strength to live by the values of the Kingdom.

It is by those who have suffered that the world has been advanced. Leo Tolstoy

Zizendorf, the 'Ecumenical Pioneer' and evangelist (1700-1760), once visited the art gallery in Dusseldorf and was arrested by Domenico's masterly painting *Ecce Homo* portraying Jesus as Pilate presented him to the crowd after his scourging. Christ is clothed in purple, bound with ropes, and crowned with thorns.
Zizendorf stood before it in awe. The eyes of Christ seemed to penetrate his heart, while the words of Christ written in Latin above and beneath the painting seemed to be addressed directly to him: "This I did for you; what are you doing for me?"
"There and then," writes A.J. Lewis, Zizendorf's hagiographer, "the young Count asked the crucified Christ to draw him into 'the fellowship of his sufferings' and to open up a life of service to him."

> **We are healed by the punishment he suffered, made whole by the blows he received.** Is 53.5

Suggestions

What is Christ saying to you as you contemplate him in his Passion? What is your response?

Read meditatively **Jn 19.4-16**.

Ask for the grace to be totally one with Christ in his suffering.

> **The way of the Cross winds through our towns and cities, our hospitals and factories, and through our battlefields; it takes the road of poverty and suffering in every form. It is in front of these new Stations of the Cross that we must stop and meditate and pray to the suffering Christ for strength to love him enough to act.** M. Quoist

On September 11, 2002, terrorists hijacked commercial planes soon after take-off, then rammed them into the twin towers of the World Trade Center in New York. Apart from crashing to the ground, burying thousands of people in the debris and injuring numberless other, the towers turned into infernos since the planes were loaded with fuel. The fire-fighters who rushed to the scene were hailed as heroes for their brave acts in rescuing the victims.

Amanda Voysey, a patient advocate at Lawrence Hospital in Bronxville, N.Y. shares this story: ... we realised that one of our own surgeons was at a meeting that morning in one of the World Trade Center towers. We waited and prayed until we finally word that he had escaped unharmed. "I saw the most remarkable things on my way down the stairs," he later told us at the hospital. "It was the face of the fireman coming up. He was bent over carrying a coil of hose." Tears filled the surgeon's eyes. "And what I saw was the image of Christ carrying the cross." (*Guideposts*, April 2002)

Let us keep our eyes fixed on Jesus...
Think of what he went through... Heb 12.2-3

Suggestions

Are you magnanimous enough to empathise with the limitations and sufferings of others?

Read prayerfully **Lk 23.26-31**, contemplating the face of Jesus. And **Rom 6.1-14** – on the response expected of one who desires to identify with Christ sufferings.

Ask for the grace to be totally one with Christ in his sufferings.

O Lady Mary, they bright crown
Is no mere crown of majesty;
For with the reflex of His own
Resplendent thorns Christ circles thee.
  The red rose of this Passion-tide
  Doth take a deeper hue from thee
  In the five wounds of Jesus dyed,
  And in they bleeding thoughts, Mary!

The soldier struck a triple stroke,
That smote they Jesus on the tree;
He broke the Heart of Hearts, and broke
The Saint's and Mother's heart in thee.
  Thy Son went up the angels' ways,
  His passion ended; but, ah me!
  Thou found'st the road of further days
  A longer way of Calvary.

On the hard cross of hope deferred
Thou hung'st in loving agony,
Until the mortal-dreaded word
Which chills our mirth, spake mirth to thee...

Francis Thompson

And sorrow, like a sharp sword, will break your own heart. Lk 2.35

Suggestions

Stay with Mary, Jesus' Mother, in silence. Observe her expression. Feel her pain.

Ask her to beg for you the grace to show compassion to others in their sufferings – grief, heartaches, sicknesses and to resignedly bear up your own sorrows, sufferings, as our Blessed Mother did.

Anton Lang, the distinguished actor in the world-famous *Oberammergaŭ Passion Play*, entranced audiences with the depth of intensity with which he portrayed Christ. One night, after his sensational performance a foreign couple went backstage to congratulate Lang. After a brief chat he posed with them for a photograph.

Then the gentleman saw the large stage cross leaning against the wall. "Snap a shot of me carrying the cross," he told his wife. He briskly approached it as she prepared the camera.

With both arms he tried to lift it to his shoulder, only to discover that he was unable to make it budge. Embarrassed, he gave it another mighty heave but could not move the solid wooden cross even one inch. Now truly humiliated, he blushingly said to Lang, "I thought it would be hollow. Why do you carry such a heavy cross?"

The muscular actor silently smiled for a moment and replied, "If the cross were not heavy, I could not play the part."

Take my yoke and put it on you,
and learn from me. Mt 11.29

Suggestions

How convinced are you that the cross of Christ – his pain, and sorrow, and suffering – were for real?

Read meditatively **Lk 23.26**.

Ask for the grace not to succumb under the weight of your own cross, but to reach out and help others bear their crosses, through patient listening and understanding, through compassion, through selfless service to the needy.

The way of the cross
  is not a dead past.
It's not a plaster ritual
  of Christ's demise,
not a unique folly
  across the centuries.
The crucifixion
  is everyday reality:
  the protracted inhumanity of man,
  the power of sin unchecked.
The poor and the powerless
        are betrayed by profits
        condemned by indifference,
        scourged by ideologies.
Daily they drag their crosses
  up a million calvaries
  there to die with thirst
  unquenched.
They die unseen.   Anon

Christ is like a single body which has many parts... If one part of the body suffers, all the other parts suffer with it. Rom 12.12,26

Suggestions

Do you understand how you are linked to the world of suffering? What is your response?

Read reflectively **Mt 27.32**.

Ask for the grace of a deeper understanding of the mystery of suffering and for greater awareness of your responsibility in helping others lift up their crosses.

In Mogadishu (Somalia) during the famine, we saw this little boy.... he had worms and was malnourished. Our photographer gave the boy a grapefruit. He was so weak he didn't have the strength to hold it, so we cut it in half for him. He picked it up, looked at us as if to say thanks, and began to walk back towards his village....

There on the ground was a little boy, eyes completely glazed over as if dead. It turned out to be his younger brother. The older brother knelt down, bit off a piece of the grapefruit, and chewed it. Then he opened up his younger brother's mouth, put the grapefruit in, and worked his brother's jaw up and down. We learned that he had been doing that for his younger brother for two weeks.

A couple of days later the older brother died of malnutrition, but the younger brother survived.... I wonder if this is what Jesus meant when he said that there is no greater love than to lay down our life for somebody else. Jack Kelley (summarised)

Help to carry one another's burdens. Gal 6.2

Suggestions

In what ways do you help alleviate the suffering of others?

Read meditatively **Gal 6.1-6**.

Ask for the grace to be heart-broken for the heart-broken Christ in humanity.

If you were arrested for being a Christian, would there be enough evidence to convict you? Kenneth E. Kirk

THE EXTRA MILE

Dear Lord, I find it hard to give
As you have told me to
To make the smallest sacrifice
Sometimes is hard to do
So grant me, Lord, the gift to give,
And through my self denial,
Lord Jesus, in my love for you,
I'll walk the Extra Mile.

Lord, give my eyes the gift to see
The other person's need
And take from me my selfishness,
Self-centredness and greed,
And make my ears attentive
To the hard cry of despair.
Lord, grant that I will go without
While others have my share.

My hands, dear Lord, are idle
And I offer them to you
That you may use them as you will,
There's so much they can do.
And guide my feet that I will walk
With those who walk alone.
And may my footprints on this earth
Lead to your Heavenly Throne.

Oh Lord, if I can live this way
My life will be worthwhile,
For then I'd know that in your name
I walk the Extra Mile
For I remember long ago that day on Calvary,
Those many many extra miles, dear Lord,
You walked for me. Amen. **Bernard Boon**

PHASE TWENTY-THREE

CALVARY RE-VISITED

I listen to the agony of God –
I who am fed,
who never went through a hungry day
I see the dead –
the children starved for the lack of bread –
I see and try to pray.

I listen to the agony of God –
I who am warm,
who never yet lacked a sheltering home
in dull alarm
the dispossessed of hut and farm
aimless and transient roam.

I listen to the agony of God –
But I know full well
That not until I share their bitter cry –
Earth's pain and hell –
Can God within my spirit dwell
to bring the Kingdom nigh.

George H. Harkness

In this phase you will contemplate Jesus as he faces the depth of degradation. You must vibrate with his feelings of rejection, loneliness, despair and dejection.

"Even the darkest forms of prayer make sense because Christ makes sense. It was in Jesus' own darkest hour, in his failure and his death, that God vindicated him and raised him up. The strength of God was manifested in the weakness of Jesus' passion, the glory of God in the foolishness of his love." William McNamara S.J.

Kilian Healy in *Walking With God* records the experiences of Fr Titus Brandisma, a university president in Holland during World War II. Fr Titus was arrested by the Nazis and shunted to a concentration camp. To punish him, they captors isolate him by locking him up in a dog kennel. Every now and then, as his guards passed by the kennel, they amused themselves by ordering him to bark like a dog.

Fr Titus felt extremely lonely and abandoned. But he kept his faith and hope strong. He used an old prayer-book as a diary; between the lines of print he wrote about his ordeal and his reflections. After he died from torture, his prayer-book was preserved. One entry in it, which was a prayer addressed to Jesus, is very inspiring. He wrote:

"The lonely way that you once walked, has made me sorrow-wise... Your love has turned to brighter light this night-like way of mine.... Stay with me, Jesus, only stay; I shall not fear if, reaching out my hand, I feel that you are near."

My God, my God, why did you abandon me? Mt 27.46

Suggestions

Have you experienced the pain of loneliness? What has been your response to it?

Read reflectively **Mt 27.45-50**.

Ask for the strength to always find consolation and inspiration in the Cross of Christ and to help others do the same in times of loneliness and despair.

In 1984 Fr Martin Jenco, OSM, an American, was appointed Director of Catholic Relief Services in Beirut. In 1985, he was abducted by Muslim extremists and held hostage for 594 days, in an unfinished building in Beirut. He endured beatings, illness and heartbreaking periods of loneliness – as he disclosed in his book, *Bound To Forgive* (1995).

Another prisoner, journalist Terry Anderson was imprisoned in the same building. Terry persuaded his captors to allow him to go to confession to Fr Jenco. For months after that, Terry and other hostages joined Fr Jenco daily to offer the Eucharist with bread saved from the morning meal. Through this spiritual union they eventually developed courage to forgive their captors.

"Just look at the madness that goes on in the world today," notes Fr Jenco in his book. "We lug our hates and our bigotry and prejudices from generation to generation and we pass [them] on.... We [must] stop and look at each other and say, 'I am so sorry for the hurt I caused you. I ask your forgiveness.'... We're all bound to forgive."

Father, forgive them. Lk 23.34

Suggestions

Does the example of give you inspiration and courage to forgive those who hurt you?

Read prayerfully **Lk 23.32-34**.

Ask for the grace to forgive from the depth of your heart all those who do you harm.

To attract the world's attention to Argentina's desperate economic straits, during Lent in March 2002, Fr Jesus Olmedo crucified himself in a barren corner of the country's border with Bolivia. Fr Olmedo, a Spanish-born priest who arrived in Argentina in the 1970s, took to a makeshift cross along with a dozen Coya Indians in the Andean region of LaPuna, where unemployment is now over 60 percent and one in every two children in malnourished. Among those taking part in the protest were men and women of all ages who tied themselves with cloths and ropes to wooden electricity pylons.

"I ask the Government to hear the voices of the crucified of LaPuna", Fr Jesus told a crowd.... "This is not theatre. This is the world of God." Speaking from his improvised cross, the priest told them, "I have learned above all here, in LaPuna, that you are the Christs crucified by pain, hunger, misery and suffering."

Don't cry for me, but for yourselves and your children. Lk 23 28

Suggestions

Are you aware of the "crucifixions" taking place daily in the world around you? What is your response?

Read meditatively **Lk 23.27-31**.

Pray for the grace of compassion and for strength to reach out to Christ who suffers in the poor, the oppressed, the marginalised, the rejects of society.

Someone ought to do it, but why should I?
Someone ought to do it, so why not I?
Between these two sentences lie whole
centuries of moral evolution. Annie Besant

Christians of various denominations in Britain celebrate *Prisoner's Week* early November. It provides an opportunity for people to examine their attitudes towards law-breakers. A leaflet published in 1990 on the occasion stated: "It (the week) also encourages us to pray for a just and Christian response to crime, its victims, and families of prisoners, offenders, and those who work in this area of life which affects us all – an area many people prefer to pass by."

To put across their idea more poignantly, they highlight the painting of the "*Crucifixion*" by an unnamed artist. The main feature of this picture of Calvary, is not the crucified Christ but one of the two thieves, with a distressed women and two children at the foot of *his* cross.

"The painting reminds us of the humanity of the men who suffered the same death as Jesus," explains the leaflet. "Then – as so often now – the despair and isolation of the prisoner's family is being ignored by everyone."

They crucified Jesus there, and the two criminals. Lk 23.33

Suggestions

Are you aware of innocent people who suffer shame and disgrace for the misdeeds of their kith and kin? Do you remember to pray for them or console them?

Read meditatively **Jn 19.23-27**.

Ask for the grace to be sensitive to all who suffer in silence, or who cannot voice their grievances because of their social condition against the injustices meted out to them.

I used to wonder how the canonization of the Good Thief would have been. The following events might have taken place. People gather in thousands in the Vatican square. The Holy Father reads out a homily like this, "Dear Brothers, today we are going to canonize a unique person. His whole life was marked with high treason and murder. Even today he is a much wanted man by the police. Every word which he uttered, except the very few last ones, were blasphemous. By a special mandate given me by Christ I declare him a saint."

An uneasy silence descends over the crowd. A pious participant in the crowd whispers to his neighbour, "How can the church accommodate such brand of saints? Saints are of a different brand. It's a tilted halo."

Fr Paul Kachapilly, S.D.B.

Today you will be in Paradise with me. Lk 23.43

Suggestions

What is your attitude toward "criminals"? Are you condemning or compassionate?

Read meditatively **Lk 23.39-43**.

Ask for the grace of an understanding heart that is slow to condemn and quick to forgive "criminals".

'Twas the thief said
the last kind words to Christ;
Christ took their kindness,
and forgave the theft.

Robert Browning

In 1991 Fr Thomas Anchanikal, the "Martyr for Justice" wrote about in *Jivan*: "The Dalits of Hazaribagh (Jharkand) are a fragmented group, economically and socially deprived, culturally impoverished, educationally backward, and religiously exploited and marginalised. Their life is characterised by poverty, illiteracy, insecurity, fear, dependence and their accompanying ill-effects.... Father Thomas was one of those who stood by them "in their struggle for dignity and equality...."

In Sirka, a village, some people had grabbed land unjustly from the Dalits. Fr Thomas, 46, had helped them recover the land, and had the land-grabbers arrested and imprisoned. In October, 1997, the ex-convicts returned to Sirka disguised as policemen. and were beating one of the villagers, when Fr Thomas happened to arrive there. They instantly recognised Father, surrounded him, and took him away at gunpoint. Three days later, Father's decapitated and battered body was seen in a river bed not far from Sirka.

Fr Thomas' martyrdom was a source of inspiration to everyone around: he had sacrificed his own life in his mission to better the life of the poorest of the poor.

> **By means of my own sufferings I am helping to complete what still remains of Christ's sufferings on behalf of his body, the church.**
> Col 1.24

Suggestions

Do you appreciate the value of "laying down one's life" for faith and justice? What is your response?

Read meditatively **Mk 8.31-38**.

Ask for the grace that like Jesus, you will have the courage to fight against injustices, even unto death.

An elderly woman, discussing her funeral service with her parish priest, made an unusual request:
"When they bury me, I want my rosary in one hand and a fork in the other?"
"I'm sorry," the priest stammered. "You want to be buried with a *fork*?"
"Yes. You see, I've attended numberless dinners in my lifetime. At the end of the best dinners, before the dirty dishes were collected, the hostess would say, 'Keep the fork.' Of course, that meant that dessert was coming. And not pudding or even ice cream – you don't need a fork for that. It meant the good stuff – like chocolate cake or home-made apple pie. When they said to keep my fork, I knew the best was yet to come! That's exactly what I want people to talk about at my funeral... When they see me in my casket in my beautiful dress, I want them to turn to one another and say, 'Why the fork?' And I want you to tell them that I kept my fork because the best is yet to come!"

Where, Death, is your power to hurt? 1Cor 15.55

Suggestions

Do you have any fear of death? Do you realise that Christ has 'conquered' death?

Read meditatively **Jn 19.38-42**.

Ask for the grace to be united with Christ in his death so that you may experience the power of the resurrection.

Out of the chill and shadow,
Into the thrill and the shine;
Out of the dearth and famine,
Into the fulness divine. M.E. Sangster

SECTION SIX

RISING TO NEW LIFE

RISING TO NEW LIFE

A boy was walking through some fields one day and came across the cocoon of a monarch butterfly. He watched it for quite awhile because the butterfly was struggling to force its way through the tiny opening in the cocoon's casing. Suddenly, it lay still. Was the butterfly stuck, the boy wondered. He pulled out a penknife from his pocket and carefully cut away the rest of the cocoon.

The butterfly emerged easily, but its body was swollen and small, its wings were shrivelled. The body waits expectantly for the creature to expand its wings and take flight – but it does not. Little did he know that the butterfly's struggle through the tiny aperture in the cocoon forces fluid from its body into the wings, giving them stability and strength so that the butterfly can fly soon after it works its way out of the hole.

The boy does not understand that the butterfly's freedom and flight are only possible after much struggle and hardship.

Nowhere in Scripture are we told how the resurrection of Jesus actually took place. There were no witnesses to the event; it remains a mystery. But the experience of the Risen Lord for 'forty days' after his death and burial is so convincing as to have become the foundation of Christianity.

The Easter experience for the disciples began with an empty tomb. Even after the assurances of the angel that "he has been raised," they walked away in disbelief and despair. Their faith seemed to be dead!

Only after they had seen the Risen Lord was their faith resurrected. Their fears turned into joy, their doubts into belief, their disappointments into hope. The confusion and fright that followed the crucifixion gave in to the conviction that Jesus was the Messiah indeed. All that Jesus had been teaching them now began to fall into place.

Jesus was alive once again, for sure. But he was radically different in appearance. (One may think of the caterpillar turning into a butterfly!). Even those who had closely associated with him before his death, found it difficult to recognise him at once. But then there were things about him – his gestures, his endearments, his expressions.. that had a familiar ring to them through which he could be identified as the selfsame Christ, their 'Lord and Master'. With this, their faith was revived.

It is significant that the Risen Christ appeared only to those who believed in him, not to the pharisees, the scribes, the crowds. He was not interested in proving anthing to the general public. He wanted only to rebuild his community of disciples, and to make their love for him powerful enough to take the world by storm. He would accomplish this through his Spirit. The resurrection of Jesus is not just an event of the past. It is a reality of the present – and the future. The Risen Lord is alive today in the Spiri everywhere. He teaches, heals and inspires. He exerts a powerful influence over the hearts of all people.

In the prayer-phases of this section you will deepen your faith in the Risen Lord and in the power of his Spirit presemt in your life. You will pray for greater commitment to Christ and a deeper desire to serve him, so that you continue his task of building up the Kingdom of God on earth.

PHASE TWENTY-FOUR

REJOICE ~ CHRIST IS ALIVE

The resurrection of Jesus is symbolically reflected in the lives of his followers. The Risen Lord enters the 'cave' which they have retreated into after his crucifixion: the cave of darkness, doubt, despair, fear and frustaration. He revives their spirits and infuses new life into them. He fills them with PEACE and JOY.

The Risen Christ now does not hide his divinity as he had done during his Passion, but manifests his divine qualities for all his friends to see and experience. He does not do so by appearing as an angel in shining armour, but most casually, as a loving master, a dear friend, a fellow-traveller, a caring host. Freed from the limitations of his physical body, the Risen Christ can go wherever he wills. He makes himself present where he is needed most – to cheer-up, to bring consolation to his crest-fallen disciples. He is Christ the Consoler.

In this phase, experience the Joy and Peace that is the fruit of the Resurrection. Get involved in the scenes where the Risen Lord makes his appearances, and draw as much inspiration as you can both by observing what he does and by experiencing the power of his Resurrection which transforms you as you contemplate him.

Pray for the grace to feel genuinely thrilled because the Lord is risen, and for courage to go out to the whole world and radiate your joy through loving service.

"Recently," confided a housewife, "I happened to wake up in the middle of a moonlight night and my gaze fell upon my only son's profile outlined against the bedroom wall. I lay still, without moving my head from the pillow towards him. I felt soaked in a loving, sharing silence that was shaped only by soft breathing. Finally I closed my eyes, knowing only too well how substantial was the silence that was shaped only by soft breathing. In fact, I had realised how substantial was any silence that cradled love."

Mary remembered all these things
and thought deeply about them. Lk 2.19

Suggestions

What did the Mother of Jesus feel during and after the Passion of Jesus?

Jesus' mother's faith was not squashed at the foot of the cross. Nor did it lie buried in the tomb of her son. She had a promise: "his kingdom will never end" (Lk 1.30). She experiences his "Easter" within her through his spiritual presence. Mary does not need 'proof of the Resurrection' as did the disciples of Christ. "How happy are those who believe without seeing me" (Jn 20.29), says Jesus. Since Jesus received his body from 'within' his mother, he is totally present to her in her heart. You may, however, take it for granted that the Risen Saviour appeared first to his mother – though this is not recorded in scripture. So contemplate Mary as she behold her Risen Son. Share her jubilation. Read meditatively **Song of Songs 3.8-14**.

Beg Mary to obtain for you the grace of truly believing that the Lord has risen and is present within you, so that you experience deep joy and consolation. Then ask for the same grace from the Christ and from the Father.

Radiating joy

A man's little daughter – an only and much-beloved child, became ill. His best efforts proved unavailing and the child died. The father was totally irreconcilable. He became a bitter recluse, shutting himself away from his many friends and refusing every activity that might restore his poise and bring him back to his normal self.

One night, in a dream, he was in Heaven witnessing a grand pageant of all the little child angels. They were marching past the Great White Throne, each carrying a candle. He noticed that one child's candle was not lighted. Then he saw that it was his own little girl. Rushing to her, he seized her in his arms, caressed her tenderly, and then asked: "How is it, darling that your candle alone is unlighted?"

"Father, they often relight it, but your tears always put it out." The man awoke from his dream and determined to change his life to normal. He mingled freely and cheerfully with his former friends and associates. No longer would his little darling's candle be extinguished by his useless tears. Strickland Gillilan (adapted)

"Woman, why are you crying," they asked her. Jn 20.13

Suggestions

Have you developed a spiritually optimistic outlook toward life through the power of Christ's resurrection? Isn't it now time for rejoicing rather than weeping?

Read meditatively **Jn 20.11-18**.

Ask for the grace to experience intimately the presence of the Risen Lord and repose with him.

Gift of peace

Mildred Normana, a US citizen, is called "The Peace Pilgrim"! She decided back in 1953 that she would devote her entire life to teaching peace. She did this by walking – back and forth across the American continent for 24 years!

She didn't have any sponsors, didn't take anything with her except a comb, a pen and a toothbrush. And to anyone who would listen she talked about the vital need for peace and the practical things that anyone could do to work for peace – peace in the world and peace within. According to Mildred, the "Symptoms of Inner Peace" are:

*An unmistakable ability to enjoy each moment.
*A loss of interest in judging other people... in interpreting the actions of others... in conflict.
*A loss of the ability to worry.
*Frequent, overwhelming episodes of appreciation.
*Contented feelings of connectedness with others and nature.
*Frequent attacks of smiling.
*An increased susceptibility to the love extended by others as well as the uncontrollable urge to extend it.

Peace be with you. Jn 20.19

Suggestions

Are you a peace-lover and a peace-maker? Do you let the 'peace of Christ' fill your being?

Read prayerfully **Jn 20.19-23**.

Ask for the grace to be united with the Risen Christ, to be filled with his Peace, and to share it with those around.

24/4 Consoling presence

In the 17th century, Ceylon (presently Sri Lanka) was occupied by staunch Dutch Calvinists. In an attempt to suppress Catholicism, they expelled all European Catholic missionaries, destroyed churches, and laid out strict rules for the native Catholics. Fr Joseph Vaz, a Goan by birth, and the founder-superior of the Institute of the Oratory of St Philip Neri in Goa, was inspired by the Holy Spirit to risk his life and go to Ceylon to cater to the needs of the oppressed Catholic flock.

In 1686, disguised as a *coolie* (porter), Fr Vaz took a boat from Tuticorin, and learned Tamil on the voyage. Then, dressed as a beggar, he roamed the island of Ceylon in search of the surviving Catholics. Admiring the courage of this priest, the Catholics rallied around him, hiding him in their houses, and holding secret gatherings at dead of night. For ten years Fr Vaz was the only priest there. He was able to build 15 churches and 400 chapels with schools, dispensaries and hospitals throughout the island. He died in 1711, and was beatified by Pope John Paul in 1995.

They saw him, but somehow did not recognise him. Lk 24.15

Suggestions

What questions, concerns do you have regarding the resurrection? How often have you met Christ on the road of Life? Do you understand that suffering is a prefix to resurrection?

Read meditatively **Lk 24.13-35**.

Ask for deep faith to be sensitive to the presence of the Risen Lord especially in the poor, and to be highly motivated to spread the good news to all.

Unshaken faith

On The Third Day, a novel by Piers Paul, is the story of a distinguished Jewish archaeologist Michal Dagan who discovers the skeleton of a first century man in Jerusalem. He invites his colleague, Fr John Lambert, a Catholic priest, to examine the find and verify what he suspects – that it is the body of Christ. During the research, one day Fr Lambert is found dead – hanging from the ceiling of a London monastery cell. Did he give up on life because of the discovery shattered his faith? The story goes on to find that out....

A similar theme is found in the movie *The World In Darkness*. An archaeologist finds a first-century mummy at the tomb of Christ which exactly the description of Jesus. The newspapers across the globe splash headlines calling the resurrection of Jesus a fraud. On his deathbed, the archaeologist confesses that the whole thing was a joke, and the mummy was not genuine.

> **If Christ has not been raised from death, then... you have nothing to believe.** ICor 15.14

Suggestions

How would you have reacted to the above discoveries? How deep is your faith in the resurrection of Jesus?

Read meditatively **Jn 21.1-14**.

Ask for a deepening of your faith in the Risen Lord, motivated by deep joy at his victory over death and darkness.

> **The gospels do not explain the resurrection; the resurrection explains the gospels. Belief in the resurrection is not an appendage to the Christian faith; it is the Christian faith.** J.S. White

Deep trust

Two young friends in Germany, Albrecht Durer and Franz Knigstein, aspired to become artists, but could not afford going to a university to. However, they decided one of them should find employment and support the other until he completed school. Then he could sell his paintings and finance the other's education.

They drew lots, and Durer got to go to an Art school while Knigstein worked and paid for Durer's tuition. Eventually, Durer turned out to be a genius whose paintings fetched a good price. He then returned home as a wealthy man in order to give Knigstein his turn at art school. To his shock he realised the great price his friend had paid. Knigstein's delicate and sensitive fingers had been ruined by his years of rugged manual labour. He had to abandon his artistic dream.

One day Albrecht saw Franz kneeling with his gnarled hands intertwined in prayer. The artist quickly sketched the "Praying Hands". Today's art galleries feature many works of the famous Albrecht Durer, but the people's favourite is the "Praying Hands".

Look at my hands. Jn 20.27

Suggestions

How trusting and loyal are you in your commitment to Christ?

Read prayerfully **Jn 20.24-29**.

Ask for the grace to share in the joy of the resurrection with fullness of heart, so as to follow Christ and serve him.

Every parting gives a foretaste of death, every union a hint of the resurrection. A. Schopenhauer

Challenging call

Thomas Merton was kneeling in the lower church at St Francis Xavier on 16th Street in Manhattan. He had just stumbled in there after wandering around all day, stunned with a notion that had suddenly and inexplicably seized him that morning: He would be a monk and a priest. It had suddenly become clear that his whole life was at a critical moment. "I looked straight at the Host," which had been exposed during a Holy Hour, "and I knew now who it was... and I said: 'Yes, I want to be a priest... If it is your will, make me a priest.'"

Then, he wrote, he quickly realised "what power I had put into motion on my behalf, and what a union had been sealed between me and that power by my decision."

"Do you love me more than these others do?" Jn 21.15

Suggestions

Is the Lord challenging you to greater commitment and service?

Read reflectively **Jn 21.1-17**.

Ask for the grace to rejoice with the Risen Lord and readily respond to his challenges.

When we walk to the edge
of all the light that we have
and take the step into
the darkness of the unknown,
we must believe that one
of two things will happen.
There is something solid
for us to stand on or,
we will be taught how to fly.

Patrick Overton

PHASE TWENTY-FIVE

EXPERIENCING CHRIST'S SPIRIT

Roll back the stone
although we fear the change;
although we are not ready;
although we'd rather weep
and run away:
Roll back the stone.
    When we are all despairing;
    when the world is full of grief;
    when we see no way ahead,
    and hope has gone away:
    Roll back the stone.
Because we're coming with the women;
Because we hope where hope is vain;
Because they call us from the grave:
Roll back the stone.

The presence of the Risen Jesus is a transforming Presence. Sadness is turned to Joy. Night to day. The heart is filled with Love. It is a love that cannot contain itself but seeks to go out of itself and share the thrill it experiences.

You must have observed that all the appearances of the Risen Lord end with his giving those present a *Mission:* to proclaim the Good News of God's Kingdom and to love and serve others so that we create a new earth where peace, freedom and justice prevail everywhere, at all levels.

Jesus commissions the women at the tomb on the first Easter morning: "Go and tell my brothers to go to Galilee" (Mt 28.10). To his apostles, he says: "As the Father has sent me, so I send you" (Jn 20.21). He instructs all his followers: "Go, then, to all peoples everywhere and make them my disciples" (Mt 28.19)

In the events related to the Resurrection of Jesus of Nazareth, the most important factor is the Holy Spirit who, as Jesus said, "will teach you everything and make you remember all that I have told you" (Jn 14.26).

Empowered by the Spirit which Jesus gifted them his disciples at Pentecost, they are so gripped by Christ and the message he has entrusted them – to proclaim to the world the "good news", that there was no stopping them. People thought them crazy, even drunk, but they willingly became "fools for Christ's sake," in order to remain faithful to their calling.

In this phase you will reflect on the commission of Jesus to the disciples, his gift of the Holy Spirit and ways in which people encounter Christ in the world today. The Spirit of the Risen Christ tranformed you, too, through Baptism, Confirmation... When you love and serve others, you become instrumental in their transformation.

Entreat the Holy Spirit to fill you with his power and enable you to recognise Christ in others, and be of service to him.

The Spirit of Jesus is *God* himself – not God in the distant heaven whom no one has ever seen but God present in our world. J. Neuner, S.J.

Easter blessing

Pamela Kay Barnet, 20, newly married, was driving to an army camp to visit her husband, Jimmy, when her car was hit head-on by a drunken driver. She suffered severe injuries on her legs, an arm and head. The doctors had little hope for her survival.

Pamela was in intensive care unit, in traction, and with damaged eyes so she could only see shadow and light. "This is too much to bear," she cried out to God one day. "Please let me know that you are here. I have never felt so alone in my life." Almost instantly she noticed a bright sunbeam sweeping across the sheets next to her face. "It seemed to quiver with energy and radiate peace and reassurance." The light remained with her all that day. "It was a simple thing, a light from a window, but it gave me comfort."

When she was released from the hospital, she told Jimmy about that consoling ray of light. With a puzzled face Jimmy said quietly: "Pam, you were in intensive care. There were no windows." (Guideposts, condensed)

Wake up, sleeper, and rise from death,
and Christ will shine on you. Eph 5.14

Suggestions

Since Christ is Light, do you let his light shine in you in times of darkness? Do you understand what it means to live in the light?

Read meditatively **Eph 5.1-20**.

As for the grace to experience the Easter Presence of Jesus and to live the Easter Joy.

Calvary Day and Easter Day,
Earth's saddest day and gladdest day,
Are just one day apart. Anon

Final delegation

The way in which Leonardo de Vinci's great career as an artist started is an interesting story. The old master he was apprenticed to fell seriously ill, so he asked the young Leonardo to complete a painting that he, the teacher, had been working on. Leonardo protested, saying that it would be impossible for him to step into his teacher's shoes. But the master insisted and convinced Leonardo to accept the job.

Leonardo took up the task as a challenge, for the sake of the master whom he loved dearly. He put in his very best and when the painting was completed there were no end of praises from all quarters. His master was so impressed by his work that he said to Leonardo in all humility, "My son, from now on there is no need for me to paint any more." And he handed over charge to Leonardo.

Go, then, to all peoples everywhere and make them my disciples. Mt 28.19

Suggestions

In what ways are you fulfilling the commission Jesus gives to his disciples at his Ascension into heaven?

Read meditatively **Mt 28.16-20**

Ask for the grace to be ready and willing to use all the power God gives you in order to accomplish the mission of Christ,

I want to be thoroughly used up when I die, for the harder I work the more I live. Life is no brief candle for me. It is a sort of splendid torch which I have got hold of for the moment and I want to make it burn as brightly as possible before handing it on to future generations. G.B. Shaw

Everlasting presence

"I walked where Jesus walked, in the towns and hills and along the seashore," reminisced Mary Amos in a *Catholic Digest* article about her tour of the Holy Land. "I imagined that I would see someone whom I considered to look the way Jesus looked as a man... Throughout the tour I kept looking for the face of Jesus among the inhabitants. No one filled my expectation."

Then Mary's perception changed – and lo, and behold, she discovered Jesus! "I found Him," she revealed ecstatically, "in Jean as she shared some medicine with others who needed it, Tory as she hugged me.... Jesus was in each one of my travelling companions in a special way.... Then I came home to a welcoming committee... Jesus was in the faces of my family that love me .... Ever since then I've thanked Jesus for letting me find Him in the faces of those who surround me every day of my life."

Build up the body of Christ. Eph 4.12

Suggestions

Do you realise that you will fulfill the mission of Christ by recognising his presence among men and women today, and helping build up unity through love and service?

Read meditatively **Eph 4.7-16**.

Ask for the grace to understand the mission of Christ, so that united with his Spirit you will be able to fulfil it.

Christ plays in ten thousand places,
Lovely in limbs and lovely in eyes not his
To the Father through the features
of men's faces. G.M. Hopkins

It begins as a piece of wood or a metal tube. Then a craftsman, using skills and tools that have been passed down for centuries, meticulously forms the wood or metal, carefully drills holes in the shaft, devises a system of stops and valves in the metal, installs an intricate system of strings, turning keys and hammers. The wood is then beautifully finished with resins and varnish; the metal is polished until it gleams. The craftsman's long hours of detailed work results in a finished flute or violin or guitar or piano.

But the completed instrument, though a beautiful work of art, remains just a piece of wood or metal until a musician takes it up and breathes into it while gliding his or her fingers across the stops or expertly manipulates the strings and keys. Then that piece of word, that tube of metal is transformed into a musical instrument, a portal for us to a world of beauty and transcendence. (*Connections*, June 2000)

He breathed over them and said,
"Receive the Holy Spirit." Jn 20.22

Suggestions

Do you experience the power of the Holy Spirit which filled every fibre of your being at your baptism and continues breathing new life into you?

Read meditatively **Acts 2.1-12**.

The Spirit is the divine wonder which does not take Jesus away from us, which makes him truly human, so that in his presence we actually begin to understand what it means to be human and what our life ought to be. At the same time it makes us feel closer to God than any other sacred celebration, so that in him we begin to realise who God is. J. Neuner, S.J.

Strains of Love

In 1994 the city of Sarajevo was under daily siege. Mortars and artillery fire instantly transformed beautiful buildings into rubble. Sarajevo's citizens were frightened, weary and increasingly despondent. Then, one February day, a mortar shell exploded in the market killing 68 civilians. Many more were wounded and maimed from the blast.

A cellist with the Sarajevo symphony could no longer stand the killing. He took his cello to the market, sat down amidst the rubble and played a symphony in memory of those killed in the blast. When he finished, he simply took up his instrument and left. Every day, for 67 days, he came to the market. Every day he played a symphony titled "Hope – your heart's music". It was his gift of love & hope to the grieving city. He did it because he felt that music is a strong motivator and his community needed hope to come up again.

I will sing with my spirit. 1Cor 14.14

Suggestions

Do you realise that through the language of the Spirit – the language of love – you can communicate God's message to everyone, everywhere?

Read meditatively **1Cor 14.7-22**.

Ask for the grace to learn well and practice always the language of love, which is a gift of the Spirit.

I can live forever withn God. Trouble, illness and death may come but my real self – my soul, will go on living in another existence with Almighty God. That is one of the plain meanings of Easter. C. Seidenspinner

Living witnesses

I'm a very logical, scientific-minded person. I need proofs for everything. Yet something has happened to me here in college that I can't explain rationally, scientifically, or even psychologically. I've become totally preoccupied with Jesus Christ, who I somehow feel is working within me.... I can't explain this feeling. It came about mainly these past few months, when I began reading about the early Christians. I was so amazed and in awe of these people that I found it impossible to question Jesus or doubt who he is – the Son of God.

In short, I guess I began to believe firmly and thoughtfully what I was taught ever since a child. I began to see what the apostles and disciples saw and loved. Jesus became real... I still have occasional doubts, but there remains that unexplainable something inside me, even in my doubts. Call it crazy, psychotic, or whatever.... I can't explain it, nor does it go away, nor did I induce it to come. It just happened. Robert Rybicki

With great power the apostles gave witness to the resurrection of the Lord Jesus. Act 4.33

Suggestions

Have you witnessed the power of the Spirit at work among Christians? Are you one of those who have been gripped by the Spirit?

Read meditatively **Acts 4.32-37** and **Acts 5.1-16**.

Ask the Spirit to fill you with the spirit of the first Christians in bearing witness to Christ.

The story of Easter is the story of God's wonderful window of divine surprise. Carl Knudsen

Joyful whirlwind

Alexei Peshkov, a Russian boy, had a very tough childhood. His father died when he was barely five years old. His uncaring mother remarried, but sent him off to his grandparents, who hated him and beat him up. Besides, the family was poverty-stricken, so there were many deprivations to be faced. Later he changed his name to Maxim Gorky (*Maxim* in Russian means maximum, and *Gorky* means bitterness) and turned out to be a famous writer!

It was the works of another famous Russian writer, Leo Tolstoy, which inspired him. He discovered in Tolstoy's stories the faith, love joy, and hope that had escaped him in life. Gorky's concluding note in his autobiography is: "And I dearly wanted to give the earth a hard kick – and myself as well – so that everything, myself included, would start spinning round in one joyful whirlwind, in a festive dance where people were in love with each other, in love with a life which had been begun for the sake of another, which was beautiful, bold and honest!"

Where the Spirit of the Lord is present, there is freedom. 2Cor 3.17

Suggestions

Do you experience freedom in the Spirit?

Read meditatively **Gal 5.22**.

Ask for the grace to be filled with the gifts of the Spirit so that you may live in joy a fully committed Christian life.

But what is freedom? Rightly understood,
A universal licence to be good. Hartley Coleridge

DEATH AND RESURRECTION

We all experience our moments
 of dying in our lives.
We get a foretaste of death
when we live in bitterness,
when loneliness enfolds us,
when fears oppress us,
when sadness overwhelms us,
and when we give in to despair.
In those moments the world is
 closing in on us, and we have
 one foot in the grave already.

But we also experience moments
 of resurrection in our lives:
when we know true love,
when we are accepted,
when we are forgiven,
when we open our hearts
 to our neighbour,
and when hope returns.
In those moments our horizon
 is widening and
we are emerging from the tomb.

Lord Jesus, may the power of your
resurrection touch whatever is dead
in us and bring it back to life.
Let the splendour of your resurrection
light up the world, scattering the shadows
of death and helping all of the Father's
children to walk in radiant hope
towards the kingdom that is to come.

Flor McCarthy, SDB

PHASE TWENTY-SIX SPLENDOURS OF LOVE

Thee God I come from – to Thee I go
All day long I like the fountain flow.
G. M Hopkins

The great mystic Meister Eckhart described God as "a great underground river that no one can dam up and no one can stop." God is the source of our life; we are 'dust and ashes' to all appearances, but nourished by God's LOVE we yield fruit for everyone to enjoy and share.

GOD IS LOVE. From Phase One on in this book, you have been unravelling the mystery of God's unconditional love –through creation, creatures, Christ!

Pause awhile and go deep within your heart – to the source of the fountain of love, life. *Feel* the streams of love flowing out of your heart, filling your bloodstream, coursing through your entire body. *Visualise* this stream overflowing, out of you, into the world. *See* it bringing freshness to those who are weary and overburdened. *Visualise* it supplying nourishment to those who are thirsty, and hungry for love. *Watch* it drown people's sorrows. *Observe* how people swim in it, fish in it, dip their pots in it to carry it to others in need....

Love necessarily consists in mutual sharing for its own nourishment and growth. Your love-roots must go deep – seeking nourishment from God, in order to bear much fruit. "I pray that you may have your roots and foundation in love" (Eph 3.17)

> Lord, You are our God. Lord, You are in all things. Lord, you do all things. You never remove Your hands from Your world, nor ever will, without end. You guide all things to the end that You ordained them for, before time began, with the same power and wisdom and love with which you made them. How could anything be amiss?"
>
> St Julian of Norwich

You have experienced growth – in your love for God-self-others – through the 'phases' of the *Spiritual Exercises*. You have accepted Creation as God's gift. You have acknowledged God's presence in Creation. You have realised that God is not merely present in his gifts, but is actually involved in keeping the gift alive and meaningful. Thus, he is constantly pouring out his love, continually re-creating all creatures. We are filled to overflowing (Rom 5.5) with his love.

You have meditated in the first few phases of this book on God's presence and power in the world. You had understood then that you cannot presume to 'find' God on your own, even though he is ever present, everywhere. It takes the eyes of faith to see God – and faith is a gift of God that enriches you even as it reveals God.

"Lord that I may see."
Open my eyes that I may see you
Give me vision to see and to find you everywhere.
Give me insight into what you are like
as I look into the ordinary things of life.
Let me share your warmth
with those whom I call friends.
Let me find you
in disappointments and frustrations.
Let me see you in my joys and triumphs.
Most of all, Lord, let me look and learn
to see you everywhere, and let me live! Anon

In this phase of your prayer, you have come a full circle – from Love to Love. You have vied the grandeur of the created universe – "its origin from God, and its being destined by God to return to himself) by contributing to his glorification through the joyful praise of those who have cooperated with his plan of creation and redemption.... The whole doctrine is summed up by St Paul: 'For from him and through him and for him all things are. To him be glory forever.

Amen (Rom 11.36)'." G.E. Ganss, S.J.

Ask for the grace to see your and the whole of God's creation as "gift", to accept them with gratitude and to respond with a loving heart by offering God all that I am and possess. You must promise to love God as he ought to be loved, and to serve him in all his creatures through Jesus Christ, his Son and our Brother.

Thou hast made me endless,
such is thy pleasure.
This frail vessel
thou emptiest again and again,
and fillest it over with fresh life.
This little flute of a reed
thou hast carried
over hills and dales, and has breathed
through it melodies eternally new.
At the immortal touch of thy hands
my little heart loses its limits in joy
and gives birth to utterance ineffable.
Thy infinite gifts come to me only
on these very small hands of mine.
Ages pass, and still thou pourest,
and still there is room to fill. Tagore

Love's records

In the book *Love*, which is part of a series of prayer guides on the *Spiritual Exercises*, the authors J.S. Bergan and S. M. Schwan, help the exercitant reall the unconditional love of God through an exercise, as follows:
I reflect how, in my life history, I have been 'carried' and sustained by the love I have received. I recall the many ways in which this love was made visible, e.g., through provision for my physical needs, through supportive relationships, through the enjoyment of life and a sense of purpose.
I become aware that these gifts have been a part of God's plan for me. I allow myself to experience the security and freedom of God's particular care and choice of me.
In light of this experience of all God has done for me, I imagine and record in my journal how the contract/ commitment God has offered to me might appear if written:

> I, God, as your creator, do hereby agree to love you, YOUR NAME_______ unconditionally. I will manifest this love within the circumstances and reality of your life.
> I will support you by ____________________
> I will nourish you ____________________
> I will give you ____________________
> I will ____________________
> The conditions of this commitment have been effective from the moment of my first thought of you. This offer is exempt from ever being terminated. Signed, GOD

How precious, O God, is your constant love. Ps 36.7

Suggestions

How often have you renewed your relationship with God? Do the above exercise, filling in the blanks in the way you experience God's involvement in your life.

Ask for the grace to be always sensitive to and grateful for the presence of God in your life.

Love's warm glow

There is a story about the father of one of America's great poets, Emily Dickinson. One evening, at the dinner hour, the fire bell started ringing madly. The people of the town rushed out of their houses, many still clutching at their forks and spoons and knives, all looking about them for the fire.

Near the bell stood Mr Dickinson. He had just seen a glorious sunset and did not want his neighbours to miss it; he had rung the fire-alarm furiously in order to get them out before it was too late.

Most of the people returned to their cottages shaking their heads and talking about what that "weird Dickinson man, nuttier than a fruitcake."

> **Every good gift and every perfect present... comes down from God, the creator of the heavenly lights.** Jam 1.17

Suggestions

What, do you think. would happen if the sun failed to rise in day?

Pray **Ps 113**.

Consider how God is a present everywhere, to everyone (see Mt 5.45), giving life always. Bask in the warmth of God's love.

Ask for the grace to love and serve God in all things.

> **The whole world and all creatures will be to you nothing else that an open book and a living Bible, in which you may study, without any previous instruction, the science of God and from which you may know his will.**
>
> Sebastian Franck

Love's refreshing stream

A newly initiated disciple approached the great Zen Master on the banks of the river, and requested him to teach him how to 'enter the way'. "Do you hear the river flowing?" asked the Master.
The disciple bowed his head in profound silence, then replied, "Yes, Master, I do."
"That is the way to enter," instructed the Master.

The angel showed me the river of the water of life, sparkling like crystal, and coming from the throne of the Lamb and flowing down the middle of the city's street. Rev 22.1-2

Suggestions

Do you experience the fountain of life that flows from God bubbling within you?

An enlightened person is "like a tree growing near a stream and sending out roots to the water. It is not afraid when hot weather comes, because its leaves stay green; it has no worries when there is no rain; it keeps on bearing fruit."
Jer 17.8

Ask that you take seriously the assurance of Jesus: "Whoever believes in me, streams of life-giving water will pour out from his heart" (Jn 7.38).

Accustom yourself gradually to carry prayer into your daily occupations. Speak, move, work, in peace, as if you were in prayer, as indeed you ought to be. Do everything without excitement, by the spirit of grace. As soon as you perceive your natural impetuosity gliding in, retire quietly within, where is the kingdom of God. Listen to the leadings of grace, then say and do nothing but what the Holy Spirit shall put in your heart. You will find that you will become more tranquil, that your words will be fewer and more effectual and that, with less effort, you will accomplish more good. Francois Fenelon

"The Ballerina Who Danced Her Way to God", was the heading of an media interview with Liliana Cosi, a former first ballerina of Milan's La Scala Theatre who has consecrated herself to God in the Focolare movement. "Classical dance is a way to find and follow God, as well as his infinite beauty," says Cosi.

"Dancing is something that demands much effort and discipline, but I experience it as a great purification and immolation, through which I come closer to perfection, offering a performance of beauty to others," she said. "For me, this is a way of bringing God to the world."

Cosi began her career in La Scala at age 9. When she was about 20, she read St Catherine of Siena's *Dialogue of Divine Providence*, and St Catherine's life. "I thought I had to leave the world, my present and future family, my career, and give everything to God." In 1965 she met an exceptional person, Chiara Lubich, foundress of the Focolare movement. "I was 23. I was already in La Scala's ballet corps and acclaimed in the Bolshoi. She advised me not to go into a convent but to live my vocation as a ballerina on stage."

If we live in truth and in love, we shall grow in all ways into Christ. Eph 4.15

Suggestions

Do you realise that God can be worshipped in the here and now – through your daily activities?

Read reflectively **Eph 4.15-16**.

Ask for the grace to find God in all you do.

Love's rainbow

Living God, You call us out of our separate and separated flowerpots to bloom together in the multicoloured glory of your herbaceous border. Bless you for your gifts of difference and colour we pray.

Colour us *red*, Passionate God, for the anger of the oppressed, for those who hunger and thirst for justice and peace, for our mother and grandmothers and all who labour to give birth to love. Colour us *yellow*, Resurrection God, for the achievement of the decade, for those who light up our lives, for all who dwell in the shadows of death and long for the morning. Colour us *green*, Creator God, for the integrity of creation, for seeds planted this weekend and leaves for the healing of the churches and nations, for all who need a new way forward to grow. Colour us *blue*, Incarnate God, for all who weep, for faith to walk and even dance upon the water, for all who need heaven to be torn open that they may hear God's affirming word: you are my son, my daughter, whom I love. Colour us *purple*, Holy God, for those whose needs and gifts are ignored, overlooked, rejected, for the silent who need a voice and the powerful who need to listen, for imagination and wisdom. Colour us your *rainbow* people of hope, Deep Loving God. Lead us forward to your promised community through Jesus Christ, your beloved and ours. Amen

C. A. Hepburn

How broad and long, how high and deep, is Christ's love. Eph 3.18

Suggestions

Are you a 'rainbow' personality?

Read meditatively **Eph 3.14-20**.

Ask for the grace of colouring the world with the rainbow of love.

Love's gifts

Rev James McKarns compares the seven-fold gifts of the Holy Spirit with the criteria provided by the famous psychologist William Menninger for emotional balance in a mature person.

1. *The ability to deal constructively with reality.* This comes through the gift of WISDOM: it enables us to distinguish reality from fantasy and live accordingly.
2. *The capacity to adapt to change.* It comes from the gift of UNDERSTANDING: It helps us to accept changes, seeing them as being for the common good. Most do not like change but favour progress. There can be no progress without change.
3. *Relative freedom from symptoms that are produced by tensions and anxieties.* COUNSEL leads us to delve beyond the visible to discover the hidden causes and symptoms of tensions and fears.
4. *The capacity to find more happiness in giving than in receiving.* PIETY warms us against selfishness.
5. *The capacity to relate to people in a consistent manner, with mutual satisfaction and helpfulness.* KNOWLEDGE gives consistent direction to our lives, lest we be shattered by every passing emotion.
6. *The capacity to direct our instinctive hostile energy into creative and constructive outlets.* FEAR OF THE LORD is beneficial and prods us to accomplish good deeds which otherwise may be left undone. This fear is reverential, as a child fears/respects his loving father.
7. *The capacity to love.* FORTITUDE is necessary for true love, for it gives us courage to make a solemn commitment in sprit of the risk of being rejected.

Do not restrain the Holy Spirit. 1Thes 5.19

Suggestions

How many of the above qualities/gifts do you possess? Reflect on the above gifts.
Ask the Holy Spirit to give you in fulness the gifts that you need most.

My little Cambodian sister,
your search for freedom is mine.
Your yearning for sanctuary
resounds in the depths of my heart.
Until you are liberated, I am enslaved.
Until you find a homeland, I am a pilgrim.
For together we walk to God.

My anguished Guatemalan brother,
your isolation is mine.
Your struggle for justice stirs my spirit.
I am alone until you breathe equity.
I am confined, for together we walk to God.

My uprooted Ugandan friend,
your desperation is mine,
while your hospitality overwhelms my being.
Until you are respected, I am in dishonour.
Until you are nourished, I am hungry.
For together we walk to God. Joan Metzner, M.M.

His power working in us is able to do so much more than we can ever ask for, or even think of. Eph 3.20

Suggestions

How far is your vision for the spread of God's Kingdom?
How deep is your solidarity in the sufferings of humanity?
How deep is your trust in God's power within you?

Read meditatively **Eph 1.18-23**.

Ask for the grace to experience God's power within you that gives you a new perspective on all reality and moves you to love and serve him so as to make Justice and Peace a reality.

PHASE TWENTY-SEVEN
UNCONDITIONAL LOVE

In this last phase you will find seven stories centred on experiences of "love". Take each of them for reflection. Link them to your favourite Gospel passages. Revive the spiritual experiences you have had through all your prayer periods in the past several months.

1. Understanding Love

Miss Stone was the super-efficient nurse at St Luke's General Hospital. Though only thirty-six years old she had reached the top position in her profession thanks to her intelligence, dedication and sheer hard work. She was a perfectionist and a 'slave-driver', she never smiled at anyone and was not interested in making friends. She was nicknamed "The Great Stone Face". Miss Stone lived alone.

After undergoing a series of medical tests for weeks, when she insisted that she be told the facts, she was informed that she suffered terminal cancer and had from six months to a year to live. She felt so frustrated, that one evening, taking a box of sleeping pills to her bedroom, she decided to end her life.

Suddenly the telephone started ringing. She ignored it. But the caller persisted. She thought, Well, if I *am* to die in peace, I shall just have to get rid of the caller. She heard an extraordinarily deep and resonant Voice which said, "Peace to you Agatha Stone, this is God. And I am asking you not to commit suicide." Nurse Stone was stunned. The voice asked her to recall certain incidents of her past. One was when she was 15 years old; her mother had died in a car crash and she had cursed God.

"But I never cursed *you*," said the Voice. "I have always loved *you* and will always love you."

The Voice then reminded her of her past shameful actions, her teenage affair with a student, her furtive abortion and consequent guilt, and so on. The Voice gave such details of her various secrets – things which nobody else in the world knew – that she realised the Voce was indeed that of God's. Marshalling all her strength to regain her composure, she finally uttered in a barely audible whisper: "What is it you want of me?" After a pause God said, "I entreat you to give up your idea of suicide. Furthermore, I entreat you to live up to your name from now on in a totally different way, Agatha Stone."

She asked how, and God explained that instead of being like a stone that is hard to herself and others, hating herself, unforgiving, she should become a rock of security and comfort to all she met, especially those who were gravely ill and facing death. She must spend the last few months of her life bringing strength and serenity to others. God gave her his personal assurance that he would be with her. Then he hung up.

Agatha hung up, too, and sat motionless. She realised that God was giving her a second chance, a possibility of changing defeat into victory. She realised it would be hard, especially if she was going to be in pain herself, but it would be a good way to make repentance for her past sins. She slept peacefully that night.

When she crossed the lobby of her apartment building the next morning she saw a notice on the bulletin board. It informed the tenants that the Telephone Company had cut off all connections for the past 24 hours, for repairs. Agatha smiled to herself, knowing that *her* telephone line was certainly not dead!

A tenant who noticed her smile froze in his tracks. "My God!" he thought, "I must be dreaming! The terrifying Miss Stone is actually smiling!"

[Condensed form of *A Second Chance* by Fr Nil Guillemette, S.J., from his book *Greater Than Our Hearts*]

2. Caring Love

In a bustling village there was a plaza surrounded by trees where the collectors gathered. These were people who made a living buying and re-selling things that people had discarded: glass bottles, shoes, pots and pans, stamp collections, hats, books, and so on. One day an old man, carrying a large pack which seemed empty, arrived at the plaza, and settled down in a corner. When asked what he had in his pack, he said it contained nothing but his lunch and raincoat. "Aren't you a collector?" people asked. "Oh, yes," he said, "I'm very much a collector. But what I collect does not fit in a pack or a box. I collect people's cares."

Everyone found this a strange idea. The care-collector explained that from his long experience he had found that the things everybody has too many of and constantly tries to get rid of, are cares, trials, burdens, sorrows, difficult times – all kind of things that weigh them down and make their lives sad. So he had offered to collect these cares from the people and they felt better. That was all.

Someone asked him how he went about collecting cares. "Well, there is probably something in your life that bothers you – some care that you have. Just tell me about it and I will add it to my collection." The inquirer asked curiously how that would help. "Can you make the problem go away just because I tell you about it?"

"No," said the care-collector, "but you will feel better about it. Try it."

The person told the old man about a problem he was faced with. When he finished, the care-collector nodded his head deeply a few times, and then put his hands together as if to scoop up something heavy. He pretended to put it into his pack. "There, I have put it away. How do you feel?"

"Why, I do feel better. I think I can handle the problem much better now. It really works."

Word spread. Soon there was a throng of people who came to give their cares to the care-collector. His spot eventually became the most popular one in the square.

One day, when a woman who seemed to be carrying a very heavy burden came to the village, the people immediately took her to the care-collector. She said she had come from a city that had more hurt and cares than anywhere else in the world. The care-collector looked very solemn. He stood up and lifted his pack in a gesture that was slower and more painful than anyone had ever seen before. After a long silence, he spoke slowly. "I must go there."

There was a great protest from everyone. They did not want to lose their care-collector. The kind gentleman slipped away in the middle of the night. He did not want his departure to be a burden and a sorrow for the people he had helped.

[Condensed version of *The Care Collector* (first part) by Leo Remington

Love, they say, is patient,
Love, they say, is kind;
Love sees beyond another's faults
For love, they say, is blind.

Love takes away the me and mine,
Instead it's us and we,
Yours and mine is ours now
For love is unity.

Love will not diminish
Or rust or fade with years,
But it will gain its strength
From time, from laughter, joy and tears.

Love is God's own gift to us,
A present from above.
He gives us peace, he gives us joy,
But first he gives us love. Anon

3. Unsolicited Love

The Menninger Clinic in Topeka, Kansas (USA) is an institution dealing in human relations. It believes that love is the best medicine. One of the standard prescriptions used by the physicians there for mental illness is "love' unsolicited". Patients suffering from illnesses that spring out of a lack of love in their lives are given special treatment by the clinic's staff – psychologically, by way of unconditional love.

Take this case of a patient whom we shall call Mr D. To begin with, Mr D had been an 'unwanted child' by his parents. As would be expected, he was neglected all though childhood. He developed multiple complexes, which turned him into a 'lone wolf' incapable of establishing emotional ties with anyone. He existed in a world of lovelessness, and began having mental problems.

He was referred to the clinic sometime after his thirty-fifth birthday. A series of tests and diagnoses revealed that Mr D was "schizophrenic" – he had retreated from the real world into a delusional one of his own making. He was admitted to the clinic for treatment. There he would lock himself in his room, refusing to budge out under any pretext. Even at common activities he made not the slightest effort to communicate with other patients.

The medical staff discussed the case and prescribed "love unsolicited" in heavy doses. The staff, including doctors, nurses and others, had been trained to administer this 'treatment': making it appear natural, even casual; being sensitive to how much the patient could take at a given moment; being discreet so as to cause no discomfort or pressure.

From that moment on, Mr D, who had not the slightest suspicion that he was the object of a 'conspiracy of love', began to receive big or small doses of affection and warmth from all quarters. A nurse or ward-boy took time off to play checkers with him. Doctors and attendants would constantly give him positive strokes at every single opportunity. One would say, "You look very well today, Mr D." Another, "It gives me such please to be in your company, Mr D." And so on.

One fine morning, Mr D walked out into the garden unbidden. The staff eyed each other contentedly, passing on the message that their prescription was taking effect. Gradually, the suffusion of love he received made Mr D more confident of and comfortable with the real world. He began to communicate with others, to get out of his shell. He was on the way to complete recovery.

4. Free love

Dead Man Walking is a critically acclaimed best-seller by Sister Helen Prejean. It is the true story of a catholic nun battling for the soul of a convicted killer on Death Row. The story begins one day in 1982 when the Prison Coalition of Louisiana, U.S.A., asked Sr Helen who lived and worked among the New Orleans poor to correspond with Patrick Sonnier, a death-row inmate and convicted killer of two teenagers. The book was recently made into a movie with the same title and widely televised.

In one of the sequences of the film we find Sr Helen urging the convict to read the Bible. She tells him, "The truth shall set you free."

"Uh huh? What is that Sister?" he asks.

"The truth is Love. The truth is Jesus came to tell us that prostitutes, tax collectors and other criminals have a dignity that no one can take away...."

"Love, huh, Sister? Turn the other cheek and all that... As simple as that, huh?"

"Not that simple.... It requires a lot of strength to turn the other cheek. Love is dangerous. That is why Jesus was killed by the people who found his message of dignity and love for all threatening..."

In the final scene the prison warden barks *"Dead Man Walking"*, as the convict makes his way to the death chamber for the lethal injection. Just before he enters the chamber, Sr Helen pleads: "I want you to remember love, remember that the last thing you ever saw is the face of love."

5. Timely love

Once upon a time, there was an island where all the feelings lived: Happiness, Sadness, and all of the others including Love.

One day it was announced to the feelings that the island would sink, so all repaired their boats and left. Love was the only one who stayed. Love wanted to persevere until the last possible moment. When the island was almost sinking, Love decided to ask for help.

Richness was passing by Love in a grand boat. Love said, "Richness, can you take me with you?"
Richness answered, "No I can't. There is a lot of gold and silver in my boat. There is no place for you here."
Love decided to ask Vanity who was also passing by in a beautiful vessel, "Vanity, please help me!"
"I can't help you Love. You are all wet and might damage my boat," Vanity answered.
Sadness was close by so Love asked for help, "Sadness let me go with you."
"Oh...Love, I am so sad that I need to be by myself!"
Happiness passed by Love too, but she was so happy that she did not even hear when Love called her!

Suddenly, there was a voice, "Come Love, I will take you." It was an elder. Love felt so blessed and overjoyed that he even forgot to ask the elder her name. When they arrived at dry land, the elder went her own way. Love realizing how much he owed the elder, asked Knowledge, another elder, "Who helped me?"

"It was Time", Knowledge answered.

"Time?" asked Love. "But why did Time help me?"

Knowledge smiled with deep wisdom and answered, "Because only Time is capable of understanding how great Love is."

6. Sensitive love

Two men prayed, and went their separate ways. One gathered wealth and power, and became famous, but there was no peace in him. The other saw the hearts of men; he too had found richness and power: but his wealth, his power, was love. When simply, kindly, tenderly he touched his fellow-men with all the richness and power of this love, the light within grew clear and bright with courage and with peace.

Both men one day stood before that golden door through which all humans must pass to the greater life beyond. The angel in the soul of each asked, "What do you bring with you? What is your gift to God?"

The one who was famous recounted his exploits. Why, there was no end to the people he knew, and the places he had been, and the things he had done – and the things he had accumulated. But the angel answered, "These are not acceptable. These things that you did, you did for yourself. I see no love in them." And the famous one sank outside the golden door and wept.

Then the angel in the soul of the other asked, "And what do you bring? What is your gift to God?"
And he answered, saying, "No one knows my name. They called me the wanderer, the dreamer. I have only a little light in my heart – nothing else, just a little light in my heart; and that which I have, I have shared with the souls of men."
Then the angel said, "Oh, blessed one, you have the greatest gift of all. It is love. Always and always, there is enough and to spare. Enter."

Then said the wanderer, "But first let me give the extra measure to my brother, that we may both walk through the door." The angel was silent; for in that moment a great light shone around the simple wanderer like a radiant mantle, enveloping both himself and his friend. The golden door was opened wide and they walked through it together.

7. Overwhelming love

The short story called *Somebody's Son* by Richard Pindell, opens with David, a boy who has run away from home, sitting by the side of a road and writing a letter to his mother, in which he expresses the hope that his old-fashioned father will forgive him and accept him again as his son. Then he informs his mother: "In a few days I'll be passing our property. If dad will take me back, ask him to tie a white cloth on the apple tree in the field next to our home."

Days later David is on a train that will go past his house. He is nervous with suspense, wondering whether the white cloth will be there or not. As the train is about to arrive at the spot from which his house will be visible, David cannot bring himself to look at it, so he turns to the man sitting next to him and says:

"Mister, will you do me a favour? Around this bend on the right, you'll see a tree. Tell me if there's a white cloth tied to it."

As the train rumbles past the tree, David stares straight ahead. Then, in a shaky voice he asks the man, "Mister, is a white cloth tied to one of the branches of the tree?" The man answers in a surprised tone of voice: "Why, son, there's a white cloth tied to practically *every* branch."

PARE AND RECEIVE, O LORD

Take, O Lord! In spite of all the reasons,
giving is not natural to me as it is to You.
Take, through Your grace, what I am too niggardly to give. Take; anyway all is Yours; You gave it all. Take, because I wish to give; I wish that all.
You have given, I, in my turn may give to You,
a real gift, an offering, a surrender of all,
henceforth to be administered by You in me,
to be disposed of, by me for You alone.

Without Your gifts I have nothing to give.
The day will come when without disposition of mine,
all will be withdrawn.
I may die slowly, inch by inch, stroke, paralysis,
loss of speech, coma;
life holding out in some final shattered corner
of doubtful consciousness, a moral nullity,
a human cipher.
Now since my powers are intact,
while they are still intact,
I make my gift of them all to You.
I offer them while they may still be used,
while You may still be served by them.

Take, O Lord, and receive.
I give in mush affection and willingness;
Lord, increase my affection.
Sufficient Your love and Your grace.
All that I have or possess, You have given me.
In death You will recall the loan,
You will resume the powers given in trust to me.
Now I wish to give then all to You.
I would say with your disciples, "Look, we
have left everything and followed You." **(Mt 19.27)**

All my life I have held back or taken back.
Now I wish in integrity to give, to give everythinhg.,
to give all. Take, O Lord, and receive! **T.F. Doody, S.J.**

NOTES

THE SPIRITUAL EXERCISES OF ST IGNATIUS LOYOLA

Introduction

The *Spiritual Exercises* is the Retreat Manual of St Ignatius of Loyola, founder of the Society of Jesus – widely known as the Jesuit Order. The manual was formally approved by Pope Paul III in 1548, after it had been effectively used by St Ignatius for well over twenty years. It was originally composed during his 'long retreat' in the Cave at Manresa, Spain (March 1522 to February 1523), where he lived like a hermit after renouncing a promising military career.

At the Cave, Ignatius had to battle against temptations, scruples, discouragement, despair and even the urge to commit suicide. But he clung to God for dear life, spending "seven hours" each day in prayer, abstained from meat, fasted and did severe penances. "He busied himself helping in spiritual matters certain souls who came there looking for him. All the rest of the day he spent thinking about the things of God that he had meditated upon or read that day. But when he went to bed, great enlightenment, great spiritual consolations often came to him... God treated him at this time just as a schoolmaster treats a child whom he is teaching." [Autobiography nn 26, 27].

At Manresa, God gifted Ignatius with the greatest mystical experience of his entire life. As he sat in meditation by the river Cardoner, "the eyes of his understanding began to be opened; not that he saw any vision, but he understood and learnt many things, both spiritual matters and matters of faith and of scholarship and this with so great an enlightenment that everything seemed new to him" [30]. He felt like a new man. All these spiritual experiences form the core of the *Spiritual Exercises*.

Ignatius narrated to his secretary cum biographer how "he had not composed the *Exercises* all at once, but that when he noticed some things in his soul and found them useful, he thought they might also be useful to others, and so he put them in writing" [99]. The final version of the text which was submitted to the Pope for approval, bears the stamp of Ignatius' further experiences in giving the *Exercises* as well as his theological training in Paris.

The Structure

The *Exercises* are dialectically arranged into four stages of a conversion process, leading to total service of God.

There is an introductory stage, which Ignatius entitled *Principle and Foundation*, where the exercitant (the one making the *Exercises*) is made aware that humankind has an end beyond the self in the "Creator and Lord"- a term Ignatius uses both for God and for Jesus Christ. Its goal is to work "for the greater glory of God" (a well-known Jesuit motto, *A.M.D.G.*), expressed in the *Exercises* in the phrase "to praise, reverence and serve God."

The second stage is a series of contemplations on Christ. These cover the whole range of Christ's life from his conception, birth and infancy to his Public Ministry. It also includes some 'key meditations': *The Call of the King*, *The Two Standards*, *The Three Classes of Men*, and *The Three Degrees of Humility*. The purpose of this stage is to get the exercitant to know Christ more intimately so as to love him more deeply and follow him more closely.

The third stage is contemplation on the Passion and death of Jesus. The fourth stage links up with the Resurrection and final commission of Jesus to his disciples. There is a concluding stage called *The Contemplation to Attain Divine Love*. It sums up the whole mystery of Christ, of the process of the *Exercises*, of realising that God's love challenges us to love him in return - not in words but in deeds.

Duration

St Ignatius structures the *Spiritual Exercises* for a 30-day Retreat to be done in seclusion and silence, However, not all those who went to him for guidance and were eager to go through the *Exercises* could afford the exclusivity it demanded, because of their professional commitments and responsibilities. So St Ignatius made provisions for such people to do the *Exercises* over an extended period, and in their familiar settings. They were instructed to reserve a fixed block of time during the course of a normal day, for formal prayer. Each day they took a fraction of the *Spiritual Exercises,* and progressively completed it over several months. This adaptation is commonly known today as *The Exercises in Daily Life.*

An extended Retreat of this type has its own advantages. The short periods spent in intimate contact with God daily help create a prayerful atmosphere that influences the whole life of the 'daily retreatants', permeating their work and rest hours. Moreover, given the structure and gradation of the *Exercises*, the retreatants eventually arrive at a state where, as St Ignatius put it, they can "find God in all things and all things in God."

Please note: The author gratefully acknowledges and is deeply indebted to the following authors for their respective works which have helped in the next section:

* **Bethy Oudot**, "Guidelines for Prayer from the school of St Ignatius", *Progressio*, Supplement No 47-48-49, November 1997. Publication of the World Christian Life Community, C.P. 6139, Borgo S. Spirito, Rome-Italy. (Quotes from this work are referred to as "Oudot")
* **John Veltri, S.J.**, *Orientations, Volume 2*. Found on the Internet. (Quotes from this work are referred to as "Veltri")

GUIDELINES FOR FORMAL PRAYER

Properly understood, the whole of life is prayer – an offering to God of all we and all we possess in a spirit of faith.

A. Formal Prayer

'Formal prayer' refers to those 'concentrated time-periods' of conscious contact – in a 'face-to-face' intimate communion. This is in contrast with the 'moments' of 'informal' encounters with God during the working or resting hours, or a constant awareness (even though 'unconscious') that one is in the presence of God. "Formal", therefore, means time set aside with deliberate intent for communing with God – away from the hustle and bustle of life.

Formal prayer must not be forced if it is to remain meaningful. You must enter into prayer with a willing, happy heart – to 'let go and let God'. Forced prayer, as someone commented, is like a bird in a cage, even if it is a golden cage – a prison. A spontaneous attitude to prayer uplifts the heart, away from the earth's gravitational pull, into a space of detached weightlessness – without a past hanging on your neck or a future blocking your vision.

B. Preparation for prayer

a. Planning

Plan the time and the length of your prayer. As far as possible keep a fixed time daily or on certain days of the week, for it makes it easier to remember. A prayer period should be a minimum of 40 minutes – if you want to do justice to it – extended to an hour. This, besides the 'transition' time at the beginning and the review at the end.

A word of caution: do not allow your moods to run your prayer-life. You may keep postponing prayer waiting for the right mood to strike, or you may easily give up prayer when the mood changes. Also beware of the general excuse that you are too "busy" with other things. As a matter of fact, you will always be busy if you do not pray!

Let your decision for devoting time for formal prayer be firm, enthusiastic. Remember, you do not pray for your own pleasure but because you want to be present to God. And this encounter needs time and regularity if it is to increase intimacy between you and God.

b. Place

Any place that lends itself to prayer is good enough. Generally one associates a 'secluded spot' with formal prayer, Remember the Lord's instruction: When you pray, go to your room, close the door, and pray to your Father who is unseen (Mt 6.6). But this may not always be possible or convenient. The next best thing would be to find an environment that is conducive for prayer, within the limited options available. Should even these be 'impossible' then one must develop, cultivate silence in ones heart, to create space for God by shutting off the distractions and disturbances of the 'world' around. This will come with practice. After all, prayer is made in the heart. And God looks to the heart of the beloved.

> "The absence of external noise is not enough. It can even reveal our inner hubbub. It would be an illusion to hope to empty our mind of all its clutter by all sorts of preliminary techniques. Praying is not about *creating a vacuum!* Praying means to be authentic and present. it means to be united with the living God, just as I am, with all that I am and all that I carry with me. *God doesn't join us in a 'sterilised' part of ourselves.* I become calm, quiet in faith, I become aware of Him Whom I want to encounter in love." Oudot

To make your prayer-area more conducive to prayer, here are some suggestions:
- Clear the table of 'work' that is pending, or other sources of 'distraction'.
- Place objects that help create a prayerful atmosphere – like a crucifix, a holy picture, your Bible, of course. You may even light a candle if it helps.

c. Posture

There are no hard and fast rules for postures to be adopted during formal prayer. Standing, sitting, squatting, kneeling, lying prostrate... hand folded, arms outstretched or placed across the breast... are some of the commonest postures.

However it is important to understand that it is not only your 'soul' that prays, but your whole being. Your body, in particular, is your 'partner' in prayer. A posture that is conducive enhances the effectiveness and seriousness of prayer. You must adopt a posture that externalises your interior attitudes, and stay with it for as long as necessary. This may require a certain amount of self-control.

> "Once one has adopted a position in prayer and the prayer is going well, one should not readily change position. The outward restlessness or shifting of position can jar the inner calm of prayer. One should remain with the posture while one is finding what one desires. Remain with it until there has been a sense of completion 'for now.'" Veltri

"Walking, too, may lend itself to praying well if it can dispose one for the relaxation and the openness of the heart needed for the prayer exercise. On the other hand, walking often interferes with such openness by its restless effect upon one's inner being. Often a certain rhythm of kneeling and sitting, standing or lying prostrate may help one keep in harmony with the variety of moods being expressed within the prayer exercise." Veltri

Through practice and experience you will arrive at the posture most suited to you during prayer. An 'ideal' posture is one that combines reverence before God who is present and bodily relaxation. The important principle behind right posture is that of remaining physically still – so that your mind and heart can get focussed. Deep prayer requires a still body.

d. Personal approach

Do not rush into prayer. Put yourself in the proper frame of mind and heart for it. You are going to meet a 'significant person': What do you expect from the meeting? Is there anything important you would like to ask? Don't you think that 'significant person' is looking forward to the meeting with you – and is also thinking about expectations and questions?

> In the *Spiritual Exercises* [75] St Ignatius offers this suggestion: "A step or two away from the place where I will make my contemplation or meditation, I will stand for the length of an Our Father, I will raise my mind and think how God our Lord is looking at me, and other such thoughts. Then I will make an act of reverence or humility."

The reason behind such an act of reverence is to make you aware that prayer is a 'living encounter' with a living God. God is not an object, a 'thing' but a person. Prayer is a person-to-person relationship. You are united with the living God just as you are, with your whole being, and all that is part of your being.

Prayer does not consist chiefly in the mental effort of 'always thinking' about God. It is something deeper, more real and substantial than a mere mental recollection of God: it is the whole person that must become one with God – a fundamental union! It is from this deep union that like a spring of living water, prayer slowly surges up to the surface, progressively invading the will, the intellect, the memory; both the sub-conscious and the whole consciousness.

e. Preliminaries

■ Take a few minutes at the start of a prayer-period to quieten yourself down, to relax. Do some deep rhythmic breathing. Settle down into a comfortable prayerful position. Let go of all your preoccupations, your pressing cares and concerns. Tune-in to the Lord.

■ Do not get anxious or upset if there are noises or distractions. Accept them, by first becoming aware of them and then letting go of them, offering them to God and begging God to help you keep your focus.

■ Say a prayer that expresses your faith in God's presence. Tell him that you adore him; thank him for his gifts, especially the gift of life. Ask for grace that you respond fully to the Spirit that prays within you.

■ At the start of every prayer period you could, wherever possible, and if you find it helpful, show some physical reverence for God's presence, like prostrating momentarily or kissing the floor.... Do not strain your imagination so as to turn this act into an exercise! If you prefer, even a simple vocal or mental expression of faith in God's Presence will suffice.

C. Dealing with the topics

Meditation is the exercise of the mind; prayer is the expression of the heart – the will, the emotions. Meditation is the basis for prayer. This book offers you points for meditation, and suggestions for prayer. But prayer itself, intimate communication with God, is personal and only you can do it as you feel inspired to, with the help of God's grace. So consider the exercises in this book only as a means of putting you in direct contact with God. Do not be in a hurry to complete each unit of a phase, as if you were doing a project with definite time-limits. The moment you feel inspired to communicate directly with God while reading through the points, stop, let go of the book, and let God take over.

THE IGNATIAN APPROACH TO UNION WITH GOD

In the context of using your mind and heart at prayer, St Ignatius has some concrete guidelines. Note that some of the points appearing above are reiterated here.

A. Introductory explanations

St Ignatius offers the retreatant some useful suggestions for drawing the maximum benefit out of the *Spiritual Exercises*. Below are some reflections based on his 'introductory explanations':

1. Just as the physical exercises we perform help keep us fit and healthy through improved circulation, breathing and muscle tone, so these *spiritual exercises* improve our spiritual fitness and health and make us more open to receive God's abundant graces. There is a difference, though, between physical and spiritual exercises. Physical exercises demand a certain rigidity of practice, a 'drill' that may lead to exertion. The spiritual exercises are performed without straining oneself, without tension or nervousness, in an easy and relaxed manner. In both cases, it is extremely helpful to have a coach or a guide.

2. The *Exercises* involve several activities like meditation, contemplation, vocal prayer, and so on. We must avoid the tendency to go through an exercise merely for the sake of completing it. The *Spiritual Exercises* is not a project to be accomplished but a process to be experienced. Any little point that helps the process is to be valued and cherished to the maximum.

There are many 'points' offered for each day's prayer; not all of them need be covered at one sitting. It is necessary to relish and digest the inspirations that come up in prayer – slowly, without haste, and to build up our convictions on them. If any idea strikes us, we must stay with it for as long as it appeals, even for the entire duration of prayer if necessary. This may turn out to be a prayer of deeper quality than one that is crammed with 'bright ideas' or inspirations.

3. "When the going gets tough, the tough get going." In prayer, we need to keep this saying in mind. When all is smooth sailing, we enjoy spending hours in prayer. In 'stormy weather' (temptations, distractions, dryness... in prayer) we may feel like running away from God. It is important that we counteract this feeling by deliberately spending the entire time assigned to prayer and *a few minutes more* just to remind ourselves that God is present even in the storm though he is not easily seen, and he will get us through it. Indirectly, we give a message to our subconscious mind that we mean business when it comes to prayer, and we will not give up. Gradually, we learn to bring things under control faster and get into the rhythm of prayer, through the grace of God.

4. We must surrender ourselves to God in prayer with great generosity of spirit. We must offer all our desires and our freedom to God, so that he can make us of all we posses in whatever way corresponds most to his holy will.

In spite of all our personal efforts to pray, we must be aware of the fact that we ultimately depend on God's Grace for whatever happens in prayer. So we must learn to be 'actively receptive' to God's communication. Activity implies our cooperation with grace, the effort we make to keep our heart 'pure' to 'see' God, and the means we employ to prepared body and soul to 'receive' in openness whatever God has to offer. To be receptive is to go to prayer without pre-conceived notions or ideas, so that we are open to what God has to offer in his own unique way, especially during the time of formal prayer.

5. God is eager to communicate with us directly. Occasionally, he may, of his own good pleasure, communicate himself in person to us, inflaming our hearts with his love and praise, and directing us as to how best to serve him and to do his holy will. This is a special privilege, a gratuitous gift of God.

Ordinarily, though, God stands outside our 'door' and knocks, waiting for us to invite him in. (Rev 3.20)

It is important that we unclutter our minds and hearts of things that draw our attention away from God and prevent us from hearing God's knocking at the door. The more attached we are to things and persons, the less attached we are to God, the less open and generous in prayer.

6. Our involvement in the process of the *Spiritual Exercises* is bound to give rise to 'spiritual movements' – interior experiences, such as thoughts, impulses, inclinations, moods, urges, Consolations, Desolations, etc. They are proof that the *Exercises* are working, that the 'medicine' is having its effect. Movements can be towards God or away from God.

> These interior reactions include all the feelings and spontaneous thoughts that occur within us – boring, angry, exciting, fearful, depressed, anxious, challenging, insightful, meaningful, etc. What makes these very human interior experiences 'spiritual movements' is their meaning through the perspective of faith along with the direction that is perceived as part of or within them. Veltri

There are three main factors that cause these movements: *concentration*, *strong attachments*, *generosity*. All three combine to create this interior movement. If one is missing, there will be no movement. We will be 'neither hot nor cold'. In our 'review' of prayer, we must check for these movements, and the direction they are taking us, and the factors influencing them.

B. Preparatory Prayer

St Ignatius Loyola suggests that those doing the *Spiritual Exercises* begin each prayer period asking God "for the grace that all my intentions, actions and operations may be ordered purely to the service and praise of the Divine Majesty." [S.E.46]

As noted earlier, your turning to God and opening yourself to him is very much a *grace*. Since you believe it is so, you ask for this grace. In Ignatius' suggestion, you are made of your *personal* involvement in prayer. There are your "intentions" – desires, enlightenment; your actions – external works; your activities – reflecting, loving, questioning, enjoying...

> This preparatory prayer is a fundamental act, and it depends on the attitude of the one who prays. It is of no importance whether I feel pleasure and enlightenment afterwards or dryness and aridity – battling for faith or the joy of union – none of these are important in themselves....In prayer as in my daily life, the essential lies in uniting my will to the will of God, in that orientation of desire which reunites and is in communion with the Spirit within me. Oudot

C. The Composition of Place

St Ignatius instructs: "When a contemplation or meditation is about something that can be gazed on, for example a contemplation of Christ our Lord, who is visible, the composition will be to see in imagination the physical place where that which I want to contemplate is taking place. By physical place I mean, for instance. a temple or mountain where Jesus Christ or our Lady happens to be, in accordance with the topic I desire to contemplate." [SE 47]

> Literally, 'composition, seeing the place' (Mullan). In each prayer exercise, the Composition is the 'prelude' which instructs a directee to settle into the prayer exercise by composing (gathering together) oneself to become interiorly stilled and as present as possible to God through the material of the prayer exercise. Ignatius suggests that this be done by making use of one's imaginative powers; that is, by recalling and making oneself present to certain aspects of the mystery upon which one is contemplating or meditating. This helps a directee at prayer to disregard what is going on around oneself and to give oneself to the exercise with a relaxed but focused attention. Veltri

To do this effectively you must let your imagination be aided by actual pictures, paintings, movies you have seen of the Holy Land. Or, you can use symbolic images – for instance, when meditating on sin, you can visualise yourself in prison, or seeing the gentleness of God as reflected in some person or human experience. The purpose is for you to let your mind get hold of a concrete setting (synagogues, countryside, towns and villages in the Holy Land, the sea of Galilee, mountains, a statue, painting) from where to launch into prayer. The 'composition of place' is a tangible point of entry to the mystery of God you have decided to pray on.
The composition of place helps in the following ways:

a. **To focus** your imagination together with your whole being at the service of prayer. Visualisation enhances inner silence. In case your attention wanders, you can return to this anchor point, this image.

b. The text or mystery you are praying on is **reality** – not a product of your imagination. Thus, the composition of place need not be an exact reconstruction but a symbolic one.

c. Being in **a particular and specific place** – where the mystery of God was enacted – during your time of prayer, is like becoming a **"pilgrim"**, (as St Ignatius was), trying to see and touch the spots on the earth where God revealed Himself.

> "Every scene in the Bible uncovers 'God among us' who reveals Himself in the reality of our humanity, in our neighbourhoods. So the region where we live takes on a biblical, divine dimension. The composition of place helps us discover God, not in thin air but in our reality (houses, roads, towns, deserts...)." Oudot

"Ignatius recommends the 'composition of place' in the *Spiritual Exercises*: that is, we reconstruct the place where the scene we are about to contemplate occurred. What he really speaks of, however, in the original Spanish text, is not a *composition of place*, but a *composition, seeing the place*. In other words, it is not the place that you compose but yourself when you see the place in fantasy." A de Mello, S.J

D. Ask for Grace

> The term "Grace" has been commonly used by Christians "over the centuries to denote and connote God's personal relationship and consequent activity with humankind as a whole and with each person individually. Since earliest times, we Christians have believed that anything we do that has any relationship whatsoever to our salvation or to our growth in God's love comes as a result of God's initiatives. 'It is by God's favour [grace] that we have been saved' (Eph 2:5). 'It is not we who love God but God loved us first...' (1Jn 4:10; Rom 5:8). Grace is a freely given and unearned gift. It refers to the abiding presence of God's life within us, which, in Roman Catholic theology, has been called sanctifying grace. It also refers to those impulses, initiatives, inspirations, etc., that ultimately encourage us into deeper involvement in God's life which, in Roman Catholic theology, has been called 'actual grace(s).'" Veltri

St Ignatius instructs: "Ask God our Lord for what I want and desire." [Sp Ex 48] Genuine desire is of great importance in Ignatian spirituality. It is not for anything at all that you ask for – but something you really want or need! This means you must be attentive to your real needs.

> **What I want or wish**: Rather than begging or putting your hand out, it is a matter of really living in the prayer, of being someone who knows what he/she wants, who has the right to 'want' something for his/her life; someone who yearns, who has longings: in other words, an authentic human being. Therefore, I have to make a quick tour of the profound desire of my heart, and **to ask God for this grace**, for it is a grace, not a right or the result of my efforts. Oudot

The graces you ask for may be in accordance with the *mystery* you are meditating or contemplating. You may ask God for healing, or for virtues that enable you to lead a more intense Christian life. Specific desires may unfold during prayer.

Why ask

In each prayer exercise, the directee is instructed to 'ask for grace' – that is, to express his/her desires to God. We know that, ultimately, it is only from God and not from one's own effort that one can receive what one desires in the prayer exercises. The very asking for a Grace or the articulation of one's desires for a deepening of one's relationship with God in some particular way, comes from God. The initial impulse, the consequent shift in one's consciousness, the openness to the gift, the reception of the gift, the presence of God's self in one – all this is grace. Veltri

♦ When you ask, you become receptive: open to receive the Word, the Spirit, inspiration from God. You thus surrender yourself to divine action – allowing the Spirit to pray, speak and act in you. You forget yourself. You ask to rise above your personal interests so that you may submit yourself more and more interiorly to God, and love and serve him the better.
♦ Your desires bring out the 'human' side of you, expressing your freedom before God. Your desires highlight your uniqueness as a person.
♦ Asking forces you to "sort" through your desires in prayer and recognise what you need to be open to God. You then 'direct' your desires towards God – therefore looking beyond yourself. There remains no scope for your cheating either yourself or God.
♦ "Little by little, the Spirit will change my petitions, helping me discover what I need and what I truly want, My petition will become closer and closer to the will of God in me." Oudot
♦ Jesus himself encourages people to ask, and he grants the requests at the deepest level.

Asking is an **act of faith** in the Lord who is all gift. It is acknowledging that *everything comes from Him,* not from our acts, acknowledging that even prayer is a gift from God. It is believing that God (as He has told us) wants to fill us to overflowing with the best there is, and to send us the *Spirit.* Oudet

E. Understand and Savour Interiorly

St Ignatius instructs: "For, what fills and satisfies the soul consists, not in knowing much, but in our understanding the realities profoundly and in savouring them interiorly." [S.E. 2]

The Psalmist says: "This word is on my lips and in my heart", "Taste and see...", "Open your mouth and I will fill it". ...

Biblically 'knowing' God does not mean having knowledge, but gaining in personal experience of God. To achieve this, you must
"– *take a little time*: a word, a verb, an attitude;
– *take the time*: to relish, savour and discover all its facets, to reflect on its significance, to let the word release its flavour; to stay with it until this word sinks in, resounds and is really welcomed and understood." Oudot

You may sometimes discover that words lose their flavour, if you are not attentive to them, or if you merely rattle them off without allowing them to "speak" to you. Rather than use your mind for discovering new insights, use your emotions to feel and to savour. God also speaks through your emotions. When a word 'awakens' my emotions, it is a sign that God is working in you, touching you.

> It is not by chance that *the language of the senses* can evoke this reality: that God truly touches and changes us in prayer. For it is truly in our reality – body, emotions, understanding, and not in the imaginary – that God speaks, and communicates with us. And it is through this reality that I become aware of this fact. What I feel and savour is not God Himself, but a sign, an indication that His word is working in me, touching me. In internalising such a passage, *in taking it to heart*, the Word nourishes me, 'becomes incarnate' and enlightens me." Oudot

It is important to note, however, that like all prayer, this process of savouring does not depend on you alone but is also God's initiative.

F. Colloquy

"A colloquy is made, properly speaking, in the way one friend speaks to another, or a servant to one in authority – now begging a favour, now accusing oneself of some misdeed, now telling one's concerns and asking counsel about them. [Sp Ex 54]

In every prayer period, it is helpful to have a dialogue with God. Sometimes the word "colloquy" is used as a fancy name for this dialogue. It is a term that describes the intimate conversation between God and me, Jesus and me, and so on. This conversation happens on the occasion of my putting myself as totally as I can into the setting of the prayer; I will find that I speak or listen as God's Spirit moves me – sometimes as sinner, sometimes as child, at other times as lover or friend, and so on. As with all conversations, the colloquy goes both ways. I say something to Jesus and then I give Jesus time to say something back to me. Sometimes it even may be helpful to imagine Jesus responding as if he were sitting beside me. At times, this little technique really helps establish the two-way flow of conversation. A colloquy takes place at any time during the period of prayer. Veltri

The colloquy helps us to progress in a more personal, true and humble *relationship* with the Lord. It is accepting that *God makes us His sons and daughters, friends...* with whom He establishes a relationship. It is *responding* to the Word and letting it take shape, expressing it in these few words or in this silence... It is *preferring the relationship itself to what I have or have not received*. It is loving....
What I express or fail to express to God shows *me more clearly what I want* and what I am not yet living. Thus, it is a way of progress. I can *compare* what I express to God in the colloquy with what I asked Him for *as a grace at the beginning*: is there any change, alteration, confirmation? Perhaps the Lord has already granted the grace asked for in the beginning. Oudot

F. Application of the Senses

When you contemplate a scripture passage you approach the scene and the mystery through the senses of seeing and hearing (looking at the characters, listening to their words). The other senses come into play successively, when you narrow down your view of a scene, or proceed from the external (reasoning) to the more internal (feeling).

The dynamics involved in your use of the senses is to shift your perspective from the farthest to the nearest. For instance, you see a person coming in the distance, but you do not *hear* the footsteps till the person approaches you. Likewise, you can **smell** a flower from a distance, but you get 'closer' to it when you **touch** it. Of course, when you **taste** something you get even closer to it. You move from the exterior to the more intimate. In a similar fashion, we use the **inner senses** to contemplate spiritual realities.

Following are a summary of practical approaches to contemplation with the sense suggested by Oudot:

◊ Imagine the *place* and decide your entry point from the exterior to the interior. Then enter into what you *see* and let what you see enter into you.

◊ Let the words and the silence penetrate your inner *ears*. Try quietly to enter more and more profoundly into the mystery through the physical aspect of the scene.

◊ *Feel, touch, taste* as if you were present: objects, the atmosphere, the "sweetness and charm" of God according to the character that you are contemplating.

◊ "Using the sense of touch, I will, so to speak, embrace and kiss the places where the persons walk or sit. I shall always endeavour to draw some profit from this." [Sp Ex 125]

◊ End with a concrete gesture: a personal prayer to the Lord, an act of thanksgiving, or a prayer of the Church.

In suggesting how to apply the senses of smell and taste, Ignatius writes: 'to smell and to taste, with the sense of smell and the sense of taste, the infinite fragrance and sweetness of the Divinity'. This implies that he includes something deeper than the physical imagining of tasting, smelling, seeing, touching, etc., something more intuitive – called by some 'the spiritual senses'.

The Application of Senses is not so much the active application of one's senses but more the passive reception of deep intimacy. In the Exercises journey, this is helped by the use of Repetition which fosters a passive and gradual simplification of the mystery that one is contemplating. Veltri

THE DYNAMICS OF CONTEMPLATION

Introduction

Ordinarily, when we refer to "contemplation" we mean that state silence – no talking – while we observe, listen, and keep our minds and hearts open to the object that draws our attention (a painting, a sunset, a waterfall, the stars, a child....). We admire, relish, and are emotionally touched by the sights or sounds. Deep contemplation makes us one with the object. In the *Spiritual Exercises*, St Ignatius recommends that we "contemplate" Christ during our periods of prayer. He wants us to do this not as an 'exercise' of prayer, but as *a way of being with Christ himself.*

You must, therefore, make a conscious effort so to project yourself into the time and space of Jesus as to recreate a scene from his life, and *become part of the action*. You must get involved in the scene, seeing how Jesus relates to people, listening to what he says feeling his nearness, and even interacting with him every now and them.

Procedure

In contemplation, we enter into the life event or story passage of the Scriptures by way of imagination, making use of all our senses. Following are some ways to do it effectively:

◊ Briefly recall the biblical scene (event/story). Do not visual it as a "Holy picture" but as a "movie" – in its historical setting (sea, hillside, field, street, house...) or an atmosphere (crowds shouting, merchants bartering, joyful children, the Last Supper...) You must genuinely *fantasize* and not just *remember* the scene or event.

The difference between *fantasy* and *memory* is that in fantasy you actually re-live the event. You are no longer conscious of our present surroundings. As far as your consciousness is concerned, you are actually in your fantasy place. Thus, if you are reliving a scene on the seashore, it is as if you hear once again the roar of the waves, you feel again the sun beating on your bare back, you feel the touch of the hot sand under your feet... and, as a result, you re-experience all the feelings you had when that scene first took place.

◊ Enter the scene. Observe what clothes and other paraphernalia people are wearing. Listen to what they are saying, what they are doing. Join them and get involved in whatever is going on. Assume the role of one of the persons, and get involved in conversation or doing something.

◊ Focus on an individual in the scene: what does he/she experience? With whom is he\she relating, conversing? Is there a message that applies to me, to my family or society? At times, if it seems appropriate, imagine you are the person who is directly involved with Jesus in the passage (the lame man, the Samaritan woman, a disciple...). Put yourself in the skin of these people... so as to feel what they did about Jesus. Place yourself in the crib, in the boat, on a tree... so that you understand better...

◊ Respond to those who speak to you: take in the intonation, the meaning that their words convey. What do the words reveal about the person (*Give me a drink!... Today I am coming to your house!... I know very well who you are... Are you going to wash my feet?...*)

> Their gestures, attitudes, actions, reactions (words). Are these acts God's, or those of men and women (therefore, mine) in relation to God? I can experience their meaning or some sense of my own, my desire, my denial, or discover there another face of God. I can touch them, rather than merely theorize about them! Perhaps I may embrace these gestures: Stretch out your [withered] hand... and I discover that I am withered, thirsting to be cured; I am paralysed or walking beside *Jesus, tired by the journey, sitting down by the well*, near Mary, who bowing her head says: *I am the handmaid of the Lord.* Oudot

After each phase of contemplation it will be good to pause and reflect on what impressions have been stamped on your mind: What was the spiritual experience like? What deeper wisdom have you acquired about God's action or my own relationship within God. This could be just a 'silent pause'.

You may repeat your contemplation of a scene – going even deeper. That is, not just seeing and hearing, but even smelling, tasting, and touching. When you thus engage all your senses in prayer, you make it simple, unified – letting the word of God speak through your body, your senses.

Contemplating Christ

When contemplating a scene in which Christ is present:
- through your imagination, make the scene come alive.
- place yourself next to him, ready to do what he bids.
- become deeply aware of his nearness. Try to understand, feel, know from the inside, like St John who says: *what we have seen with our own eyes; ... what we have touched with our own hands: the Word, who is life...*
- Listen eagerly; savour the words he utters. Dialogue with him.
- Become permeated by the scene so as to relish the mystery of it a little, and let it reverberate in you.

Contemplating Christ transforms you from within into his image.

PRAYING THE SCRIPTURAL WORD OF GOD

Reading Meditatively:

All through the book we have 'suggested' that you "read meditatively". This is a method of prayer in which you listen with your heart to God's word in the scriptures. In earlier times this method has been referred to partially *as Lectio Divina* which developed as a key form of meditation in the monasteries. It is a natural process which, when one begins to 'listen' with the heart (reading), moves through a pondering or reflection with the heart (meditation)), through a response of the heart (praying) to a resting in God (contemplation).

Praying with Scripture:

Following are some ways of praying over a passage of Scripture.

a. Once you have 'settled down' for prayer, read through the passage of Scripture that you have selected, slowly and attentively. Certain words or phrases will carry special meaning for you personally. They might seem to leap right off the page to embrace you, as if they were placed there because they have something specific to convey to you. Savour such words or phrases. Turn them over gently and carefully in your heart. Do not be in a hurry to go to the next word or phrase in the passage till you feel fully satisfied.

b. Be in touch with your thoughts and more importantly with your feelings as you take in deeply the word or phrase that has struck you. Pause to speak to God, to tell him *exactly* how you feel joyful, hopeful, anxious, angry, surprised, etc. Feel the touch of God as he 'speaks' to you in his Word.

c. At the end of the prayer-period have an intimate conversation with God, summing up all the graces you have received from reading the particular passage of Scripture.

Pondering The Scriptures With Your Heart (Veltri):

A very good way of pondering a passage of scripture with your heart is to approach the scripture text as you would a love letter. Read the passage slowly, aloud, or in a whisper....
Let the words wash over you.... Savour each phrase or word.... Re-read the passage lovingly as if you were reading a letter from a dear friend.... Stay with the words or phrases that especially catch your attention.... Absorb them the way the thirsty earth receives the rain.... Allow your heart to be moved; when a thought or feeling resonates deeply, stay with it.... Allow it to penetrate your being.... Express it to God.... Occasionally you might want to ask yourself questions concerning this passage: why? how? when? how might this apply to me now? Let further feelings and thoughts well up in your heart as you ponder to find deeper meaning or understanding or a different way of seeing things. Respond authentically and spontaneously as in dialogue.

THREE METHODS OF PRAYING

St Ignatius proposes three simple methods of praying, which can be used any time, particularly in preparing/reviewing formal prayer.

First Method: On a Series of Points

Take up 'topics' that go in a series. St Ignatius suggests the Ten Commandments, the 7 capital sins, the 7 Virtues, the 3 Powers of the soul (will, memory, understanding), the 5 senses. But one can add one's own list: for example, the 8 Beatitudes, the 3 theological virtues (faith, hope and love), the members of one's family, one's friends, colleagues....

The method of prayer

- *Ask questions*: How have I experienced this point today?
- *Pray*: what can I *give thanks* for on this point? What do I need to *ask pardon* for? How can I make progress *tomorrow*?
- *Conclude* with a short prayer: the Our Father, Hail Mary...
- Then go on to the next point.

An example: **Praying on the 5 Senses:**

Sight

- What have I seen with my eyes today? How have I looked at other, the world, myself?
- What have I seen to give thanks for, or to wonder at?
- What did I shut my eyes to, whom or what did I refuse to see. Ask pardon.
- How will I see tomorrow, whom, and with what aim?
- Short vocal prayer, then go on to the next point.

Hearing

- How have I listened, and what have I understood today?
- What have I heard to give thanks for? What have I understood, or refused to understand?
- What have I shut my ears to, or what will I open them to tomorrow...

*

Example: **Praying on my Family members/Friends/...**
Take each one and ask yourself:

- What can I give thanks for with regard to this person?
- What do I need to ask pardon for in this relationship?
- What should I ask of the Lord for myself in relation to this person and for him/her? How do I continue the relationship in the days to come?
- Concluding prayer....

*

Example: **Praying on my Body**
My feet: Whom did I go toward today? Who came to meet me? From whom did I turn away?
Whose footsteps did I follow? Did I have my feet on the ground?...
My head: What was I thinking of? Was I preoccupied? What or whom did I not think of enough? Do I live only in my head? What have I created, devised? ....

NOTE: On each point you can also do the following:
Contemplate or imagine how *Jesus* or *Mary* look at people. To whom did they listen and how? What did they do with their hands? How did they live each of these points, this beatitude, this commandment....?

Second Method: The Meaning of the Words

Content
Could be one of your favourite prayers, a biblical text, or a Psalm you know by heart.

Method
Contemplate the meaning of each of the words.

- Choose a prayer you know well (Our Father....), or memorise one.
- Say the first word or phrase, then begin to search for its meaning, for you...Stay with it as long as you are drawing something for it by way of nuances in significance, relish, comparisons, etc. You need not complete the text chosen at one sitting.
- Conclude the session by saying out the prayer chosen,
- In the next session, you can take up the same prayer/text, recite the first words which you have previously prayed over and then contemplate the meaning of the word or words following them using the same method.

Third Method: Rhythmic Breathing

Content
A prayer you know by heart.

Method
Praying to the rhythm of your breathing.

- Choose a prayer you usually recite by heart.
- Recite the prayer *mentally, very slowly, to the rhythm of your breathing*: at each exhalation, pronounce, or interiorly 'slip in', one word or a few words.
- Or, in the brief silence following and accompanying the *exhalation*, keep your mind and heart centered *on the meaning* of the word you have just said, or *on the person* you are addressing (the Father, Mary...), or *let the feelings* aroused by this word *ascend to God*: admiration, love, my own smallness...
- Conclude your prayer in the way you feel best.

(Based on Bethy Oudot's explanations)

REVIEW OF PRAYER

St Ignatius suggests: "After finishing the exercise, for a quarter of an hour, either seated or walking about, I will examine how well I did in the contemplation or meditation. If poorly, I will seek the reasons; and if I find them, I will express sorrow in order to do better in the future. If I did well, I will thank God our Lord and use the same procedure next time." [Sp Ex 77]

> The focus of the review is what happened during the prayer exercise itself – not so much what finished ideas you had but rather what heart-felt understandings were emerging. In other words the interior reactions of the heart. Therefore, the movements of consolation, desolation, fear, anxiety, boredom, distractions, especially if they were deep or disturbing. Veltri

Following are question to help you make the review:

What was your mood at the beginning of prayer (happy, sad, peaceful, anxious, loving, doubtful, trusting...)?
Did the mood change during the prayer? Why, or why not?
Did you find the topic of prayer appealing? In what way?
Did you feel any resistance to praying on the topic? Why?
Was there any particular word or phrase that you found striking, inspirational?
Were you continuously aware of God's presence?
Is there some point that you need to return to in the next period of prayer?

If you want to have a longer review, you may ask further questions:
What are my moods, feelings, inspirations... telling me about my relationship with God?
What connections do I see between my life and my prayer?
What must I do to intensify my awareness of God all through my busy day?

You may keep a written record of the review for future reference.